CHEF
SCHOOL

LEITH'S SCHOOL
OF FOOD & WINE

First published in Great Britain 1998
Bloomsbury Publishing Plc, 38 Soho Square,
London W1V 5DF

Text copyright © 1997
by Leith's School of Food and Wine

The moral right of the authors has been asserted

A CIP catalogue record for this book is available
from the British Library

ISBN 0 7475 3903 0

10 9 8 7 6 5 4 3 2 1

Designed by Carroll Associates
Photographers: Patrick Rowe, Robin Allison-Smith,
Andrea Heselton, Lawrence White
Home Economists: Belinda Kassapian,
Jacqui Thomas, Vivien Pidgeon, Netty Nicholson,
Puff Fairclough, Janey Bevan

Printed in Great Britain by
Butler and Tanner Ltd, Frome

CHEF SCHOOL

LEITH'S SCHOOL OF FOOD & WINE

FOREWORD BY

CAROLINE WALDEGRAVE

FOREWORD

BY CAROLINE WALDEGRAVE

Leith's School of Food and Wine opened in 1975 and has remained ever since a very successful school, training cooks for a large variety of jobs. During the 1990s the number and popularity of TV food programmes increased enormously. Delia Smith had opened the floodgates. Now not a day goes by without someone quizzing a famous chef or celebrity about the virtues of 25-year-old balsamic vinegar, the advantages of one risotto rice over another, or the best way to make a good sour-dough bread. I suppose it wasn't surprising that several TV companies began to approach us to say that they wanted to make a programme about Leith's School. Each company produced a proposal better than the last one. Laminated leaflets with seductive mock-up photographs were biked over on an almost daily basis showing what stars we could be.

I read the proposals and realized that life at Leith's would make a rather good soap – a culinary rival for *Neighbours*; but we resisted the temptation and settled back to our core business. Then yet another proposal arrived, this time from Sarah Caplin on behalf of Granada Television. Her idea was very different. She wanted to film at the school every day for the first term of the 3-term diploma and make the course accessible to viewers at home. After several discussions I agreed, for two reasons. First, I liked and trusted her commitment to education. Second, I thought that the idea of making what we offer available to a far wider audience was itself exciting and original. If food is to become ever more fashionable and popular, it is no good just knowing where to buy the best Dijon mustard and when to plant your rocket seeds. You need to be able to *cook*.

This book and the accompanying TV series is about real cooking, not just the latest fads. It may well be anathema to 'foodism'. It is a systematic attempt to teach the basic techniques. If you cook your way through this book you will be able to approach other cookery books, however exotic, knowing that you can cook the recipes they offer properly. If you want to make goat's cheese soufflés, sear scallops and serve them with rocket and balsamic vinegar, make a salad of grilled vegetables and serve them with Parmesan and chive crisps, make triple chocolate bavarois and garnish it with cages made from spun sugar and chocolate shapes made from tempered chocolate, you must know the basics first.

Students at Leith's who join us for Term 1 of the 3-term diploma will spend, in total, 45 days learning how to cook. Half their day will be spent watching a cookery demonstration or listening to a talk and half the day will be spent cooking. The TV series is only 24 programmes, so we have had to combine 2 days at Leith's into half an hour of television time. Each chapter of the book reflects one of the 24 programmes.

The presentation is almost in note form – the notes a student might take. If you follow the series and have this book to hand we will try to enable you to do a Leith's course of your own, although of course we can't give the constant hands-on advice that the school offers. The book will also stand on its own without the TV series – if you follow it you will cover all the basic techniques which have been derived from fundamental recipes. It is the recipes that have been chosen to illustrate the techniques throughout the book; in other words, if you want to know about whisking egg whites, simply look up meringues which is the fundamental

recipe chosen to illustrate the techniques and principles of cooking with egg whites.

Most of the recipes and much of the information in this book have been taken from *Leith's Cookery Bible* (written by Prue Leith and myself, published by Bloomsbury) but it has been put together in such a way as to stand as a cookery course in its own right. Cook your way from the beginning to the end and something that may once have been a chore can become a pleasure. Many of the recipes that were on the school curriculum in 1975 are in this book. Fashion in food may be as fluid as fashion in clothes, but the essential basic skills of the trade which are needed in order to create new and original ideas remain the same. This book has been written for both the enthusiastic amateur and the potential professional.

Enjoy cooking. Enjoy eating.

ACKNOWLEDGEMENTS

First and foremost I am grateful to Belinda Kassapian who has put this book together – she has had to do it in an enormous hurry and it has been done with skill and energy. Most of the information for the book existed in some form or other but Belinda has had to prise lecture notes from all of us at the school and turn ideas and student key fact sheets into something accessible for the general public. I am also very grateful to all the teachers, especially CJ Jackson, Alison Cavaliero, Emma Crowhurst, Eithne Swan, Sue Spaull and Puff Fairclough, who have allowed their demonstration notes to become more widely known. We have had contributions also from some of our guest lecturers and I am most grateful to Roz Denny, Peter Gordon and Jane Namazee for allowing us to publish their recipes.

Making the television programme to accompany this series was great fun and we all enjoyed working with executive producer Sarah Caplin, lighting cameraman Patrick Rowe, director Mandy Temple, series producer Rachel Goodwin, and sound recordists Simon Pinkerton and Dave Calvert. The school will seem empty without Patrick constantly eyeing us through the video-recorder.

The person without whom this book would not have been possible is the editor Helen Dore who had to cope with a constant stream of information and notes from all directions. She has put this book into the form that now exists and I am in awe of her talents.

I am also very grateful to Annie Simmonds, Emily Ackroyd and Judy van der Sande who have had to type many illegible manuscripts.

The food for the photographs was cooked beautifully by Belinda Kassapian assisted by Jacqui Thomas, Vivien Pidgeon and Netty Nicholson. The photographs were styled and taken by Patrick Rowe and Andrea Heselton. The action shots of the school were taken by Robin Allison Smith and Lawrence White with much useful advice from Puff Fairclough. I think they help to bring the school alive. Many thanks also to David Reynolds at Bloomsbury for supporting this project and to Monica Macdonald for co-ordinating it.

I am particularly grateful to Prue Leith, the founder of Leith's School – many of her words of wisdom have been incorporated into this text.

Staff of both past and present and some of our outside lecturers have contributed to this book. I cannot acknowledge them all, but I am grateful to Karen Sorensen for her section on nutrition, to Philippa Carr for her wine chapter and to Fiona Burrell, Sally Procter and Caroline Yates who have contributed recipes.

Finally, I would like to thank Carroll Associates who designed the book.

Caroline Waldegrave

CONTENTS

CONVERSION TABLES

The tables below are approximate, and do not conform in all respects to the conventional conversions, but we have found them convenient for cooking. Use either metric or imperial measurements. But do not mix the two.

WEIGHT

Imperial	Metric	Imperial	Metric
1/4 oz	7–8g	1/2 oz	15g
3/4 oz	20g	1oz	30g
2oz	55g	3oz	85g
4oz (1/4 lb)	110g	5oz	140g
6oz	170g	7oz	200g
8oz (1/2 lb)	225g	9oz	255g
10oz	285g	11oz	310g
12oz (3/4 lb)	340g	13oz	370g
14oz	400g	15oz	425g
16oz (1lb)	450g	1 1/4 lb	560g
1 1/2 lb	675g	2lb	900g
3lb	1.35kg	4lb	1.8kg
5lb	2.3kg	6lb	2.7kg
7lb	3.2kg	8lb	3.6kg
9lb	4.0kg	10lb	4.5kg

LIQUID MEASURES

Imperial	ml	fl oz
1 teaspoon	5	
2 scant tablespoons	28	
4 scant tablespoons	56	
1/4 pint (1 gill)	150	5
1/3 pint	190	6.6
1/2 pint	290	10
3/4 pint	425	15
1 pint	570	20
1 3/4 pints	1000 (1 litre)	35

USEFUL MEASUREMENTS

Measurement	Metric	Imperial
1 American cup	225ml	8fl oz
1 egg, size 3	56ml	2fl oz

1 egg white	28ml	1fl oz
1 rounded tablespoon flour	30g	1oz
1 rounded tablespoon cornflour	30g	1oz
1 rounded tablespoon caster sugar	30g	1oz
2 rounded tablespoons fresh breadcrumbs	30g	1oz
2 level teaspoons gelatine	8g	1/4oz

30g/1oz granular (packet) aspic sets 570ml/1 pint liquid.

15g/1/2oz powdered gelatine, or 3 leaves, will set 570ml/1 pint liquid. (However, in hot weather, or if the liquid is very acid, like lemon juice, or if the jelly contains solid pieces of fruit and is to be turned out of the dish or mould, 20g/3/4oz should be used.)

WINE QUANTITIES

Imperial	ml	fl oz
Average wine bottle	750	25
1 glass wine	100	3
1 glass port or sherry	70	2
1 glass liqueur	45	1

LENGTHS

Imperial	Metric
1/2in	1cm
1in	2.5cm
2in	5cm
6in	15cm
12in	30cm

OVEN TEMPERATURES

°C	°F	Gas mark	AMERICAN	AUSTRALIAN
70	150	1/4		
80	175	1/4	COOL	VERY SLOW
100	200	1/2		
110	225	1/2		
130	250	1	VERY SLOW	
140	275	1		SLOW
150	300	2	SLOW	
170	325	3	MODERATE	MODERATELY SLOW
180	350	4		
190	375	5	MODERATELY HOT	
200	400	6	FAIRLY HOT	MODERATE
220	425	7	HOT	MODERATELY HOT
230	450	8	VERY HOT	
240	475	8		HOT
250	500	9		
270	525	9	EXTREMELY HOT	
290	550	9		VERY HOT

INTRODUCTION TO THE SCHOOL AND THE BEGINNER'S CERTIFICATE
CHAPTER 1

Techniques Covered
Chopping an onion
Crushing garlic

This one-term autumn course gives students a full introduction to kitchen techniques and most styles of cooking. It is designed for the interested amateur and the potential professional. Students will become proficient in family and party cooking, learning to understand recipes, plan time efficiently and cook with relaxed confidence.

Fundamental cooking methods are practised thoroughly and on many days three-course meals are cooked, which are either eaten for lunch or taken home in the evening. The day is divided between the practical preparation and cooking of food and watching expert demonstrations. The dishes prepared are interesting and uncomplicated, balanced between classical cuisine and modern recipes.

❷ Cookery Terms
Allumette: Potato matchstick.
Brunoise: Evenly diced vegetables.
Jardinière: Vegetables cut into even batons.
Julienne: Vegetables or citrus rind cut into thin matchstick lengths or very fine shreds.
Mise en place: Putting into place – preparation done in advance prior to cooking, e.g. if parsley or onion needs to be chopped for more than one recipe, do them all at the same time.
Paysanne: Evenly cut, thin pieces of vegetable – triangular, circular or squared.
To turn: To shape vegetables, e.g. carrots or potatoes, to a small barrel shape. To cut mushrooms into a decorative spiral.

Timeplans
A timeplan can help you make the most of your time. By taking a little time to plan an order of work, you can maximize your output within a minimum timespan.

Students use the following guidelines to write a timeplan for each practical cookery session:

1. MENU
Write down what is to be cooked, with the recipe page numbers, and list the quantities of ingredients to be used.
2. COLLECT INGREDIENTS
Bracket the ingredients for each individual recipe together so that you can see at a glance which ingredient is for which recipe.
3. ORDER OF WORK
Note down the order in which the food is to be prepared and cooked. When a recipe has not

been attempted before, more detail can be added.

4. REMINDERS

Put in reminders to yourself to wash up, clear up and empty the rubbish bin – it is easy to forget these things, which make all the difference to successful and efficient cooking.

5. TIMINGS

Timing notes can be helpful, e.g. 'Put in the oven by 11.25 a.m.' *or* 'Don't put in the oven before 11.25 a.m.' Do not include timings for every single item, however.

6. HIGHLIGHTING

A highlighter pen can be used to remind you not to forget things that are in the oven, etc.

7. FINAL REMINDER

Remind yourself to collect dishes and plates for serving, and to warm them if necessary. Also include a list of everything to be served so that nothing is forgotten.

❶ Health and Safety

HYGIENE ADVICE

1. Wash hands thoroughly before cooking and when changing tasks. Use an alcohol-based gel if possible.
2. Avoid touching cooked food with your hands.
3. Keep separate chopping boards for raw foods and cooked foods or raw foods that require no cooking (e.g. salad). Rinse boards with cold water, then wash after preparing meat or fish. Scrape and sanitize boards regularly.
4. Never lick fingers or taste off wooden spoons.
5. Keep nails clean and short, avoiding nail varnish and excessive jewellery that might trap bacteria.
6. Keep hair tied up and away from the face.
7. Do not smoke.
8. Do not cook if you have diarrhoea.

SAFETY ADVICE

1. Keep a First Aid box at close hand.
2. Wipe up spills on the floor immediately.
3. Never leave glasses or knives in the sink.
4. Carry knives at your side with the blade pointing down.
5. Only touch electric plugs with dry hands and always turn off switches before removing or inserting plugs.

EQUIPMENT AND UTENSILS

When buying kitchen equipment, the basic rule for standard items is to buy the best that you can possibly afford. Good kitchen equipment will probably last for 15 years and is worth the investment. When buying small or specialist equipment that may be used once only, be as economical or extravagant as your purse dictates.

The following is not intended to be a complete list of the kitchen equipment available, but includes all the utensils that the home cook could possibly want, while excluding certain specialist items like preserving and cake-decorating equipment, barbecues, smokers and storage equipment.

Utensils

The following items of equipment are essential for any cook.

1 cook's knife with 18cm/7in blade

1 cook's knife with 7.5cm/3in blade

1 filleting knife with 14cm/5in blade
1 fruit knife
1 carbon-steel knife
1 palette knife
1 large saucepan 21cm/8in diameter with lid
1 medium saucepan 19cm/7in diameter
  with lid
1 small saucepan 12cm/5in diameter
1 frying pan with 20cm/8in diameter base
1 colander
2 wooden spoons
1 fish slice
1 rubber spatula
1 sieve (bowl strainer)
1 potato peeler
1 set of scales
1 measuring jug
1 pair poultry shears
3 gradated pudding basins
1 cheese grater
1 wooden board
1 roasting tin
1 salad bowl
1 whisk

KEEPING KNIVES SHARP

Sharp knives are essential for cutting, chopping and slicing.

Take a carbon steel in one hand and the knife in the other. Place the base of the blade of the knife at the base of the steel. Slide the blade of the knife along the top of the steel at a 30-degree angle until the tip of the knife reaches the tip of the steel. You have sharpened one side of the knife and will now need to repeat the action with the blade at the same angle but with the knife blade under the steel.

Repeat the above until the knife is sharp.

This technique takes some practice, and getting the pressure right is essential – too much or too little and the blade will remain blunt. The blade of a sharp knife will feel slightly rough.

FOOD PRESENTATION

If food looks delicious, people are predisposed to find that it tastes delicious. If you have spent a long time cooking, it is a shame just to dump the food on a plate. At Leith's School we have gradually developed a set of rules which can be used as guidelines when presenting food. Fashion may dictate the method – be it stylish nouvelle cuisine or chunky real food – but the guidelines are the same.

1. Keep it simple

Over-decorated food often looks messed about – no longer appetizing, but like an uncertain work of art. The more cluttered the plate, the less attractive it inevitably becomes.

2. Keep it fresh

Nothing looks more off-putting than tired food. Sprigs of herbs used for garnish should always be absolutely fresh. Pot herbs now widely available in supermarkets make this easy to ensure. Salad wilts when dressed in advance; sautéed potatoes become dull and dry when kept warm for hours, and whipped cream goes buttery in a warm room, so don't risk it.

3. Keep it relevant

A sprig of fresh watercress complements lamb cutlets nicely. The texture, taste and colour all do something for the lamb. But scratchy sprigs of parsley, though they might provide the colour, are unpleasant to eat. Gherkins cut into fans do nothing for salads, tomato slices do not improve the look of a platter of sandwiches – they rather serve to confuse and distract the eye. It is better by far to dish up a plate of chicken mayonnaise with a couple of suitable salads to provide the colour and contrast needed, than to decorate it with undressed tomato waterlilies or inedible baskets made out of lemon skins and filled with frozen sweetcorn.

4. Centre height

Dishes served on platters, such as chicken sauté, meringues, profiteroles or even a bean salad, are best given 'centre height' – arranged so the mound of food is higher in the middle with sides sloping down. Coat carefully and evenly with the sauce, if any. Do not overload serving platters with food, which makes dishing up difficult. Once breached, an over-large pile of food looks unattractive.

5. Contrasting rows

Biscuits, petits fours, little cakes and cocktail canapés all look good if arranged in rows, each row consisting of one variety, rather than dotted about. Pay attention to contrasting colour, taking care, say, not to put 2 rows of chocolate biscuits side by side, or 2 rows of white sandwiches.

6. Diagonal lines

Diamond shapes and diagonal lines are easier to achieve than straight ones. The eye is more conscious of unevenness in verticals, horizontals and rectangles.

7. Not too many colours

As with any design, it is easier to get a pleasing effect if the colours are controlled – say, just green and white, or just pink and green, or chocolate and coffee colours or even 2 shades of one colour. Coffee icing and hazelnuts give a cake an elegant look. Adding multi-coloured icings to a cake, or every available garnish to a salad, tends to look garish. There are exceptions of course: a colourful salad Niçoise can be as pleasing to the eye as a dish of candy-coated chocolate drops.

8. Contrasting the simple and the elaborate

If the dish or bowl is elaborately decorated, contrasting simple food tends to show it off better. A Victorian fruit epergne with ornate stem and silver carving will look stunning filled with fresh strawberries. Conversely, a plain white plate sets off pretty food design to perfection.

9. Uneven numbers

As a rule, uneven numbers of, say, rosettes of cream on a cake, baked apples in a long dish, or portions of meat on a platter look better than even numbers. This is especially true of small numbers. Five and three invariably look better than four, but there is little difference in effect between 11 and 12.

10. A generous look

Tiny piped cream stars, or sparsely dotted nuts, or mean-looking chocolate curls on a cake look amateurish and stingy.

11. Avoid clumsiness

On the other hand, the temptation to
cram the last spoonful of rice into the bowl, or squeeze the last slice of pâté on to the dish leads to a clumsy look, and can be daunting to the diner.

12. Overlapping

Chops, steaks, sliced meats, even rashers of bacon, look best evenly overlapping. This way, more of them can be fitted comfortably on the serving dish than if placed side by side.

13. Best side uppermost

Usually the side of a steak or a cutlet that is grilled or fried first looks the best, and should be placed uppermost. Bones are generally unsightly and, if they cannot be clipped off or removed, they should be tucked out of the way.

14. Individual plating

Until the advent of nouvelle cuisine in the 1970s it was considered a caterer's short-cut trick to plate dishes individually. Suddenly it became the only way to present food. When plating individually the same rules apply to presentation. Keep it simple and keep it relevant. We add two extra caveats. First, think of the rim of the plate as a picture frame: do not put any food on the 'frame'. Second, stick to your original idea. If a dish has been plated up and then changed, it will inevitably look messy

Chopping an onion

1. Slice the unpeeled onion lengthwise through the core, then peel both halves. Do not remove the root end, which will serve to hold the 'leaves' together when chopping.
2. Put one half of the onion flat on the board. Using a thin, sharp knife make horizontal parallel cuts towards the root, without cutting through to the root end.
3. Make a series of parallel vertical cuts down to the board, again avoiding the root end.
4. Finally, slice the onion, making the cuts at right angles to the previous two sets of cuts. Put the root end into the stock pot or chop it separately like parsley.

Crushing garlic

1. If using many cloves, split a head of garlic with a solid punch of the fist. (Put greaseproof paper on the board if you want to avoid having to scrub the board later.)
2. To skin a single clove, place it near the edge of a chopping board and lay the flat of a heavy knife over the clove with the handle overlapping the edge of the board. Use the palm of your hand to push down on the knife to crush the clove slightly and loosen the skin.
3. The papery skin of the half-crushed garlic clove can now be easily peeled off.
4. To make garlic paste, use the tip of a firm knife and a little salt to crush the clove, working from the tip to the root end.
5. Continue the process of crushing and mixing until the paste is smooth.

EGGS

CHAPTER 2

Techniques Covered
Beating eggs
Making an omelette
Making an emulsion oil-based sauce
Separating an egg

❓ Cookery Terms

Baveuse: Soft texture, used to describe the inside of a perfectly cooked omelette.
Boil: To heat a liquid to 100°C/200°F, at which point the liquid boils at a rapid, bubbling pace.
Emulsion: A stable suspension of fat and other liquid, e.g. mayonnaise, hollandaise.
Liaison: Ingredients, e.g. egg yolk and cream, for binding together and thickening sauce, soup or other liquid.
Napper: To coat, mask or cover, e.g. hardboiled eggs 'nappés' for Egg Mayonnaise (see Chapter 1).
Pass: To strain or push through a sieve.
Poach: To cook very gently in a barely moving liquid just below boiling point.
Prove (a pan): To make a frying pan non-stick: Heat a tablespoon of oil and salt in the pan to a high temperature. Tip out the excess, then rub the salt and oil around the pan with plenty of kitchen paper to make the surface of the pan smooth. Wipe away excess salt. Do not wash the pan before use.
Scald: Of milk: to heat until on the point of boiling, when some movement can be seen at the edges of the pan but there is no overall bubbling.
Season: Of food: to flavour, generally with salt and pepper. Of iron frying pans, griddles, etc.: to prepare new equipment for use by placing over high heat, generally coated with oil and sprinkled with salt. This prevents subsequent rusting and sticking.

Recipes
Crème Anglaise
Mayonnaise
Plain French omelette
Poached eggs on toast

Points to Remember
Nutrition
Eggs are very nutritious, containing protein, fat, vitamins A, B, D and E, iron and mineral salts.

Cooking

Eggs need to be cooked slowly at low temperatures to prevent the protein from toughening. Hardboiled eggs should really be hard-simmered eggs.

Boiling an egg

Eggs are often boiled, yet there is considerable confusion about the correct method of doing this. The easiest and most foolproof is as follows:

1. Prick the rounded end of the egg with an egg-pricker or a needle to allow air to escape.
2. Bring a pan of water to the boil. Have the eggs at room temperature. (If chilled, add 30 seconds to cooking time.)
3. Carefully lower the eggs into the water on a perforated spoon.
4. Time the cooking from the moment of immersion, keeping the water simmering or gently boiling, and not boiling too vigorously, which tends to crack the shells and toughen the whites. Three minutes will cook a medium-sized egg until the white is barely set; indeed, the white closest to the yolk will still be slightly jelly-like. Four minutes give a runny yolk and a just-set white. Six minutes give a well-set white and moist but runny yolk (set on the rim and thick but wet inside). Twelve minutes give a nicely hardboiled egg. Fifteen minutes will give a yellow-green rim to the dry yolk and make the white tough and unpalatable.

     Alternatively, to hardboil eggs, place in cold water, bring to the boil and simmer for 10 minutes.

Structure

An average egg weighs around 55g/2oz (yolk 25g/scant 1oz: white 30g/1oz). A brittle fragile shell contains a white and a yolk which are held in place by a chalaza (cord).

Shell
The shell is porous and pervious to air, water and smells. The colour of the shell is dependent on the colour of the chicken.
White
The albumen (egg white) is thick, viscous, transparent and made up of 88 per cent water and 9 per cent protein. When fresh it is very viscous and gelatinous. As the egg stales the white becomes runnier.
Yolk
Yolks are yellow in colour, varying in depth depending on the diet of the chicken. Yolks consist of 16 per cent protein, 30 per cent fat and 51 per cent water.

Storage
Store eggs in a refrigerator in the box in which they were bought to prevent transfers of tastes and smells. Always store eggs pointed end downwards so that the air pocket in the rounded end is uppermost. Use within 2 weeks of purchase.

Coagulation
Eggs coagulate at a low temperature so great care must be taken when cooking with them.
Temperatures at which coagulation occurs:

White:	60–65°C
Yolk:	62–65°C
Whole egg:	69°C
Whole egg with added milk and sugar (e.g. crème anglaise):	80–85°C
Curdling:	88°C

Uses of egg in cooking

Yolks:	Elasticity	e.g. cakes and soufflés
	Emulsion	e.g. mayonnaise
	Thickening	e.g. crème anglaise
	Enriching	e.g. rich shortcrust pastry
	Glazing	e.g. bread
Whites:	Setting	e.g. baked egg custard
	Lightening	e.g. chocolate mousse
	Raising	e.g. soufflés
	Whisking	e.g. meringues
	Clearing	e.g. aspic
Whole egg:	Binding	e.g. stuffing
	Glazing	e.g. pastry
	Sealing (glue)	e.g. fixing pastry

NOTE: The taste of a free-range egg is better than that of a battery egg. Free-range eggs are naturally more expensive, but are increasingly preferred to battery eggs.

Consumption of raw eggs or uncooked dishes made with them, such as home-made mayonnaise, mousse and ice cream, carries the risk of food poisoning. However, this is minimal if you use only the freshest free-range eggs, if the dishes are eaten as soon as possible after they are made, and if they are never left for more than 1 hour at room temperature.

Healthy people run little risk from eating cooked eggs, however they have been prepared – boiled, fried, scrambled or poached. Vulnerable people such as the elderly, the sick, babies, toddlers and pregnant women should only eat eggs that have been thoroughly cooked until both white and yolk are solid. They should avoid eating egg recipes which require light cooking, such as meringues and hollandaise sauce.

Lightly cooked egg dishes should be eaten as soon as possible after cooking and if not for immediate use should be stored in the refrigerator after cooling. Pasteurized egg, either dried or in frozen yolk form, which is free from harmful bacteria, is often used by caterers in these dishes and is available as a useful alternative in the home.

Separating an egg

You will need 2 clean bowls. Hold the egg in one hand and crack it sharply across the middle against one of the bowls. Gently pull the shell apart, keeping the yolk in one half and letting the white fall into the bowl. Carefully tip the yolk from one half of the shell to the other, letting the rest of the white fall into the bowl. Use the broken edge of the shell to cut away any of the white that won't fall. Drop the yolk into the other bowl.

Do not separate an egg over an already separated egg white in case the egg yolk splits. If some yolk does fall into the white, use a clean half-egg shell to scoop it out carefully – the white must not then be used for meringues.

CRÈME ANGLAISE (ENGLISH EGG CUSTARD)

290ml/¹/₂ pint milk
1 vanilla pod or a few drops
*   of vanilla essence*
2 egg yolks
1 tablespoon caster sugar

1. Heat the milk and vanilla pod, if using, and bring slowly to the boil.
2. Beat the yolks in a bowl with the sugar. Remove the vanilla pod, and pour the milk on to the egg yolks, stirring steadily. Mix well and return to the pan.
3. Stir over a low heat until the mixture thickens sufficiently to coat the back of a spoon (about 5 minutes). Do not boil. Strain into a chilled bowl.
4. Add the vanilla essence, if using.

MAYONNAISE

2 egg yolks
salt and freshly ground white pepper
1 teaspoon dry English mustard
290ml/1/2 pint olive oil, or 150ml/1/4 pint
each olive and salad oil
a squeeze of lemon juice
1 tablespoon white wine vinegar

1. Put the yolks into a bowl with a pinch of salt and the mustard and beat well with a wooden spoon.
2. Add the oil, literally drop by drop, beating all the time. The mixture should be very thick by the time half the oil is added.
3. Beat in the lemon juice.
4. Resume pouring in the oil, going more quickly now, but alternating the dribbles of oil with small quantities of vinegar.
5. Season to taste with salt and pepper.
NOTE: If the mixture curdles, another egg yolk should be beaten in a separate bowl, and the curdled mixture beaten into it drop by drop.

PLAIN FRENCH OMELETTE
SERVES 1
3 eggs
salt and freshly ground black pepper
a pinch of freshly grated Parmesan cheese
(optional)
1 tablespoon cold water
15g/1/2 oz butter

1. Break the eggs into a bowl and with a fork mix in the seasoning, Parmesan cheese and water.
2. Melt the butter in a heavy 15cm/6in omelette pan and swirl it around so that the bottom and sides are coated. When foaming, pour in the egg mixture.
3. Hold the pan handle in your left hand and move it gently back and forth over the heat. At the same time, move the mixture slowly, scraping up large creamy flakes of egg mixture. As you do this some of the liquid egg from the middle of the omelette will run to the sides of the pan. Tilt the pan to help this process. Leave over the heat until the bottom has set and the top is creamy. Remove from the heat.

4. With a fork or palette knife fold the nearside edge of the omelette over to the centre and then flick the whole omelette over on to a warmed plate with the folded edges on the underside. Alternatively, fold the omelette in two and slide it on to the plate.
NOTE: Grated cheese, fresh chopped herbs, fried mushrooms or other flavourings can be added to the basic omelette mixture.

POACHED EGGS ON TOAST
SERVES 4
4 very fresh cold eggs
4 slices of fresh toast, buttered
salt and freshly ground black pepper

1. Fill a large saucepan with water and bring to simmering point.
2. Crack an egg into a cup and tip into the pan, holding the cup as near to the water as possible.
3. Raise the temperature so that the water bubbles gently. Stir the water with a wooden spoon to create a small 'whirlpool'.
4. With a slotted spoon, draw the egg white close to the yolk.
5. Poach each egg for 2–3 minutes.
6. Lift out with the slotted spoon, drain on absorbent kitchen paper while still on the spoon and trim the egg whites if they are very ragged at the edges.
7. Place each egg on a piece of toast and sprinkle with salt and pepper. Serve immediately.

Causes of Failure
Curdled crème anglaise: Milk allowed to boil.
Curdled mayonnaise: Oil added too quickly, more vinegar or lemon juice needed.
Black ring round the yolk of a hardboiled egg: Egg overcooked or not cooled down quickly enough after cooking.
Rubbery omelette: Overcooked egg.
Watery liquid separating from scrambled egg: Overcooked egg.
Poached egg not holding its shape in the water: Stale egg or water boiling too fast.

PASTRY I
CHAPTER 3

Techniques Covered
Rubbing fat into flour
Lining a flan ring
Covering a pie dish
Baking blind

❷ Cookery Terms
Bake blind: To bake a flan case while empty. In order to prevent the sides from falling in
or the base bubbling up, the pastry is usually lined with paper and filled with 'blind beans'.
See below.
Blind beans: Dried beans, peas, rice and pasta used to fill pastry cases temporarily
during baking.
Relax or rest: Of pastry: to set aside in a cool place to allow the gluten (which will have
expanded during rolling) to contract. This lessens the danger of shrinking in the oven.
Of batters: to set aside to allow the starch cells to swell, giving a lighter result when cooked.
Sweat: To cook gently, usually in butter or oil, but sometimes the food's own juices,
without frying or browning.

Recipes
Rich shortcrust pastry

Quiche Lorraine
Apple and orange crumble

Points to Remember
The Ingredients
FATS
Butter: Gives a crisp, rich shortcrust pastry with excellent flavour.
Solid margarine: Gives a similar result that is slightly less rich and flavourful.
Lard: Gives very short but rather tasteless pastry.
FLOUR
Plain (all-purpose) flour is normally used. Wholemeal flour produces a delicious
nutty-flavoured crust, but is more absorbent than white flour and will need more liquid,
which makes it harder and heavier. For this reason, a mixture of wholemeal and white flour,
usually half and half, is generally used to make 'wholemeal' pastry.
    The flour must be sifted, even if it has no lumps in it, to incorporate air and give the
pastry lightness.
LIQUIDS
The less liquid used in pastry-making the better.
Water: Gives the pastry crispness and firmness. Too much makes the pastry easy to handle
but gives a hard crust that shrinks in the oven. Too little makes the pastry difficult to handle
and dry to taste.
Egg or egg white: Gives a firm but not hard crust.
Egg yolk: Gives a rich, soft and crumbly crust.

The rubbing-in method

The fat is rubbed into sifted flour and other dry ingredients with the fingertips, then the liquid ingredient is added to bind the pastry together.

RUBBING IN

1. Keep everything as cool as possible – if the fat melts the finished pastry may be tough.
2. The fat must be firm and cold but not hard.
3. Cut the fat into tiny pieces with a small knife and floured fingers.
4. Rub in the fat using your fingertips.
5. Keep your hands about 25cm/10in above the bowl, dropping the floury flakes from a height – this cools the fat and aerates it, making the finished pastry lighter.
6. Shake the bowl regularly so that big unrubbed pieces of fat come to the surface.
7. Stop rubbing in when the mixture resembles very coarse – not fine – breadcrumbs.

ADDING LIQUID

1. Add only as much water as is needed to hold the pastry together.
2. Sprinkle the water, 1 teaspoonful at a time, over as large a surface as possible.
3. Mix with a table knife so it is handled as little as possible. Stop mixing as soon as the mixture holds together in lumps.
4. Lightly flour your hands and quickly and gently gather the dough into a ball, rolling it around the bowl to pick up crumbs.

RELAXING AND ROLLING OUT

This allows the cells to swell and absorb the liquid evenly. The pastry will not shrink drastically or unevenly.

1. Chill the pastry for 30 minutes before   rolling it out, or at least before baking.
2. Wrap it in clingfilm to prevent it from drying out.

3. Lightly dust the work surface with flour – too much can alter the proportion of flour to other ingredients.

Lining a flan ring

1. Roll out the pastry on a floured surface to a round 5cm/2in larger than the flan ring. Lay the rolling pin gently on the pastry and fold one side over it.
2. Lift up the pastry on the rolling pin. Brush off excess flour.
3. Drape the pastry carefully over the flan ring by turning the rolling pin slowly to allow it to fall gently over the ring. Do not let the rolling pin touch the ring or it may cut through the pastry. Do not stretch the pastry or it will shrink back once in the oven.
4. Ease the pastry into the corners with the back of a finger.
5. Alternatively, you can use a small ball of pastry dough to push it well into the corners.
6. Roll the pin over the top of the flan ring to cut off the excess pastry.
7. Gently dislodge the pastry edge with a finger if it sticks to the flan ring – this will prevent it sticking in the oven.

Covering a pie dish

1. Roll out the pastry on a floured board. Cut a band of pastry wider than the rim of the pie dish.
2. Wet the rim and press the band on all the way round. Brush with water.
3. Lay over the rolled-out pastry. Trim the edges, press down firmly and mark with a fork, or press into a frilly edge with fingers and thumb.
4. Shape pastry trimmings into leaves. Brush top of pie with water and deco rate with the pastry leaves.

Baking blind

Line the raw pastry case with a piece of kitchen foil or a double sheet of greaseproof paper and fill it with baking blind beans. This is to prevent the pastry bubbling up during cooking. Bake in the oven preheated to 200°C/400°F/gas mark 6. When the pastry is half cooked (about 15 minutes) the blind beans can be removed and the empty pastry case further dried out in the oven. The beans can be used indefinitely.

RICH SHORTCRUST PASTRY
170g/6oz plain flour
a pinch of salt
100g/3 1/2 oz butter
1 egg yolk
very cold water to mix

1. Sift the flour with the salt into a large bowl.
2. Rub in the butter until the mixture resembles coarse breadcrumbs.
3. Mix the egg yolk with 2 tablespoons water and add to the mixture.
4. Mix to a firm dough, first with a knife, and finally with one hand. It may be necessary to add more water, but the pastry should not be too damp. (Though crumbly pastry is more difficult to handle, it produces a shorter, lighter result.)
5. Chill, wrapped, in the refrigerator for 30 minutes before using. Or allow to relax after rolling out but before baking.

NOTE: To make sweet rich shortcrust pastry, mix in 1 tablespoon caster sugar once the fat has been rubbed into the flour.

QUICHE LORRAINE
SERVES 2
110g/4oz flour quantity rich shortcrust pastry (see above)
For the filling
1/2 small onion, finely chopped
55g/2oz rindless bacon, diced
7.5g/1/4 oz butter
5 tablespoons milk
5 tablespoons single cream
1 egg
1 egg yolk
30g/1oz strong Cheddar or Gruyère cheese, grated
salt and freshly ground black pepper

1. Roll out the pastry and use to line a 15cm/6in flan ring. Refrigerate for about 45 minutes to relax – this prevents shrinkage during baking.
2. Preheat the oven to 200°C/400°F/gas mark 6. Bake the pastry case blind (see page 22) and remove from the oven.
3. Fry the onion and bacon gently in the butter. When cooked but not coloured, drain well.
4. Mix together the milk, cream, egg and egg yolk. Add the onion, bacon and cheese. Season with salt and pepper (the bacon and cheese are both salty, so be careful not to overseason).
5. Reduce the oven temperature to 150°C/300°F/gas mark 2.
6. Pour the mixture into the prepared flan case. Bake the flan in the centre of the preheated oven for about 40 minutes.
7. Remove the flan ring and bake for a further 5 minutes to allow the pastry to brown. The top of the quiche should be pale and set.
8. Serve hot or cold.

APPLE AND ORANGE CRUMBLE
SERVES 4
900g/2lb cooking apples
3 oranges, segmented (see page 39)
3 tablespoons demerara sugar
a pinch of ground cinnamon
For the crumble
170g/6oz plain flour
a pinch of salt
110g/4oz butter
55g/2oz granulated sugar

1. Peel and core the apples. Cut into chunks. Mix with the orange segments and their juice. Add the sugar and cinnamon. Tip into an ovenproof dish.
2. Preheat the oven to 200°C/400°F/gas mark 6. Preheat a baking sheet.
3. Sift the flour with the salt into a bowl. Rub in the butter and when the mixture resembles coarse breadcrumbs mix in the sugar. Sprinkle the mixture over the apples and oranges.
4. Bake on the baking sheet for 45 minutes or until hot and slightly browned on top.

NOTE: If using wholemeal flour for the crumble topping, use 140g/5oz melted butter. Instead of rubbing it into the flour, mix briskly with a knife.

Causes of Failure
Shrinkage: Over-handled, stretched too much during rolling, not chilled sufficiently, not cooked on top shelf.
Tough texture: Too much water, over-handled, heavy-handed rolling.
Greasy appearance: Over-worked, hot hands, cooked at too low a temperature.
Grey appearance: Not baked blind for long enough, or not covered well in the refrigerator.

VEGETABLES AND RICE
CHAPTER 4

Techniques Covered
Preparing and cooking vegetables
Cooking potatoes
Cooking rice

❷ **Cookery Terms**
Blanch: Originally to whiten by boiling, e.g. to boil sweetbreads or brains briefly to remove traces of blood, or to boil almonds to make the brown skin easy to remove, leaving the nuts white. Now commonly used to mean parboiling, as in blanching vegetables prior to freezing, or pre-cooking so that they have only to be reheated before serving.
Concasser: To chop roughly.
Croûtons: Small evenly sized cubes of fried bread used as a soup garnish and occasionally in other dishes.
Refresh: To hold boiled green vegetables under cold running water, or to immerse them immediately in cold water to prevent their cooking further in their own steam, and set the colour.

Recipes
Mashed potatoes
Coleslaw with raisins and walnuts
Caesar salad

Vichy carrots
Warm basmati salad with vegetable ribbons
Nori sushi with Thai jasmine rice

PREPARING VEGETABLES
Always wash vegetables before preparing them. Vegetables are an excellent source of vitamins and minerals but these can easily be leached if the vegetables are cut up too far in advance of cooking, if they are left to soak in cold water (vitamin C particularly is lost in this way), if they are cut up with a blunt knife, which damages the cells, or if they are cooked with bicarbonate of soda in an attempt to preserve colour.

Fresh green vegetables
BLANCHING AND REFRESHING
This method of cooking vegetables is commonly used in restaurants where some advance preparation is vital. It is worth doing when coping with a large selection of vegetables.
BOILING
Boil the vegetables separately: bring the water to a good boil and drop in the vegetables. Use enough water to barely cover them and add 1 teaspoon salt for each 570ml/1 pint water. Boil as rapidly as you dare (delicate vegetables like broccoli can break up if too rapidly boiled). As soon as they are tender, drain them and serve or rinse under cold running water to prevent further cooking and to set the colour. This is called refreshing. Just before serving, toss the vegetables separately in melted butter over a good heat.
    As the cooking liquid contains most of the vitamins and minerals it should, if possible, be preserved and used for soups or sauces.
SWEATING
Put the prepared vegetables into a heavy saucepan with 1 tablespoon butter or oil. Cover

tightly with a lid. Cook over a very low heat. Shake the pan frequently until the vegetables are tender. Season with salt and dish up.

STEAMING

Steaming in a proper steamer is an excellent method of cooking root vegetables, but is less successful with green ones as their bright colour is sometimes lost. It is nutritionally superior to boiling – although vegetables take longer to cook, there is no leaching of vitamins or minerals into the water.

STIR-FRYING

This cooking method, much beloved of Chinese cooks, is excellent for green vegetables. It preserves vitamins and minerals, and the vegetables remain bright in colour. The disadvantage is that you must stand over the vegetables while they cook, but cooking time is short.

Slice the vegetables as thinly as you can, then put into a large deep-sided frying pan (a Chinese wok is perfect) with a splash of oil. Toss the vegetables in the hot oil over a fierce heat. Shake the pan, and stir and turn the vegetables continually until they are just tender. Sprinkle with salt and serve.

Fresh non-green vegetables

BOILING

Put the vegetables into cold salted water and bring slowly to the boil. Cook, covered, until completely tender. With the exception of carrots (which are good with a bit of bite to them), root vegetables should be cooked until tender. Drain and brush with melted butter if required. New potatoes are usually put into boiling salted water.

REFRESHING

It is sometimes advisable to rinse carrots briefly in cold water after cooking, as this sets the bright colour, but it is not necessary.

SWEATING OR HALF-STEAMING

Slice the vegetables fairly thickly. Cook them slowly in butter or oil in a covered saucepan. They will absorb more fat than green vegetables. This is a very good method for mushrooms.

STEAMING

This is excellent for all root vegetables, particularly for large potatoes, which might otherwise break up while boiling.

POTATOES

In Britain potatoes are often classified according to when they are harvested:

First earlies (new): end May–July

Second earlies (new): August–March

Main crop: September–May

The growing season for early potatoes is short. They are harvested when the tubers are immature; the skin is not 'set' and can be rubbed off easily, and they should be eaten soon after purchase as they do not keep well.

Main crop varieties are lifted when fully mature and will keep through to next year's harvest if correctly stored.

The three most popular varieties of main crop potatoes grown in Britain are, in descending order, Maris Piper, Record and Cara.

Buying and storing

Look for potatoes that are well-shaped, firm and free from blemishes. Avoid those with green patches as these indicate exposure to light and the production of toxins (non-deadly poisons) under the skin. Buy new potatoes in small quantities as they do not keep well.

Always remove potatoes from the plastic bag in which they have been sold.

Main crop potatoes will keep well if they are stored, unwashed, in a dark, cool, frost-free, airy place away from smells. Light turns potatoes green, and warmth and dampness can cause them to sprout, shrivel and rot.

RICE

by Roz Denny

Rice is an excellent food for a well-balanced, healthy diet. For a start, it is a complex carbohydrate starchy food, and as such one of the foods nutritionists and doctors tell us we must eat more of. In fact, half our daily calorie intake should come from starchy foods such as rice. A good 55g/2oz portion (uncooked weight) which swells to 150g/5oz cooked weight provides approximately 170 calories, with useful amounts of B group vitamins, a small amount of easy-to-digest protein, the minerals iron and zinc and useful amounts of fibre. The starchy carbohydrate in rice does not give the body immediate energy. Rather, the energy is released slowly into the bloodstream. In other words, it is better-value energy and keeps us going longer. Rice is therefore an invaluable food for athletes and sportsmen and women.

Cooking methods

Allow 55g/2oz uncooked rice per person

Choosing the right grain for a dish is the secret of successful rice cooking. It is hard to make a pilaf with a risotto rice, or a risotto with an easy-cook rice. Also, many grains need differing amounts of water and cooking times: most brown rice, for example, needs considerably longer cooking than white. The best guide is to follow instructions on the pack. There are four main methods (see below) of cooking rice, apart from risotto and pudding rices: The first method, the open-pan, is quick and easy and so ideal for inexperienced cooks. Note that all rice benefits from a standing time of about 5 minutes after cooking and draining so that excess water is absorbed back into the grain. Allow for this before serving. In addition, basmati rice benefits from rinsing and sometimes a little pre-soaking. This is not essential but does give a lighter, more traditional result (see box below).

1. OPEN-PAN/FAST BOILING

Suitable for basmati, easy-cook basmati, brown basmati and other brown rices, long-grain, wild rices and wild rice blends.

Allow 1.2 litres/2 pints water and 1 teaspoon salt for each 110g/4oz rice.
Bring a saucepan of water to a rolling boil. Add salt, then stir in the rice. Return to a medium boil and cook for the following times:

- *Basmati and Thai rices*: 10 minutes
- *American long-grain*: 12 minutes
- *Easy-cook basmati and easy-cook long-grain*: 15 minutes
- *Brown basmati and wild rice with white rice blends*: 20–25 minutes
- *Brown long-grain rices*: 25–30 minutes
- *Wild rice*: 40–50 minutes

Drain in a large sieve and rinse in hot water. Allow to stand in the sieve for 5 minutes before forking through with melted butter or oil.

2. COVERED PAN/ABSORPTION METHOD

Suitable for Thai rice, sushi rice, basmati (rinsed), brown basmati, brown rice, wild rice, wild rice with white rice blends, easy-cook rices. A measured amount of water is absorbed during cooking, so there is no need to drain. Follow the instructions below according to the rice variety.

Put rice, water and salt to taste into a saucepan. Bring to the boil, stir once, then cover and lower the heat to a gentle simmer. Do not lift the lid.

After the calculated cooking time (see below) remove from the heat, still uncovered, and allow to stand 5 minutes before forking through with butter or oil.

For each (225ml/8fl oz) cup of rice allow:
- *Thai and sushi rice*: 1¼ cups water. Cook for 10–12 minutes.
- *Basmati rice*: 1½ cups water. Cook for 10–12 minutes.
- *Brown basmati, wild rice with white rice blends, easy-cook rices*: 2 cups water. Cook for 20–25 minutes.
- *Wild rice and brown long-grain rice*: 2½–3 cups water. Cook for 40–50 minutes.

3. STEAMING/MICROWAVE

Suitable for basmati, long-grain and Thai rices.

Rinse first if using basmati. Par-boil in plenty of boiling salted water for 5 minutes. Drain in a sieve and rinse under cold running water for a good minute or two. Drain again.

Place in a non-metallic heatproof bowl. Cover with clingfilm and vent the side very slightly.

Microwave on full power (100%) for 5 minutes (Thai and basmati), 7 minutes for long-grain rice.

Allow to stand (still covered) for 5 minutes before forking through with butter or oil.

4. PILAF

Suitable for basmati, easy-cook basmati and long-grain rices. Rinse first if using basmati.

Fry 1 chopped onion and 2 crushed cloves of garlic in 3 tablespoons sunflower or olive oil for 5 minutes.

Stir in 250g/9oz rice and cook gently for 1–2 minutes, stirring occasionally.

Pour in 450ml/¾ pint stock or water for basmati, 600ml/1 pint for other rices.

Add salt and pepper to taste. Bring to the boil, then cover and simmer gently for 10 minutes for basmati, 12–14 minutes for long-grain rices and 20 minutes for easy-cook basmati.

Allow to stand, still covered, for 5 minutes, then fork through with butter or oil.

5. COOKING PERFECT BASMATI RICE

Good basmati rice is light and fragrant with a delicate texture. High-quality basmati is sold in perfect condition free from grit with a pronounced aroma and few broken grains. The name 'basmati' means fragrant in Hindi. There are a number of ways of cooking basmati.

The *Quick and Easy* way to cook basmati is in a large pan of boiling water for 10 minutes, then drain and rinse in boiling water.

But the best way to bring out the famed basmati charm and true aroma is the *Combination Method*. First, you need to rinse and soak the rice, then par-boil in bubbling water, then finish cooking by steaming, either in a saucepan or microwave oven.

Rinsing and soaking: Not for hygiene reasons but to bring out the best in the grain in terms of lightness and delicacy. Rinsing is done to remove any fine surface starch.

The traditional Indian and Middle Eastern way of rinsing is to pour the basmati into a large bowl. Run cold water over the grains, shaking them with your hand, then tip the water out. The wet grains remain at the bottom. Repeat this four more times. With practice, you can do this very quickly. Soak the grains for 20 minutes in the last rinsing water, then drain in a sieve, not a colander.

1. Boiling: Put a large pan of salted water on to boil. When the water starts to roll, add the rice. Stir once, return to the boil and cook for 5 minutes. Drain in a sieve and hold the rice under cold running water. Drain again. If liked, the rice can be stored in the refrigerator at this stage ready for reheating later.

2. Steaming: Put the drained rice into a saucepan with a little heated oil on the bottom. Place a well-fitting lid on top, wrapped in a clean tea towel, if liked. Cook over high heat for 1–2 minutes, then turn the heat down to the lowest setting and cook for 15 minutes.

3. Serving: Remove the pan from the heat but do not lift the lid or you will let out precious steam. Leave to stand for 5 minutes, then fork the rice through gently with some oil or melted butter and serve hot and steaming. A few chopped fresh herbs may be stirred in too.

MASHED POTATOES
SERVES 4
675g/1¹/₂lb potatoes, peeled
salt and freshly ground black pepper
about 100ml/3¹/₂fl oz milk
55g/2oz butter
a little freshly grated nutmeg

1. Boil the potatoes in salted water until tender. Drain thoroughly.
2. Push the potatoes through a sieve or mouli. Return them to the dry saucepan. Heat carefully, stirring to allow the potato to steam-dry.
3. Push the potato to one side of the pan. Set the exposed part of the pan over direct heat and pour in the milk. Add the butter, salt, pepper and nutmeg. Tilt the pan to allow the milk to boil and the butter to melt.

4. When the milk is boiling, or near it, beat it into the potato. Check the seasoning.
NOTE: This recipe is for soft mashed potatoes. If you want a stiff consistency, add less milk.

COLESLAW WITH RAISINS AND WALNUTS
SERVES 4
225g/8oz firm white cabbage, very finely shredded
3 small carrots, coarsely grated
3 tablespoons mayonnaise (see page 20)
1 teaspoon French mustard
1 teaspoon sugar
salt and freshly ground black pepper
1 tablespoon raisins
1 tablespoon chopped walnuts

1. Toss the cabbage and carrots together in a bowl.

2. Mix the mayonnaise with all the remaining ingredients and combine it with the cabbage and carrots.

NOTE: Mayonnaise for coleslaw is delicious made with cider vinegar.

CAESAR SALAD

SERVES 4

2 large cloves garlic, slivered
150ml/¼ pint olive oil
2 tablespoons lemon juice
pinch of dry English mustard
freshly ground black pepper
1 egg, boiled for 1 minute
2 anchovy fillets, finely chopped
2 slices of bread, crusts removed, cubed
1 cos lettuce
2 tablespoons freshly grated Parmesan cheese

1. Mix the garlic with the oil. Leave to stand for 10 minutes. Strain off 3 tablespoons of the oil to make the dressing.
2. Add it to the lemon juice, mustard, pepper and egg. Whisk well. Add the anchovies.
3. Pour the remaining oil and the garlic into a frying pan. There should be at least 1cm/½ in oil. Heat slowly. When the garlic shreds begin to sizzle, remove, add the bread cubes and fry, turning frequently with a fish slice or spoon, until the croûtons are crisp and brown. Using a perforated spoon, lift out the croûtons and drain and allow to cool on absorbent kitchen paper.
4. Toss the lettuce in the dressing. Sprinkle over the croûtons and cheese.

VICHY CARROTS

SERVES 4

560g/1¼ lb carrots
2 teaspoons butter
½ teaspoon salt
1 teaspoon caster sugar
freshly ground black pepper
2 teaspoons mixed chopped fresh mint
and parsley

1. Peel the carrots and cut them into sticks or even-sized barrel shapes; or if they are very young leave them whole.
2. Put all the remaining ingredients except

the pepper and herbs into a saucepan, half-cover them with water and boil until the water has almost evaporated and the carrots are tender. Then turn down the heat and allow the carrots to brown slightly in the remaining butter and sugar, watching to make sure they do not burn.

3. Season with pepper and mix in the herbs.
NOTE: It is important not to oversalt the water. When the water has evaporated the entire quantity of salt will remain with the carrots.

WARM BASMATI SALAD WITH VEGETABLE RIBBONS
by Roz Denny
SERVES 4
2 medium carrots, peeled
15cm/6in length daikon/mooli radish, peeled
15cm/6in length cucumber, washed
about 6 large radicchio, washed and dried
3 salad onions, peeled and trimmed
sea salt and freshly ground black pepper
250g/9oz top-quality basmati rice
For the dressing
2 tablespoons olive or groundnut oil
3 tablespoons soy sauce, preferably light
2 tablespoons rice wine vinegar
1 fat clove garlic, crushed
small knob fresh root ginger, grated finely
2 teaspoons sesame oil
1 teaspoon clear honey
2 teaspoons toasted sesame or black cumin seeds

1. Prepare the vegetables. Slice the peeled carrots and daikon/mooli into long thin ribbons using a vegetable peeler. Wash the cucumber and slice thinly.

2. Cut the cores from the radicchio, roll up the leaves and slice into thin shreds. Cut the salad onions into thin strips. Mix all the vegetables in a bowl, season well and chill.

3. Boil the basmati for 10 minutes in a large pan of salted water, timing from when the water returns to the boil after the rice has been stirred in. Drain and allow the rice to rest for 5 minutes.

4. Meanwhile, shake all the dressing ingredients together in a screw top jar. Then toss into the rice as it cools. Mix the chilled ribbons of vegetables into the hot, dressed rice and serve in a large attractive bowl. Sprinkle with the sesame or cumin seeds and serve as soon as possible.

NORI SUSHI WITH THAI JASMINE RICE
by Roz Denny
Thai jasmine rice, with its fragrance and light sticky grains, makes simply stunning Japanese style sushi, ideal for canapés at a drinks party. Nori and Konbu seaweeds and rice wine vinegar can be bought from specialist food stores.
MAKES 40-50
200g/7oz Thai jasmine rice
450ml/³/4 pint water
2 'knots' Oden Konbu seaweed
¹/2 cucumber
2 eggs
1 tablespoon light soy sauce
freshly ground black pepper
a little oil, for frying
6–8 sheets nori seaweed
For the dressing
2 tablespoons rice wine vinegar
1 ¹/2 tablespoons caster sugar
1 teaspoon sea salt
For dipping
dark soy sauce

1. Boil the rice with the water and konbu either in a rice cooker or according to the covered pan method on the pack instructions. Stand, still covered, for 15 minutes, remove the konbu, stir in the dressing ingredients and cool until tepid.

2. Cut the cucumber into long thin pencil lengths. Beat the eggs with the soy sauce and pepper and make a flat omelette using a little oil. Cut into strips.

3. Lay a sushi mat or thick napkin out on the worktop. If you have a gas cooker, pass a sheet of nori quickly over the flames. Lay it on the mat and spoon a layer of rice over two-thirds of the sheet, up to the edges.

4. Arrange two cucumber strips and one omelette strip horizontally along the rice, then roll up firmly like a Swiss roll, using the sushi mat or napkin to help you.

5. Press the roll to compress, then unroll the mat. Make up the rest of the sushi rolls. Cut each roll crossways into 5–6 pieces and arrange on black or dark plain plates or trays. Put soy sauce in a little dish and serve on the same plate for dipping.

Causes of Failure

Gluey mashed potato: Too much potato pushed through the sieve at once, overbeaten.

Grey-looking mashed potato: Cold milk stirred into the potato instead of hot.

Oily croûtons: Fat not hot enough when frying, not drained on kitchen paper immediately after frying or sprinkled with salt to absorb excess oil.

Collapsed salad leaves: Salad dressed too early.

SETTING METHODS AND NURSERY PUDDINGS
CHAPTER 5

Techniques Covered
Using gelatine (powdered and leaf)
Using eggs and chocolate to set a mousse
Melting chocolate
Whisking egg whites
Segmenting an orange
Degorging a cucumber

❷ Cookery Terms

Bain-marie: A roasting tin half-filled with hot water in which terrines, custards, etc. stand while cooking. The food is protected from direct fierce heat and cooks in a gentle, steamy atmosphere. Also a large container that will hold a number of pans standing in hot water, used to keep soups, sauces, etc. hot without further cooking.

Degorge: To extract the juices from meat, fish or vegetables, generally by salting then soaking or washing. Usually done to remove indigestible or strong-tasting juices.

Fold: To mix with a gentle lifting motion, rather than to stir vigorously. The aim is to avoid beating out air while mixing.

Loosen: To stir a spoonful of whisked egg white into a mixture before folding in the majority. This allows the main bulk of the whisked egg white to be incorporated more easily, thus avoiding loss of volume.

Purée: Liquidized, sieved or finely mashed fruit or vegetables.

Slake: To mix flour, arrowroot, cornflour or custard powder to a thin paste with a small quantity of cold water.

Zest: The skin of an orange or lemon, used to give flavour. It is very thinly pared without any of the bitter white pith.

Recipes

Cucumber mousse
Chocolate mousse
Orange jelly and orange segments
Queen's pudding

Meringues (Swiss meringues)
Bread and butter pudding
Apples and blackberries in cassis syrup

GELATINE

Gelatine, available powdered and in leaves, is obtained from the bone and connective tissue of certain animals. Connective tissue is a physical harness of muscles, made up of three basic proteins – collagen, elastin and reticulin. Collagen is converted by low slow cooking into gelatine.

Acids weaken the setting powder of gelatine, so when following a recipe such as lemon soufflé an increased amount of gelatine is called for.

Using powdered gelatine
1. Pour a small amount of liquid into a saucepan.
2. Slowly sprinkle on the required amount of gelatine.
3. Leave the gelatine to 'sponge' i.e. swell, for 3–5 minutes.
4. Melt the gelatine over a very low heat. Do not allow to boil. Do not stir. It should become clear and warm.
5. Pour into the mousse/soufflé base. Stir briskly: if the base is too cold the gelatine can set quickly in streaks. Gelatine is generally poured from a height to help cool it down.
6. When the mousse has reached setting-point other light ingredients such as cream or whisked egg whites can be added. If the cream or egg whites are added too early the base mix will not support their weight and the soufflé will separate into layers. If the cream or whites are added too late the mixture has to be beaten hard to incorporate the additions and the result is heavy.

Setting-point is when the base mixture will support its own weight and when a spoon is drawn through the mixture the bottom of the mixing bowl will remain visible for 2–3 seconds.

Using leaf gelatine
1. Soak the leaves in a small amount of cold water for 5 minutes.
2. Dissolve over a gentle heat until liquid.
3. Use as powdered gelatine.

GELATINE CONVERSION TABLE

1 level teaspoon	5–7g	1/4oz	1 1/2 leaves
3 level teaspoons	15g	1/2oz	3 leaves
6 level teaspoons	30g	1oz	6 leaves

AGAR AGAR

Agar agar, a seaweed, is cooked, pressed, freeze-dried and then flaked or powdered for use as a setting agent in vegetarian cooking. 1 teaspoon powder has the setting power of 1 tablespoon flakes. Agar agar's setting qualities are affected by the nature of the food to which it is added, and so required quantities will vary, but as a general rule 1 teaspoon powder or 1 tablespoon flakes will set 570ml/1 pint, and twice the quantity should be used to set a firm jelly.

Using agar agar

1. Soak the agar agar in the full liquid measurement specified in the recipe, in a saucepan; leave powder for 5 minutes, flakes for 10–15 minutes.
2. Dissolve the agar agar in the pan over a medium heat, stirring continuously. Turn up the heat and boil for 2–3 minutes, continuing to stir to prevent sticking. Use as required. (Agar agar may be re-boiled without impairing its setting ability.)
3. If properly prepared, agar agar sets quickly on contact with anything much cooler than itself. Therefore, the ingredients to which it is added must be no colder than room temperature. To test whether it is ready for use, spoon a small quantity on to a cold plate: a skin should form very quickly, and wrinkle if a finger is pulled over the surface.

MERINGUES
Whisking egg whites

1. An electric mixer, hand-held electric beater or balloon whisk may be used.
2. Both bowl (ideally copper) and whisk (ideally balloon) must be scrupulously clean, dry and free from grease.
3. Do not use a plastic bowl as plastic tends to retain traces of fatty material on the surface.
4. When the egg yolks are separated from the whites, no specks of yolk must be allowed to remain in the whites: the fat in the yolk can reduce the whisked volume by up to two-thirds.
5. When the whites are half-whisked, the addition of a little caster sugar (15g/1/2oz per 4 whites) will assist efficient whisking and reduce the possibility of overwhisking.
6. When making Swiss meringues (see page 40), once the whites are stiff, add half the total sugar quantity if using a powerful electric mixer, whisk again until very shiny, then add the remainder and whisk lightly until just incorporated. If using a hand-held electric beater, once the whites are stiff add the sugar a tablespoon at a time. If using a balloon whisk see recipe for meringues (page 40).
7. Ideally egg whites are whisked by hand with a balloon whisk in a clean copper bowl (see note). A chemical reaction takes place between the egg whites and the copper which means that the egg whites are stabilized and will thus hold their shape for several minutes without separating. Egg whites whisked in a copper bowl also give you a greater volume of smooth-textured egg white foam. This foam is easy to fold into soufflé bases and makes for excellent meringues. It is difficult to overwhisk whites in a copper bowl.
8. Acid, usually in the form of cream of tartar, is often added to stabilize the foam. Although it has no effect on the volume of foam produced, it makes it less prone to overwhisking and resulting lumpiness, draining and collapse. Only a minute amount of acid is necessary to make a significant difference – about 1/16 teaspoon per egg white.

NOTE: A copper bowl must be cleaned before use. Rub the inside with half a lemon dipped in a generous quantity of salt. Wipe thoroughly and use immediately. The clean bowl is essential;

once the copper becomes oxidized the chemical reaction between the egg whites and copper bowl is weakened. The acid in the lemon also helps to increase the volume of egg white.

Cooking meringues

Once the foam is formed it is baked to coagulate the protein, dry out the sugar to the point where it is more solid than liquid, and so leave the structure strong enough to stand up for hours.

Soft meringues are typically baked at 180°C/350°F/gas mark 4 for 15 minutes. This crisps the surface but leaves the centre moist and chewy.

Hard meringues are baked at 110°C/225°F/gas mark 1/2 for an hour or two, or put into a hot oven with the heat turned off, and allowed to dry for several hours. Meringues can also be baked in an airing cupboard. They come out uniformly dry and crisp.

Baking at too high a temperature may coagulate the proteins so rapidly that the moisture squeezed out may not be able to evaporate before beading up into tears of syrup on the

surface. Weeping can also be a problem in humid weather. When the sugar in a well-dried meringue absorbs moisture from the air and dissolves into droplets of syrup, it makes the meringues sticky and limp.

Paper for cooking meringues: The best is silicone-coated, non-stick baking parchment. Greased and floured greaseproof paper or kitchen foil may also be used, but the great advantage of baking parchment is that meringues may be left to cool completely on it and can then be easily removed without sticking or breaking.

CUCUMBER MOUSSE
SERVES 4

1 large cucumber, peeled if preferred
110g/4 oz cream cheese
150ml/¼ pint double cream, whipped, or
*   plain yoghurt or soured cream*
salt and freshly ground white pepper
a pinch of freshly grated nutmeg
juice of 1 lemon
150ml/¼ pint white (see page 52) or
*   vegetable stock (see page 52)*
15g/½oz powdered gelatine

1. Grate the cucumber, reserving about 2.5cm/1in to slice for decoration. Put the grated cucumber into a sieve. Leave to drain (degorge) for 15 minutes.
2. Oil a soufflé dish or mould, and leave upside down to drain.
3. Beat together the cream cheese and whipped cream, yoghurt or soured cream. Mix in the grated cucumber and season well with salt, pepper and nutmeg. Add the lemon juice.
4. Put the stock into a small saucepan, sprinkle over the gelatine and set aside for 5 minutes until spongy. Then place over a gentle heat until the gelatine is liquid and add to the cucumber mixture, mixing gently but thoroughly.
5. Pour into the prepared mould and refrigerate.
6. To turn the mousse out, invert a wetted plate over the mould and turn plate and mould over together. Give a sharp shake to dislodge the mousse. Garnish with cucumber slices.

NOTES: If a velvety texture is required, blend the cucumber with the yoghurt or cream in a blender.

This mousse does not keep well. Eat within 24 hours.

CHOCOLATE MOUSSE
SERVES 4

110g/4oz plain chocolate
4 eggs

1. Chop the chocolate into even-sized pieces. Put into a heatproof bowl set over, not in, a saucepan of simmering water. Allow it to melt.
2. Separate the eggs.
3. Whisk the egg whites until quite stiff. Stir the melted chocolate into the egg yolks. Mix well. Fold the whites into the chocolate mixture.
4. Turn immediately into a soufflé dish or individual pots or glasses.
5. Chill until set, preferably overnight, but for at least 4 hours.

ORANGE JELLY AND ORANGE SEGMENTS
SERVES 4

For the orange jelly
3 tablespoons water
20g/¾oz powdered gelatine
570ml/1 pint orange juice
4 oranges, segmented (see below)

1. Start with the jelly: put the water into a small saucepan. Sprinkle over the gelatine and leave for 5 minutes to become spongy. Dissolve over a very low heat without boiling or stirring until liquid and clear.
2. Mix the gelatine with 150ml/¼ pint of the orange juice, warmed. Add the remaining orange juice and pour into a wet plain jelly mould or pudding basin.
3. Chill in the refrigerator for 2–4 hours, or until set.
4. Loosen the jelly around the edges with a finger. Invert a damp serving plate over the jelly mould, turn the mould and plate over

together, give a sharp shake and remove the mould. If the jelly won't budge, dip the outside of the mould briefly into hot water to loosen it.

5. Decorate with the orange segments.

Segmenting an orange
1. Cut 1cm/¹/₂in off the top and bottom of the orange so that the orange flesh is exposed.
2. Place the orange on one end and cut the skin off in 2.5cm/1in downward strips, following the natural curve of the orange, removing all the white pith and leaving the orange flesh exposed.
3. Turn the orange over and cut off any white pith that may have been missed.
4. Cut out the orange segments leaving behind the membranes.

QUEEN'S PUDDING
SERVES 4
290ml/¹/₂ pint milk
15g/¹/₂oz butter
140g/5oz caster sugar
55g/2oz fresh white breadcrumbs
grated zest of 1 lemon
2 eggs
2 tablespoons raspberry jam, warmed

1. Heat the milk and add the butter and 30g/1oz of the sugar. Stir until the sugar dissolves, then add the breadcrumbs and lemon zest. Allow to cool.
2. Preheat the oven to 180°C/350°F/gas mark 4.
3. Separate the eggs. Mix the egg yolks into the breadcrumb mixture. Pour into a pie dish and leave to stand for 30 minutes.
4. Place the pudding in a roasting pan half-filled with hot water (a bain-marie) and bake in the preheated oven for 45 minutes, or until the custard mixture is set. Remove from the oven and allow to cool slightly.
5. Turn down the oven temperature to

150°C/300°F/gas mark 2.

6. Carefully spread the jam over the top of the custard. (This is easier if you melt the jam first.)
7. Whisk the egg whites until stiff. Whisk in 2 teaspoons of the remaining sugar. Whisk again until very stiff and shiny and fold in all but 1/2 teaspoon of the remaining sugar.
8. Pile the meringue on top of the custard and dust the top lightly with the reserved sugar.
9. Bake in the oven until the meringue is set and straw-coloured (about 10 minutes).

NOTE: This is particularly good served hot with cold whipped cream.

MERINGUES (SWISS MERINGUES)
MAKES 50 MINIATURE OR 12 LARGE MERINGUES

This recipe assumes use of a balloon whisk; if using an electric mixer see notes on whisking egg whites (page 36).

4 egg whites
a pinch of salt
225g/8oz caster sugar
For the filling
290ml/1/2 pint double cream, whipped

1. Preheat the oven to 110°C/225°F/gas mark 1/2.
2. Line 2 baking sheets with non-stick baking parchment.
3. Whisk the egg whites with a pinch of salt until stiff but not dry.
4. Add 2 tablespoons of the sugar and whisk again until very stiff and shiny.
5. Fold in the remaining sugar.
6. Drop the meringue mixture on to the lined baking sheets in spoonfuls set fairly far apart. Use a teaspoon for tiny meringues; a dessertspoon for larger ones.
7. Bake in the preheated oven for about 2 hours until the meringues are dry right through and will lift easily off the paper.
8. When cold, sandwich the meringues together in pairs with whipped cream.

BREAD AND BUTTER PUDDING
SERVES 4

3 slices of white bread
20g/3/4oz butter
2 tablespoons currants and sultanas, mixed
2 teaspoons chopped mixed peel
2 eggs
1 egg yolk
1 rounded tablespoon sugar
290ml/1/2 pint creamy milk
vanilla essence
ground cinnamon
demerara sugar

1. Spread the bread with the butter. Cut into quarters. Arrange in a shallow ovenproof dish, buttered side up, and sprinkle with currants, sultanas and peel.
2. Make the custard: mix the eggs and egg yolk with the sugar and stir in the milk and vanilla essence.
3. Strain the custard carefully over the bread and leave to soak for 30 minutes. Sprinkle with cinnamon and demerara sugar.
4. Preheat the oven to 180°C/350°F/gas mark 4.
5. Place the pudding in a roasting pan half-filled with hot water (a bain-marie) and cook in the middle of the oven for about 45 minutes, or until the custard is set and the top is brown and crusty.

NOTE: The pudding may be baked quite successfully without the bain-marie, but if used it will ensure a smooth, not bubbly custard.

APPLES AND BLACKBERRIES IN CASSIS SYRUP
SERVES 4

4 Granny Smith apples, with stalks
*   if possible*
For the poaching liquid
225g/8oz blackberries
juice and 2 strips of zest from 1/2 lemon
1/2 cinnamon stick
2 strips of orange zest
110g/4oz sugar
150ml/1/4 pint crème de cassis
150ml/1/4 pint dry white wine
To serve
2 tablespoons of the poaching juices
*   (see above)*
plain yoghurt
225g/8oz blackberries

1. Put the poaching ingredients into a large shallow pan and simmer over a low heat until the sugar has dissolved.
2. Peel the apples, cut in half leaving the stalk on one half, and remove the cores with a melon baller or small spoon.
3. Add to the poaching liquid, cut side up, and cover with a lid.
4. Poach the apples over a low heat for about 15 minutes, or until just tender. Baste frequently, using a wooden spoon to avoid damaging the fruit. Remove the pan from the heat. Leave the fruit to cool in the liquid. The longer the apples are left in the poaching liquid the more coloured they will become.
5. Remove the apples with two wooden spoons and place, cut side down, on a plate. Strain the cooking liquid through a plastic or nylon sieve, return to a clean saucepan and simmer over a medium heat until reduced to a thick syrup. Leave to cool.
6. To serve: put 2 apple halves on each of 4 pudding plates and spoon the syrup over and around. Add a spoonful of yoghurt if wished or serve it separately.
7. Decorate with blackberries.

NOTE: This recipe also works well with pears; cook them for 20 minutes.

Causes of Failure
Jelly not setting: Overheated gelatine.
Gelatine forming stringy lumps: Gelatine added to a cold liquid, not compatible and it has set too quickly.
A cucumber mousse not turning out of mould: Mould not oiled well enough.
Dense chocolate mousse: Egg whites over-folded into chocolate and yolks.
Chocolate streaks in mousse: Chocolate too cold when added.
Chocolate goes hard and lumpy: Overheated while melting, or a splash of water has got into the bowl.
Meringues not holding shape: Egg white not whisked to a stiff peak; or sugar added too quickly.
Meringues not setting/collapsing: Undercooked.

MEAT – ROASTING/JOINTING – AND STOCKS AND SAVOURY SAUCES
CHAPTER 6

Techniques Covered
Roasting chicken, pork and accompaniments
Jointing a chicken
Making a stock
Making a flour-based sauce

❷ Cookery Terms
Baste: To spoon over a liquid (sometimes stock, sometimes fat) during cooking to prevent drying out and to promote flavour.
Deglaze: To loosen and liquefy fat, sediment and browned juices stuck at the bottom of a frying pan or saucepan by adding liquid (usually stock, water or wine) and stirring while boiling.
Depouiller: To skim off the scum from a sauce or stock: a splash of cold stock is added to the boiling liquid. This helps to bring scum and fat to the surface, which can then be skimmed more easily.
Glace de viande: Reduced brown stock, very strong in flavour, used for adding body and colour to sauces.
Gratiner: To brown under a grill after the surface of the dish has been sprinkled with breadcrumbs and butter and, sometimes, cheese. Dishes finished like this are sometimes called gratinée or au gratin.
Infuse: To steep or heat gently to extract flavour, as when infusing milk with onion slices.
Oyster: Small piece of meat found on either side of the backbone of a chicken. Said to be the best-flavoured flesh. Also a bivalve mollusc.
Parboil: To half-boil or partially soften by boiling.
Pass: To strain or push through a sieve.
Reduce: To reduce the amount of liquid by rapid boiling, causing evaporation and a consequent strengthening of flavour in the remaining liquid.
Roux: A basic liaison or thickening for a sauce or soup. Melted butter to which flour has been added.
Sear: To brown meat rapidly usually in fat, for flavour and colour.
Tammy strainer: A fine mesh strainer, conical in shape, through which sauces are passed to make them smooth and shiny.

Recipes
French roast chicken
English roast chicken
Roast pork
Roast parsnips
Roast potatoes
Apple sauce
Bread sauce

Chicken with tomato and coriander
Brown stock
White stock
White fish stock
Vegetable stock
Court bouillon
Macaroni cheese

Points to Remember

Three factors determine the toughness of a particular cut of meat: the age of the animal (the older it is the tougher it will be); the activity of the particular joint (the neck, shoulders, chest and legs are used far more than the back of a quadruped and are therefore tougher); and finally the texture of the fibres.

Muscle tissue is made up of long thin cells or muscle fibres bound together by sheets of connective tissue. Individual fibres can be as long as the whole muscle. Bundles of fibres are organized in groups to form an individual muscle. The lengthways structure of muscles is known as the grain of the meat. It is easier to carve and also to chew in the direction of the grain, which is why meat is cut across the grain. The connective tissue is the harness of the muscle and is visible as gristle, tendons, etc. Connective tissue is made up of three main proteins: collagen, which can be converted by long, slow cooking into gelatine; elastin, which is elastic and not changed by heat; and reticulen, which is fibrous and not changed by heat.

Tender cuts of meat such as sirloin steak have relatively few connective tissues and as they cook the meat fibres shrink and lose moisture. If overcooked, the juices finally dry up and a once tender piece of meat becomes tough and dry. However, a tough cut of meat such as oxtail, which has a lot of connective tissue, can become very moist during cooking. The collagen is converted into gelatine and the meat becomes almost sticky in its succulence.

As meat should be tender and juicy rather than dry and tough, it is important to cook it in such a way as to minimize fluid loss and to maximize the conversion of the tough collagen in the connective tissue into water-soluble gelatine.

It is possible to tenderize meat before cooking it. This can be done by cutting, pounding and grinding to break down the structure of the muscle bundles. It can also be done by marinating. The acid in citrus fruit or wine produces protein-digesting enzymes that can break down muscle and connective tissue.

Roasting meat
1. Weigh the joint and establish the length of cooking time (see below).
2. Preheat the oven (electric ovens take longer to heat up than gas ovens).
3. Prepare the joint for roasting; see the relevant recipe.
4. Heat some dripping in a roasting pan and if the meat is lean, brown the joint over direct heat so that it is well coloured. Pork and lamb rarely need this but many cuts of beef do.
5. Place the joint in the pan, on a grid if you have one available, as this aids the circulation of hot air; roast for the time calculated. Once the meat is cooked leave it to 'rest' in the turned-off oven for 20 minutes or so to allow the meat juice to set.

ROASTING TIMES

Obviously a long thin piece of meat weighing 2.3kg/5lb will take less time to cook than a fat round piece of the same weight. Bone is also a good conductor of heat so joints cooked on the bone cook more quickly, pro rata, than a similar piece of meat cooked off the bone. The times below are therefore meant only as a guide. The essential point is that meat must reach an internal temperature of 60°C/140°F to be rare, 70°C/170°F to be well done. A meat thermometer stuck into the thickest part of the meat, and left there during cooking, eliminates guesswork. Meat cooked on the bone generally tastes better than meat cooked off the bone.

BEEF: Beef is generally roasted in the hottest of ovens for 20 minutes to brown the meat (or it may be fried all over in fat before being transferred to the oven). Whatever the method, calculate the cooking time after the browning has been done, and allow 10–15 minutes per 450g/1lb for rare meat, 20 minutes for medium and 25 for well done, roasting the meat in an oven preheated to 190°C/375°F/gas mark 5.
LAMB: Put the lamb into the hottest of ovens for 20 minutes, then allow 20 minutes per 450g/1lb at 190°C/375°F/gas mark 5. This will produce very slightly pink lamb. If lamb without a trace of pinkness is wanted, allow an extra 20 minutes after the calculated time is up.
PORK: Pork must be well cooked. Allow 40 minutes per 450g/1lb at 170°C/325°F/ gas mark 3. If crackling is required, roast at 200°C/400°F/gas mark 6 for 25 minutes to 450g/1lb, plus 25 minutes over.
VEAL: Brown in hot fat over direct heat. Or roast for 20 minutes at maximum temperature. Then allow 20 minutes per 450g/1lb at 180°C/350°F/gas mark 4.

To joint a chicken
1. Singe the chicken, then wipe with kitchen paper to remove any hairs and pin feathers.
2. Place the chicken on a board breast side down with the parson's nose facing you.
3. Using a large cook's knife, make a cut down the backbone through the skin from one end to the other.
4. Use your thumbs to loosen the oyster pieces located at the top of each leg next to the backbone.
5. Turn the chicken over, pull the skin up tightly over the breast, then cut between the breast and the leg, cutting as close to the leg as possible, using the blade of the knife, not the tip.
6. Continue cutting the skin around the leg to the backbone next to the oyster piece.
7. Bend the leg out from the body to release the ball joint from the socket.
8. Use a knife to cut the cartilage around the ball joint.
9. Remove the leg by grasping it firmly and pulling it towards the back of the chicken. The oyster piece should come away with the leg.
10. Repeat Steps 5–9 to remove the other leg.

11. Feel for the joint between the drumstick and the thigh then cut through the joint using a large knife.
12. Place the chicken breast side up on the board, then cut through the breast meat of the chicken from one end to the other, using the blade of the knife.
13. Using kitchen scissors, cut through the breast-bone. Do not remove the bone from the breast.
14. Using scissors, cut along the fat line on the edge of the breast, cutting through the ends of the ribs then around underneath the wing to the neck of the chicken. Save the carcase for stock.
15. Tuck the wings back as shown. Place the two breasts next to each other, then cut through the meat on a slant from the 'elbow' to the 'cleavage'.
16. After cooking, use scissors to remove the pinion (wing tip) from each wing. Remove the knuckles: grasp the end with kitchen paper, then cut through the skin with a knife and using scissors push the skin back and cut through the bone. Use scissors to remove any other unsightly bits of bone from the chicken pieces.

STOCKS AND SAVOURY SAUCES

Behind every great soup and behind many a sauce stands a good strong stock. Stock is flavoured liquid, and the basic flavour can be fish, poultry, meat or vegetable. Stock cubes and bouillon mixes are usually over-salty and lack the intense flavour of properly made stock, making food taste the same. As an emergency measure, or to strengthen a rather weak stock, they are useful. But a good cook should be able to make a perfect stock.

Making a stock

The secret of stocks is slow, gentle simmering. If the liquid is the slightest bit greasy, vigorous boiling will produce a murky, fatty stock. Skimming, especially for meat stocks, is vital: as fat and scum rise to the surface they should be lifted off with a perforated spoon, perhaps every 10–15 minutes.

Rich, brown stocks are made by first frying or baking the bones, vegetables and scraps of meat until a good, dark, even brown. Only then does the cook proceed with the gentle simmering. Care must be taken not to burn the bones or vegetables: one burnt carrot can ruin a gallon of stock. Brown stocks are usually made from red meats or veal, and sometimes only from vegetables for vegetarian dishes. Brown fish stock can be very useful.

White stocks are more delicate and are made by simmering only. They are usually based on white poultry or vegetables.

The longer meat stocks are simmered the better flavoured they will be. A stockpot will simmer all day in a restaurant, being skimmed or topped up with water as the chef passes it, and only strained before closing time. However, it is important not to just keep adding bits and pieces to the stockpot and to keep it going on the back burner for days, because the pot will become cluttered with cooked-out bones and vegetables that have long since given up any flavour. At least 3, and up to 8 hours over the gentlest flame, or in the bottom oven of an Aga, is ample cooking time.

In the Aga, skimming is unnecessary – as the liquid hardly moves there is no danger of fat being bubbled into the stock, and it can be lifted off the top when cold.

Fish stocks should never be simmered for more than 30 minutes. After this the bones begin to impart a bitter flavour to the liquid. For a stronger flavour the stock can be strained, skimmed of any scum or fat, and then boiled down to reduce and concentrate it.

Similarly, vegetable stocks do not need long cooking. As they contain very little fat, even if the vegetables have been browned in butter before simmering, they are easily skimmed, and can then be boiled rapidly to concentrate the flavour. An hour's simmering or 30 minutes' rapid boiling is generally enough.

The bones

Most households rarely have anything other than the cooked bones from a roast available for stocks. These will make good stock, but it will be weaker than that made with raw bones. Raw bones are very often free from the butcher, or can be had very cheaply. Get them chopped into manageable small pieces in the shop. A little raw meat, the bloodier the better, gives a rich, very clear liquid.

Water

The water must be cold, as if it is hot the fat in the bones will melt immediately and when the stock begins to boil much of the fat will be bubbled into the stock. The stock will then be murky, have an unattractive smell and a nasty flavour. Cold water encourages the fat to rise to the surface; it can then be skimmed.

Jellied stock

Veal bones produce a particularly good stock that will set to a jelly. A pig's trotter added to any stock will have the same jellifying effect. Jellied stock will keep longer than liquid stock, but in any event stocks should be reboiled every 2 or 3 days if kept refrigerated, or every day if kept in a larder, to prevent them going bad.

Salt

Do not add salt to stock. It may be used later for something that is already salty, or boiled down to a concentrated glaze (glace de viande), in which case the glaze would be over-salted if the stock contained salt. (Salt does not boil off with the water, but remains in the pan.)

Storage

A good way of storing a large batch of stock is to boil it down to double strength, and to add water only when using. Or stock can be boiled down to a thick, syrupy glaze, which can be used like stock cubes. Many cooks freeze the glaze in ice cube trays, then turn the frozen cubes into a plastic box in the freezer. They will keep for at least a year if fat-free.

Sauces

Larousse defines a sauce as a 'liquid seasoning for food', and this covers anything from juices in a frying pan to complicated and sophisticated emulsions.

Flour-thickened sauces

The commonest English sauces are those thickened with flour, and these are undoubtedly the most practical for the home cook. The secret is not to make them too thick (by not adding too much flour), to beat them well and to give them a good boil after they have thickened to make them shine. They will also look professionally shiny if they are finished by whizzing in a blender, or if they are 'mounted' with a little extra butter, gradually incorporated in dice, at the end.

The butter and flour base of a sauce is called a roux. In a white roux, the butter and flour are mixed over a gentle heat without browning; in a blond roux, they are allowed to cook to a biscuit colour; and in a brown roux, they are cooked until distinctly brown.

Another way of thickening a sauce with flour is to make a beurre manié. Equal quantities of butter and flour are kneaded to a smooth paste and whisked into a boiling liquid. As the butter melts the flour is evenly distributed throughout the sauce, thickening the liquid without allowing lumps to form. Cornflour and arrowroot are also useful thickeners. They are 'slaked' (mixed to a paste with cold water, stock or milk), added to a hot liquid and allowed to boil to thicken it for a couple of minutes.

Emulsions and liaisons

Emulsions are liquids that contain tiny droplets of oil or fat evenly distributed in suspension. Like liaisons, they may be unstable.

Stable emulsions

Mayonnaise is the best known of the cold and stable emulsion sauces, in which oil is beaten into egg yolks and held in suspension. If the oil is added too fast the sauce will curdle.

Warm emulsions

The most stable warm emulsions, like cold emulsions, are based on egg yolks and butter. The best known is hollandaise. Great care has to be taken not to allow the sauce to curdle.

Eggless emulsions

These have become the more fashionable butter sauces. The classic is beurre blanc. Eggless emulsions curdle very easily, so great care should be taken to follow the recipe precisely.

Unstable emulsions

French dressing will emulsify if whizzed or whisked together, but will separate back to its component parts after about 15 minutes.

Sabayons

Egg yolks are whisked over heat and the flavouring ingredient is gradually whisked in. The suspension is temporary and most sabayons collapse after 30–40 minutes.

Liaisons

Egg yolk can be mixed with cream to form a liaison. It is then used to thicken and enrich sauces. The yolks must not boil or the sauce will curdle.

FRENCH ROAST CHICKEN

SERVES 4

1 x 1.35kg/3lb roasting chicken with giblets
butter
freshly ground black pepper and salt
1 slice of onion
1 bay leaf
a few parsley stalks
For the gravy

1 scant tablespoon plain flour
290ml/¹/₂ pint white stock, made
  with chicken bones (see page 52) or
  vegetable water

1. Preheat the oven to 200°C/400°F/gas mark 6.
2. Smear a little butter all over the chicken. Season inside and out with pepper only

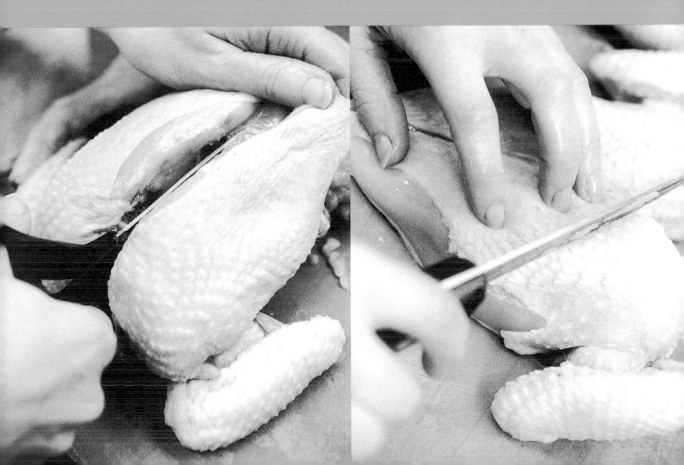

(no salt). Put the bird breast side down in a roasting pan.

3. Put all the chicken giblets (except the liver) and the neck into the pan with the chicken. Add the onion, bay leaf and parsley stalks. Pour in a cup of water. Roast in the preheated oven for 30 minutes.

4. Take out of the oven, season all over with salt, turn the chicken right side up and baste it with the fat and juices from the pan. Return to the oven.

5. Check how the chicken is doing periodically. It will take 60–80 minutes. It is cooked when the leg bones wobble loosely and independently from the body. Baste occasionally as it cooks, and cover with kitchen foil or greaseproof paper if it is browning too much. Remove the cooked chicken to a warmed serving dish and keep warm while making the gravy.

6. Place the roasting pan with its juices over a low heat. Skim off most of the fat.

7. Whisk in enough flour to absorb the remaining fat.

8. Add the stock or vegetable water and stir until the sauce boils. Simmer for 2–3 minutes. Check the seasoning. Strain into a warmed gravy-boat and serve with the chicken.

ENGLISH ROAST CHICKEN
SERVES 4
1 x 1.35kg/3lb roasting chicken
15g/1/2 oz butter
freshly ground black pepper
For the stuffing
30g/1oz butter
1 onion, finely chopped
55g/2oz fresh white breadcrumbs
1 small cooking apple, grated
2 teaspoons chopped mixed fresh herbs
grated zest of 1/2 lemon
1/2 egg, beaten
salt and freshly ground black pepper
To garnish
4 chipolata sausages
4 rashers of rindless streaky bacon
For the gravy
1 scant tablespoon plain flour

290ml/1/2 pint white stock, made from the chicken neck and giblets (see page 52)
To serve
bread sauce (see page 50)

1. Preheat the oven to 200°C/400°F/gas mark 6.

2. Start to make the stuffing: melt the butter in a saucepan and fry the onion until soft but not coloured.

3. Put the breadcrumbs, apple, herbs and lemon zest together in a mixing bowl.

4. Add the softened onion and enough beaten egg to bind the mixture together. Do not make it too wet. Season to taste with salt and pepper, then cool.

5. Stuff the chicken from the neck end, making sure the breast is well plumped. Draw the neck skin flap down to cover the stuffing. Secure with a skewer if necessary.

6. Smear a little butter all over the chicken and season with salt and pepper. Roast in the preheated oven for about 1 1/2 hours, or until the juices run clear when the thigh is pierced with a skewer.

7. Meanwhile, make each chipolata sausage into 2 cocktail-sized ones by twisting gently in the middle. Cut each bacon rasher into short lengths and roll them up.

8. After the chicken has been roasting for 1 hour, put the sausages and bacon rolls into the roasting pan, wedging the bacon rolls so that they cannot come undone.

9. Baste occasionally and check that the sausages and bacon are not sticking to the side of the pan and getting burnt.

10. When the chicken is cooked, lift it out on to a warmed serving dish. Trim off the wing tips and tops of the drumsticks, surround with the bacon rolls and sausages and keep warm while you make the gravy.

11. Slowly pour off all but 1 tablespoon of the fat from the roasting pan, taking care to keep any juices. Add the flour and stir over heat for 1 minute. Add the stock and stir until the sauce boils. Simmer for 3 minutes. Check the seasoning. Strain into a warmed gravy-boat.

12. Serve the chicken with bread sauce and the gravy.

NOTE: The chicken looks neater if it is trussed after stuffing, but it is more difficult to get the thighs cooked without the breast drying out if this is done.

ROAST PORK
SERVES 4
1.35kg/3lb loin of pork, with skin intact
oil
salt
For the gravy
2 teaspoons plain flour
290ml/¹/₂ pint brown stock (see page 51)
To serve
1 small bunch of watercress
apple sauce (see page 50)

1. Preheat the oven to 220°C/425°F/gas mark 7.
2. Score the rind (crackling skin) with a sharp knife in cuts about 5mm/¹/₄ in apart, cutting through the skin but not right through the fat.
3. Brush the skin with oil and sprinkle with salt to help give a crisp crackling.
4. Place the pork in a roasting pan and roast in the top of the preheated oven for 1 hour 40 minutes (25 minutes per 450g/1lb plus 25 minutes). After 30 minutes turn down the oven temperature to 190°C/375°F/gas mark 5.
5. Once the pork is cooked, turn off the oven, put the pork on a serving dish and replace it in the oven, leaving the door ajar if it is still very hot.
6. Tip all but 2 teaspoons of the fat from the roasting pan, reserving as much of the meat juices as possible.
7. Add the flour and stir over the heat until well browned.
8. Remove from the heat, add the stock and mix well with a wire whisk or wooden spoon. Return to the heat and bring slowly to the boil, whisking all the time. Simmer for a few minutes until the gravy is shiny. Season to taste with salt and pepper. Strain into a warmed gravy-boat.
9. Garnish the pork with watercress and serve with the gravy and apple sauce.

NOTE: Remove the crackling before carving, then cut it into thin strips with kitchen scissors.

ROAST PARSNIPS
SERVES 4
675g/1¹/₂lb parsnips
salt
oil
salt and freshly ground black pepper

1. Preheat the oven to 200°C/400°F/gas mark 6.
2. Wash and peel the parsnips. Cut them in half lengthways.
3. Boil in salted water for 5 minutes. Drain well.
4. Heat 1cm/¹/₂ in of oil in a roasting pan in the preheated oven. When the oil is hot, add the parsnips. Season with salt and pepper.
5. Roast the parsnips, basting and turning during cooking, until they are crisp and golden brown (about 30 minutes).

ROAST POTATOES
SERVES 4
900g/2lb potatoes
salt
4 tablespoons dripping or oil

1. Preheat the oven to 200°C/400°F/gas mark 6.
2. Wash and peel the potatoes and, if they are large, cut them into 5cm/2in pieces.
3. Bring them to the boil in salted water. Simmer for 5 minutes. Drain well, return to the pan and shake the potatoes.
4. Melt the dripping or oil in a roasting pan and when hot add the potatoes, turning them so that they are coated all over. Season with salt and pepper.
5. Roast, basting occasionally, and turning the potatoes over halfway through cooking. See notes below.

NOTES: Potatoes can be roasted at almost any temperature, usually taking 1 hour in a hot oven, or 1¹/₂ hours in a moderate one. They should be basted and turned over once

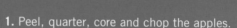

1. Peel, quarter, core and chop the apples.
2. Place in a heavy saucepan with the lemon zest, water and sugar. Cover with a lid and cook very slowly until the apples are soft.
3. Beat in the butter, cool slightly and add extra sugar if required. Serve hot or cold.

BREAD SAUCE
This is a very rich sauce. The quantity of butter may be reduced, and the cream is optional.
SERVES 4
1 large onion, peeled
6 cloves
290ml/¹/₂ pint milk
1 bay leaf
10 white peppercorns, or a pinch of freshly ground white pepper
a pinch of freshly grated nutmeg
salt
55g/2oz fresh white breadcrumbs
55g/2oz butter
2 tablespoons single cream (optional)

1. Cut the onion in half. Stick the cloves into the onion pieces and put with the milk and bay leaf into a saucepan.
2. Add the peppercorns, nutmeg, and a good pinch of salt. Bring to the boil very slowly, then remove from the heat and leave to infuse for 30 minutes. Strain.
3. Reheat the milk and add the breadcrumbs, butter and the cream, if

or twice during cooking, and they are done when a skewer glides easily into them. Potatoes roasted in the same pan as meat have the best flavour, but this is not always possible if the joint or bird is very large, or if liquid has been added to the pan.

The water in which the potatoes were parboiled can be saved and used for making gravy if no stock is available.

APPLE SAUCE
SERVES 4
450g/1lb cooking apples
finely grated zest of ¹/₄ lemon
3 tablespoons water
2 teaspoons sugar
15g/¹/₂oz butter

using. Mix and return to the saucepan.
4. Reheat the sauce carefully without boiling. If it has become too thick, beat in more hot milk. It should be creamy. Check the seasoning.

CHICKEN WITH TOMATO AND CORIANDER
SERVES 4

1 x 1.35kg/3lb chicken, jointed into 8 pieces (see page 44)
seasoned plain flour
2 tablespoons oil
2 onions, finely chopped
1 clove garlic, crushed
1 x 400g/14oz can of tomatoes
1 bay leaf
2 teaspoons tomato purée
salt and freshly ground black pepper
2 tablespoons roughly chopped fresh coriander

1. Dip the chicken pieces in the seasoned flour.
2. Heat the oil in a large sauté pan and brown the chicken all over. With a slotted spoon, take up the pieces and place them in a roasting dish or casserole.
3. Preheat the oven to 180°C/350°F/gas mark 4.
4. Add the onions to the sauté pan and cook over a low heat for 10 minutes, or until beginning to soften. Add the garlic and cook for 1 further minute. Add the tomatoes, bay leaf and tomato purée. Season to taste with salt and pepper. Bring slowly to the boil, stirring continuously.
5. Pour the mixture over the chicken pieces. Cover and cook in the preheated oven for 45–50 minutes, or until the chicken is tender. Turn off the oven.
6. Lift the chicken pieces out of the sauce. Trim them and arrange on a warmed serving dish. Keep warm in the turned-off oven.
7. Skim any fat off the sauce, then boil rapidly to a syrupy consistency. Stir the sauce well to amalgamate the tomatoes and to prevent the sauce from catching. Add three-quarters of the coriander. Check the seasoning and pour the sauce over the chicken. Garnish with the remaining coriander.

BROWN STOCK
900g/2lb beef and veal bones
1 onion, peeled and chopped, skin reserved
1 carrot, roughly chopped
1 stick of celery, chopped
green part of 2 leeks, chopped (if available)
sunflower oil
parsley stalks
a few mushroom peelings (if available)
2 bay leaves
6 black peppercorns

1. Preheat the oven to 220°C/425°F/gas mark 7.
2. Put the beef bones into a roasting pan and brown in the oven (up to 1 hour).
3. Brown the onion, carrot, celery, and leeks, if using, in the oil in a large stockpot. It is essential that they do not burn.
4. When the bones are well browned add them to the vegetables with the onion skins, parsley stalks, mushroom peelings, if using, bay leaves and peppercorns. Cover with cold water and bring very slowly to the boil, skimming off any scum as it rises to the surface.
5. When clear of scum, simmer gently for 6–8 hours, or even longer, skimming off the fat as necessary and topping up with water if the level gets very low. The longer it simmers, and the more liquid reduces by evaporation, the stronger the stock will be.
6. Strain, cool and lift off any remaining fat.
NOTE: Lamb stock can be made in the same way with lamb bones but is only suitable for lamb dishes.

WHITE STOCK
onion, sliced
celery, sliced
carrot, sliced
chicken or veal bones
parsley
thyme
bay leaf
black peppercorns

1. Put all the ingredients into a saucepan. Cover generously with water and bring to the boil slowly. Skim off any fat, and/or scum.
2. Simmer for 3–4 hours, skimming frequently and topping up the water level if necessary. The liquid should reduce to half the original quantity.
3. Strain, cool and lift off all the fat.

WHITE FISH STOCK
onion, sliced
carrot, sliced
celery, sliced
fishbones, skins, fins, heads or tails of white fish
parsley stalks
bay leaf
a pinch of chopped fresh thyme
6 black peppercorns

1. Put all the ingredients together into a saucepan, with water to cover, and bring to the boil. Turn down to simmer and skim off any scum.
2. Simmer for 20 minutes if the fish bones are small, 30 minutes if large. Strain.
NOTE: The flavour of fish stock is impaired if the bones are cooked for too long. Once strained, however, it may be strengthened by further boiling and reducing.

VEGETABLE STOCK
MAKES 290–425ml/ $^1/2$ – $^3/4$ pint
4 tablespoons oil
1 onion, roughly chopped
1 leek, roughly chopped
1 large carrot, roughly chopped
2 sticks celery, roughly chopped
a few cabbage leaves, roughly shredded

a few mushroom stalks
2 cloves garlic, crushed
a few parsley stalks
6 black peppercorns
sea salt
1 large bay leaf
6 tablespoons dry white wine
570ml/1 pint water

1. Heat the oil in a large saucepan. Add the vegetables, cover and cook gently for 5 minutes or until softening.
2. Add the garlic, parsley stalks, peppercorns, salt, bay leaf, wine and water and bring to the boil. Reduce the

heat and simmer for 30 minutes or until the liquid is reduced by half.

3. Strain the stock through a sieve, pressing hard to remove as much of the liquid as possible. Discard the vegetable pulp. Allow to cool and skim off any fat.

NOTE: The stock can be kept, covered, in the refrigerator for up to 1 week. It can also be frozen.

COURT BOUILLON

This is a lightly acidulated, concentrated liquid used for cooking fish and shellfish.

1 litre/1 3/4 pints water
150ml/5fl oz white wine vinegar or
    white wine
1 carrot, sliced
1 onion, sliced
1 stick of celery, sliced
12 black peppercorns
1 bay leaf
1 tablespoon salad oil
a pinch of salt

1. Put all the ingredients into a saucepan and bring to the boil. Reduce the heat and simmer for 20 minutes.

2. Strain the court bouillon, cool and use as required.

MACARONI CHEESE

SERVES 4
170g/6oz macaroni
20g/3/4oz butter
20g/3/4oz plain flour
cayenne pepper
a pinch of dry English mustard
425ml/3/4 oz pint milk
salt and freshly ground black pepper
170g/6oz strong Cheddar cheese, grated
1/2 tablespoon fresh white braeadcrumbs

1. Cook the macaroni, uncovered, in plenty of rapidly boiling salted water. The water must boil steadily to keep the macaroni moving freely and prevent it from sticking to the saucepan; the lid is left off to prevent boiling over. Cook the macaroni until it is just tender. Drain well and rinse under boiling water.

2. Melt the butter in a second saucepan and add the flour, cayenne pepper and mustard. Cook, stirring, for 1 minute. Remove from the heat. Pour in the milk and mix well. Return to the heat and stir until boiling. Simmer, stirring all the time, for 2 minutes.

3. Stir the macaroni into the sauce and reheat if necessary. Season the sauce to taste with salt and pepper. Stir in all but 1 tablespoon of the cheese and turn the mixture into an ovenproof dish.

4. Preheat the grill to its highest setting.

5. Mix the reserved cheese with the breadcrumbs and sprinkle evenly over the sauce; make sure that all the sauce is covered or it will form brown blisters under the grill.

6. Grill fairly quickly until the top is browned and crisp.

Causes of Failure

Roasting: Pale gravy – roux not browned enough; not enough meat juices used. Tough meat – cooked at too high a temperature for cut of meat.

Crackling not 'crackled' – temperature of oven not high enough at start; rind not scored deep enough; salt and oil not rubbed into skin before cooking; skin basted with fat during cooking; or not a thick enough layer of fat under the skin; or rind too deeply scored right into the fat.

Flavourless bread sauce – milk not infused with flavourings for long enough, not well seasoned.

Soft skinned roast potatoes – not parboiled for long enough; not shaken in the pan for long enough after parboiling to rough up the edges; fat not sizzling when the potatoes went into it.

Dry chicken breasts: Overcooked.

Stock: Pale brown stock – bones and vegetables not browned enough. Brown stock with bitter flavour – bones or vegetables burnt when browning. Cloudy stock – fat not skimmed off; stock allowed to boil.

Lumpy cheese sauce: Milk added too quickly.

Greasy cheese sauce: Cheese added to the sauce and allowed to boil.

FISH I AND PARTY PLANNING
CHAPTER 7

Techniques Covered
Scaling, gutting, filleting and skinning flat
and round fish
Pan-frying fish fillets
Cooking kippers by the 'jug' method
Making a risotto
Flambéeing
Glazing fruit tarts
Menu planning
Kitchen organization

❷ Cookery Terms
Clarified butter: Butter that has been separated from milk particles and other impurities which cause it to look cloudy when melted, and to burn easily when heated (see page 192).
Flamber: To set alcohol alight (literally, 'to flame'). Usually to burn off the alcohol and excess fat, but frequently simply for dramatic effect.

Recipes
Lemon sole with cucumber
Fish pie
Mackerel with gooseberry sauce
Jugged kippers

Risotto alla Milanese
Chicken sauté normande
Individual apple tarts/sweet rich
shortcrust pastry/apricot glaze

FISH
Freshwater fish are divided into coarse fish, fished mainly for sport and generally thrown back live into the rivers, and game fish, which are caught both for sport and commercially. Much freshwater fish in fact comes from fish farms. Many freshwater fish, such as bass, sturgeon, sea trout and salmon, spend most of their adult lives in the sea, swimming back up the rivers to spawn, but they are still classified as freshwater fish despite the fact that most of them are caught by trawl in the sea. Coarse river fish, such as roach, gudgeon and tench, are not sold commercially and are seldom eaten except by anglers' families.

Most of our fish comes from the sea. It is increasingly difficult today to get locally caught fish. Fish is frozen or deep-chilled on trawlers and immediately exported. For the cook this is sad. Fish is a valuable source of protein, vitamin D (in oily fish), calcium and phosphorus (found especially in the edible bones of whitebait, sardines, etc.), iodine, fluorine and some of the B vitamins. Fish contains very little fat, and even oily fish seldom has more than 20 per cent fat content. The fat in fish is polyunsaturated and contains essential fatty acids that cannot be obtained elsewhere.

Like meat, fish is composed of muscle fibres that vary in length and thickness according to type. For example, lobster has long and coarse fibres and herring very fine fibres.

The fibres are generally shorter than in meat and are packed in flakes with very little connective tissue between them. The fat is dispersed among the fibres. The connective tissue is very thin and is quickly converted to gelatine when cooked. Because of its structure, fish is naturally more tender than meat, and over-vigorous or overlong cooking will cause dryness and disintegration as the connective tissue dissolves and the flakes fall apart. The protein in the fibres coagulates, the fish begins to shrink and the juices are extracted – in dry heat there is a more rapid loss of juices. In moist heat soluble nutrients and flavouring minerals are lost into the liquid, making an overcooked fish dry, tough and tasteless.

Fish should be cooked quickly by grilling or frying, or slowly by poaching. If frying or grilling, the fish should be protected from the fierce heat by a coating of seasoned flour, beaten eggs, breadcrumbs or a batter. If poaching, use a well-seasoned court bouillon and then use this liquid to make the sauce so that none of the flavour is lost. Do drain fish well after it has been poached, and do not keep it warm as it will dry out and become tough and tasteless. Fish does not keep well and should be eaten as fresh as possible. A plausible theory explaining this is that as fish live in cold water, they are cold-blooded and their enzymes work at very low temperatures. Thus they continue, unlike meat, to deteriorate in the refrigerator.

Preparation for cooking
REMOVING THE SCALES
Large fish have dry scales which should be removed before cooking. To do this, scrape a large knife the wrong way along the fish (from tail to head). This can be a messy business as the scales tend to fly about; it can be cleanly done in a plastic carrier bag to prevent this. However, unless you are buying fish from a wholesale market, the fishmonger will do it for you.
GUTTING AND CLEANING A ROUND FISH
The fishmonger will probably clean the fish, but if you are to do it yourself you will need a very sharp knife. Fish skin blunts knives faster than anything else. If the fish is to be stuffed or filleted it does not matter how big a slit you make to remove the entrails. If it is to be left whole, the shorter the slit the better. Start just below the head and slit through the soft belly skin. After pulling out the innards, wash the fish under cold water. Make sure all the dark blood along the spinal column is removed. Now carefully cut away the gills. Take care not to cut off the head if you want to serve the fish whole. If you do not, cut off head and tail now. To remove the fins, cut the skin round them, take a good grip (if you salt your fingers well it will stop them slipping) and yank sharply towards the head. This will pull the fin bones out with the fin.
SKINNING AND FILLETING A FLAT FISH
Fish skin is easier to remove after cooking. But sometimes the fish must be skinned beforehand. Most whole fish are not skinned or filleted before grilling, but sole (and lemon sole, witch and plaice) are skinned on at least the dark side, and sometimes on both sides. To do this, make a crossways slit through the skin at the tail, and push a finger in. You will now be able to run the finger round the edge of the fish loosening the skin. When you have done this on both edges, salt your fingers to prevent slipping, take a firm grip of the skin at the tail end with one hand, and with the other hold the fish down. Give a quick strong yank, peeling the skin back towards the head. If necessary, do the same to the other side.

Flat fish are generally filleted into four half-fillets. To do this, lay the fish on a board with the tail towards you. Cut through the flesh to the backbone along the length of the fish. Then, with a sharp pliable knife, cut the left-hand fillet away from the bone, keeping the blade almost flat against the bones of the fish. Then swivel the fish round so the head is towards you and cut away the second fillet in the same way. Turn the fish over and repeat the process on the other side. (If you are left-handed, tackle the right-hand fillet first.)

FILLETING AND SKINNING A ROUND FISH
Round fish are filleted before skinning. If they are to be cooked whole, they are cooked with the skin, but this may be carefully peeled off after cooking, as in the case of a whole poached salmon. To fillet a round fish, lay it on a board and cut through the flesh down to the backbone from the head to the tail. Insert a sharp pliable knife between the flesh and the bones, and slice the fillet away from the bones, working with short strokes from the backbone and from the head end. Remember to keep the knife as flat as possible, and to keep it against the bones. When the fillet is almost off the fish you will need to cut through the belly skin to detach it completely. Very large round fish can be filleted in four, following the flat fish method, or the whole side can be lifted as described here, and then split in two once off the fish.

TO SKIN A FLAT FISH
Put the fillet skin side down on a board. Hold the tip down firmly, using a good pinch of salt to help get a firm grip. With a sharp, heavy, straight knife, cut through the flesh, close to the tip, taking care not to go right through the skin. Hold the knife at right angles to the fish fillet, with the blade almost upright. With a gently sawing motion, work the flesh from the skin, pushing the fillet off rather than cutting it. The reason for keeping the knife almost upright is to lessen the danger of cutting through the skin, but with practice it is possible to flatten the knife slightly, so that the sharp edge is foremost, and simply slide it forward, without the sawing motion.

TO BONE A ROUND FISH
Split the fish open completely, clean thoroughly and lay, skin side up, on a board. With the heel of your hand, press down firmly on the backbone of the fish. This will loosen it. Turn it over, cut through the backbone near the head, and pull it out with all the side bones, or nearly all the side bones, attached to it.

PINBONING FISH
This is done to remove all the irritating small bones that run along the flanks of the fish, and which are the reason why some people do not enjoy eating fish.

Any cut of fish should be pinboned before cooking. Run the tips of the fingers of one hand over the surface of the flesh to locate the ends of the small bones. Pull the bones out with tweezers or pliers. The fish is now ready for cooking.

CATERING FOR LARGE NUMBERS – TIME MANAGEMENT

Planning a party for large numbers can be daunting. If you follow through the points below it can help you plan for the event and decide realistically on the menu/venue/number of helpers needed and the time it will take to put the party together. See also costing (page 140) and entertaining (page 172).

Assess the menu
- How much time will be required to prepare the menu?
- How much time is available?
- Will any help to prepare food be available?
- Which dishes can be prepared in advance and stored in the refrigerator or frozen?
- Is there enough room in the refrigerator/freezer to store the dishes safely?

Plan the preparation
- Make a timeplan (see Chapter 1) by making a chart of the preparation time available prior to the point when you need all the food to be prepared.
- Read each recipe carefully, then slot the preparation of each into the timeplan, taking into account cooking times.
- Break the recipes up into parts. You may be able to prepare some parts (e.g. pastry) in advance.

- Be sure to allow extra time for increased quantities.
- Determine which dishes can be prepared simultaneously.
- Organize tasks so that several can be done at once.
- Allocate time for shopping and unpacking.
- Allow plenty of time on the day to cook/reheat food and arrange it on platters.
- Set aside blocks of time, at least 2 hours as a minimum, for food preparation. Try to avoid interruptions, turn on the answerphone.

To save time
- Place orders with suppliers and have food delivered if possible.
- Use assembly-line principles: if you have to make 10 sandwiches, butter 10 slices of bread, pile on filling, cover with 10 further slices and cut into stacks, rather than making individual sandwiches.
- Use the food processor, mixer, etc. Borrow extra kitchen equipment if possible.
- Determine if there is a quicker way to cook a dish (e.g. instead of poaching a whole chicken, joint it before poaching (see page 44), or for very large numbers, buy pre-cooked chickens to save time and fuel).
- Use good quality ready-made ingredients where possible.
- Make several multiples of a recipe at a time. Recipes can usually be doubled or trebled.

LEMON SOLE WITH CUCUMBER
SERVES 4
*1 large cucumber, peeled, halved
   lengthways, deseeded and thickly sliced
3 x 675g/1½lb lemon soles, filleted and
   skinned (see page 55)
seasoned plain flour
55g/2oz unsalted butter
salt and freshly ground white pepper
lemon juice*

1. Blanch the cucumber in a saucepan of boiling salted water for 30 seconds. Refresh, drain and dry well.
2. Dip the sole fillets in seasoned flour. Lay them on a plate but do not allow them to touch each other or they will become soggy.
3. Heat half the butter in a frying pan. When foaming, put in a batch of fillets. Turn them over when golden-brown (about 1 minute on each side). Dish on to a shallow platter and keep warm. Fry the remaining fillets in the same way.
4. Melt the remaining butter in the pan. Add the cucumber and fry quite briskly for 1 minute. Remove from the heat, add salt, pepper and lemon juice. Return to the heat, bring to the boil and tip over the fish. Serve immediately.

FISH PIE
SERVES 6
*900g/2lb haddock, whiting or cod fillet or a
   mixture of any of them
425ml/¾ pint milk
½ onion, sliced
6 black peppercorns
1 bay leaf
salt and freshly ground black pepper
5 hardboiled eggs, quartered
1 tablespoon chopped fresh parsley
30g/1oz butter
30g/1oz plain flour
2 tablespoons double cream
675g/1½lb mashed potatoes (see page 30)*

1. Preheat the oven to 180°C/350°F/gas mark 4.
2. Lay the fish fillets in a roasting pan.
3. Heat the milk with the onion,

peppercorns, bay leaf and a pinch of salt.

4. Pour over the fish and cook in the preheated oven for about 15 minutes, until the fish is firm and creamy-looking.

5. Strain off the milk and reserve it for the sauce. Flake the fish into a pie dish and add the eggs. Sprinkle over the parsley.

6. Melt the butter in a saucepan, stir in the flour and cook for 1 minute. Remove from the heat and gradually add the reserved milk.

7. Return to the heat and stir, bringing slowly to the boil. Season to taste with salt and pepper. Stir in the cream and pour over the fish, mixing the sauce in carefully with a palette knife or spoon.

8. Spread a layer of mashed potatoes on the top and mark with a fork in a criss-cross pattern. Or pipe the potatoes on top of the pie. Dot with butter. Place on a baking sheet and brown in the oven for about 10 minutes, or longer if the pie has been made in advance.

MACKEREL WITH GOOSEBERRY SAUCE
SERVES 4
4 x 225g/8oz mackerel
For the gooseberry sauce
340g/12oz young gooseberries
30g/1oz caster sugar
30g/1oz butter
a pinch of ground ginger
To garnish
lemon wedges

1. Preheat the grill.
2. Clean the mackerel, cut off the fins and make 2 or 3 diagonal slashes into the flesh through the skin.
3. Prepare the gooseberry sauce: top and tail the berries and place them in a saucepan with a little water and the sugar. Simmer until tender.
4. Push the gooseberries through a sieve. Beat in the butter and ginger and taste for sweetness.
5. Grill the mackerel for about 5 minutes on each side, depending on size, or until cooked.
6. Arrange the mackerel on a warmed serving dish. Garnish with lemon wedges (see opposite). Hand the sauce separately.

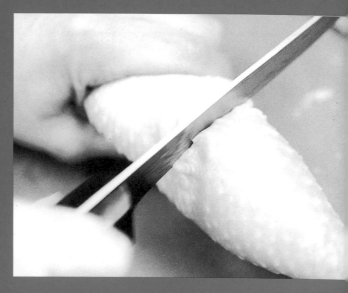

To make a lemon wedge
At Leith's we never use a slice of lemon as it cannot be squeezed; we always serve a lemon wedge.

Wash the lemon well. Trim the ends and cut it in half lengthways. Cut each half into 3 or 4 long wedges (depending on the size of the lemon) and with a sharp fruit knife cut away any thick membrane at the tip of the wedge (this will make squeezing easy). Remove any obvious pips and use as required. Lime wedges can be made in exactly the same way.

JUGGED KIPPERS
SERVES 4
4 kippers
butter
freshly ground black pepper

1. Place the kippers, tails up, in a tall stoneware jug. Pour over enough boiling water to cover the kippers and leave to stand for 5–10 minutes.
2. Serve immediately on a warmed dish with a knob of butter and plenty of pepper.

MENU PLANNING
Once a menu is planned, cooking becomes much easier. It is making the decisions that can be so daunting. Here are a few hints that may help. One of the most important things

is to make the menu relevant to the people for whom you are cooking; giving a rugger XV grilled aubergines with pesto would be as absurd as giving a ladies' lunch party carbonnade of beef with savoury crumble. The menu should stay in style throughout. The figurative leap from the south of France, with aubergine flan, to the Nursery, with steak and kidney pudding, apart from being badly balanced, would also give your guests an uncomfortable culture shock. One of the many skills of cooking is to think of the people for whom you are cooking and choose a menu that you know they will like. Here are a set of guidelines that can help:

- Never repeat the same basic ingredients in a menu – for example, do not have pastry

in two courses. However, it is perfectly acceptable to have a fish first course, such as a seafood salad, followed by a fish main course.
- Try to devise a menu that is full of colour. This is particularly important when planning a buffet party. For a conventional lunch or dinner party, always think about the appearance of the main course plate.
- Think about the balance of the menu. Do not be so inclined to generosity that you daunt your guests. If there is to be a great number of courses then serve a sorbet halfway through to refresh the palate. If you decide to serve a very rich pudding,

always offer a light alternative.
- The texture of the meal is important – it should vary.
- Try not to have too many exciting and exotic tastes in one menu. If you get carried away, sometimes the basic flavour of a delicious ingredient can be drowned. If the menu is to include a highly seasoned dish, don't follow it with a subtle dish – your guests simply won't be able to appreciate it.
- Most people love sauces, so if you serve a sauce be generous.
- We would always recommend serving a salad with any rich meal.

At Leith's there is always much discussion about the order of a meal. In England we conventionally serve the pudding followed by the cheese. In France it is more usual to serve the cheese before the pudding – the theory being that the red wine is finished with the cheese and then the pudding is served with sweet white wine. We rather like the French approach for its practicality in that it means that the host or hostess can nip off to the kitchen and do any last-minute cooking if necessary for the pudding. Finally, we would say don't overtax yourself. A dinner party is meant to be fun. Don't try to cook three hot courses and sit down to each successive course feeling slightly more flushed. Prepare as much as you can in advance – work out a timetable of how you are going to cope, and enjoy the meal with your guests.

RISOTTO ALLA MILANESE
SERVES 4
85g/3oz unsalted butter
1 large onion, finely chopped
400g/14oz risotto (arborio) rice
150ml/¼ pint dry white wine
1.75 litres/3 pints white stock (see page 52)
about 15 saffron strands
salt and freshly ground black pepper
30g/1oz unsalted butter
55g/2oz Parmesan cheese, freshly grated

1. Melt the butter in a large saucepan and gently cook the onion until soft and lightly coloured. Add the rice and wine and bring

to the boil, cook until the wine is absorbed (about 3 minutes), then reduce the heat and stir gently and continuously.

2. Meanwhile, reheat the stock in a second pan and add the saffron. Allow the stock to simmer gently.

3. Start adding the hot chicken stock to the rice a little at a time, stirring gently. Allow the stock to become absorbed after each addition. Keep stirring constantly. Season with salt and pepper, and keep adding the stock until the rice is cooked but still *al dente* (about 30 minutes).

4. Remove the pan from the heat, add the butter and the Parmesan cheese and mix well with a wooden spoon until the butter is melted and the cheese absorbed. Serve immediately, with additional grated Parmesan cheese handed separately if desired.

CHICKEN SAUTÉ NORMANDE
SERVES 4

30g/1oz clarified butter (see page 192)
1 x 1.35kg/3lb chicken, jointed into 8
   pieces (see page 44)
1 shallot, chopped
1 tablespoon Calvados
2 teaspoons plain flour
225ml/8fl oz dry cider
150ml/¼ pint white stock, made with
   chicken bones (see page 52)
salt and freshly ground black pepper
1 bouquet garni (1 bay leaf, parsley stalks
   and 4 sprigs of fresh thyme, tied together
   with string)
2 tablespoons double cream
To garnish
2 dessert apples, peeled, cored and cut
   into wedges
15g/½oz butter
a pinch of caster sugar
chopped fresh parsley

1. Heat the butter in a large sauté pan and brown the chicken pieces all over.
2. Add the shallot and sauté for 2–3 minutes.
3. Add the Calvados, light it with a match and shake the pan until the flames subside. Remove the chicken pieces.
4. Stir in the flour and cook for 1 minute.

Remove from the heat. Add the cider. Blend well and add the stock. Return to the heat and bring slowly to the boil, stirring continuously. Season with salt and pepper and add the bouquet garni. Simmer for 2 minutes.

5. Replace the chicken, cover and simmer gently for 45 minutes until tender.
6. Meanwhile, prepare the garnish: fry the apple wedges in the butter with the sugar until golden brown on each side. Keep warm.
7. When the chicken is cooked, lift it out and trim the pieces neatly. Arrange on an ovenproof platter and keep warm.
8. Strain the sauce into a clean saucepan and reduce by boiling rapidly to the required consistency. Add the cream and season to taste with salt and pepper.
9. Pour sauce over the chicken, garnish with the apple and sprinkle with the parsley.

INDIVIDUAL APPLE TARTS
MAKES 8

170g/6oz flour quantity sweet rich
shortcrust pastry (see page 24)
4 dessert apples
caster sugar
Calvados
warm apricot glaze

1. Preheat the oven to 220°C/425°F/gas mark 7.
2. Roll out the pastry and divide into 8 equal pieces.
3. On a floured work surface, roll out each piece of pastry as thinly as possible. Cut each into a 12.5cm/5in circle, place on a baking sheet and refrigerate for 20 minutes.
4. Peel the apples, if preferred. Cut in half and carefully remove the cores, using the point of a knife.
5. Slice the apples thinly and arrange the slices of half an apple on each circle of chilled pastry. Take care to pack the apples tightly to allow for shrinkage during cooking.
6. Sprinkle each tart evenly with 2 teaspoons caster sugar.
7. Bake on the top shelf of the preheated oven for 15 minutes, or until golden-brown. If

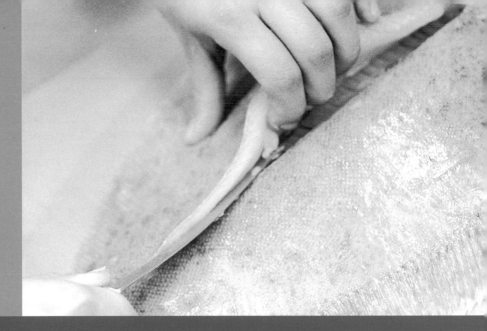

the tarts are not quite brown, place them under a hot grill for 1–2 minutes.
8. Sprinkle with a little Calvados and brush with warm apricot glaze.

SWEET RICH SHORTCRUST PASTRY
170g/6oz plain flour
a pinch of salt
100g/3 1/2oz butter
1 egg yolk
very cold water to mix

1. Sift the flour with the salt into a large bowl.
2. Rub in the butter until the mixture resembles breadcrumbs.
3. Mix the egg yolk with 2 tablespoons water and add to the mixture.
4. Mix to a firm dough, first with a knife, and finally with one hand. It may be necessary to add more water, but the pastry should not be too damp. (Though crumbly pastry is more difficult to handle, it produces a shorter, lighter result.)
5. Chill, wrapped, in a refrigerator for 30 minutes before using. Or allow to relax after rolling out but before baking.
NOTE: To make sweet rich shortcrust pastry, mix in 1 tablespoon caster sugar once the fat has been rubbed into the flour.

APRICOT GLAZE
3 tablespoons apricot jam
2 tablespoons water
juice of 1/2 lemon

1. Place all the ingredients in a heavy saucepan.
2. Bring slowly to the boil, stirring gently (avoid beating in bubbles) until syrupy in consistency. Strain.
NOTE: Use when still warm, as the glaze becomes too stiff to manage when cold. It will keep warm standing over a saucepan of very hot water.

Causes of Failure
Pale, pan-fried fish fillets: Pan and fat not hot enough; fish not dipped in flour.
Watery juices appearing in frying pan: Pan not hot enough.
Liquid appearing at the bottom of fish pie: Overcooked fish.
Apple tarts not browning on top: Oven temperature not high enough; tarts not cooked on high shelf in the oven.
Apricot glaze not spreading easily: Too thick, needs to be let down with lemon juice, or warmed up a little.
Thick and gluggy risotto: More liquid needed; or has been left waiting around before eating – must be eaten immediately after making.
Pale-looking chicken in a sauté: Colour washes off into the sauce during cooking – important to brown the chicken pieces very well at the start.

CAKES
CHAPTER 8

Techniques Covered
Creaming butter and sugar
Whisking eggs and sugar
Lining cake tins
Using self-raising flour
Using bicarbonate of soda
The all-in-one method

❓ Cookery Terms
Cream: To beat ingredients together, such as butter and fat when making a sponge cake.
Dropping consistency: The consistency where a mixture will drop reluctantly from a spoon, neither pouring off nor obstinately adhering.
Moule-à-manqué: French cake tin with sloping sides. The resulting cake has a wider base than top, and is about 2.5cm/1in high.

Recipes

Victoria sandwich
Lemon curd
Whisked sponge

Black sticky gingerbread
Old-fashioned boiled Christmas cake

CAKE-MAKING

Most cakes are made by combining fat, sugar, flour, eggs and liquid. Air or another raising agent is incorporated to make the mixture rise during baking. As it bakes, strands of gluten in the flour are stretched by the gas given off until the heat finally firms the cake. It is even rising that gives a cake a light, sponge-like texture.

Ingredients
FATS
Butter makes the best-flavoured cakes. *Margarine,* particularly the soft or tub variety, is useful for speed but has less flavour than butter. *Vegetable shortenings* are flavourless but give light cakes. *Lard* cakes are often delicious but heavy, and for this reason lard is little used in cakemaking. *Oils* are not much used as they do not easily hold air when they are creamed or beaten, and the resulting cakes can therefore be heavy.
SUGARS
The finer creaming possible with *caster sugar* makes it most suitable for cake-making. Coarse *granulated sugar* can give a speckled appearance to a finished cake unless the sugar is ground down first in a blender or food processor. *Soft brown sugars* give colour and flavour to dark cakes like gingerbread, but they give sponge cakes a drab look and too much caramel flavour.
  Golden syrup, honey, treacle and molasses are used in cakes made by the melting method.

Such cakes are cooked relatively slowly, as these thick liquid sugars tend to caramelize and burn at higher temperatures.

EGGS

Unless specified, most recipes assume a medium egg weighing 55g/2oz (UK size 3). The eggs should be used at room temperature – cold eggs tend to curdle the mixture and this results in the cake having a tough, coarse, too open texture. When using whisked egg whites in a cake, be sure not to allow even a speck of yolk into the whites. Any yolk or fat on the whisk will prevent proper whisking of the whites, reducing their air-holding ability and the lightness of the finished cake.

FLOURS

Plain white flour is used in cake-making unless otherwise specified. The high proportion of 'soft' or low-gluten wheat in European plain flour makes it particularly suitable for cake-making. In North America, plain or 'all-purpose' flour is made with more 'hard' than soft wheat, so *cornflour*, which is also weak (low in gluten), is sometimes substituted for some of the all-purpose flour, or special *soft 'cake flour'* is used. Although a little gluten is needed to allow the mixture to stretch and expand as it rises, too much would give a tough, chewy cake.

   Self-raising flour has a raising agent (baking powder) added to it and should be used only if specified in the recipe. All flours, even if labelled 'ready-sifted', should be sifted before use to eliminate any lumps and to incorporate air.

Raising agents

Air is incorporated into cake mixtures by agitating the ingredients. Methods include sifting the flour, beating the butter and beating or creaming it again with the sugar to a fluffy, mousse-

like consistency, and whisking the eggs. The heat of the oven causes the air trapped in the mixture to rise and leaven or lighten the cake, either by itself or in conjunction with other raising agents.

Steam raises some mixtures even when air has not been beaten into them. Flour mixtures with a high proportion of liquid in them, like Yorkshire pudding, will rise in a hot oven since, as the water vaporizes and the steam rises, the uncooked flour mixture rises with it. While in this puffed-up state, the mixture hardens in the oven heat with the steam trapped inside. The pockets of air created by steam are uneven and very open, so steam is not used on its own for making cakes. But steam is a contributing factor in raising wet cake mixtures such as gingerbread.

Bicarbonate of soda, or baking soda, is a powder which, when mixed into cake mixtures, quickly gives off half its substance as carbon dioxide. In a cake the trapped gas causes the mixture to puff up. Heat sets the mixture once it has risen. By the time the cake cools, the gas will have escaped and will have been replaced by air. Unfortunately, the bicarbonate of soda remaining in the cake can give it a slightly unpleasant smell and taste, and a yellowish colour. For this reason, bicarbonate of soda is most often used in strong-tasting cakes such as gingerbread and those flavoured with chocolate, treacle or molasses. The carbon dioxide reaction is speeded up by acidic substances, so bicarbonate of soda is usually used in cake mixtures with ingredients such as sour milk, vinegar, buttermilk, soured cream, cream of tartar and yoghurt. This makes it especially suitable for quickly mixed items like fruit cakes, scones, soda bread and gingerbread. It also gives them a soft texture and spongy crust with a deep colour. Unfortunately the process destroys some of the vitamins present in the flour.

Baking powder in commercial forms consists of bicarbonate of soda and an acid powder that varies according to the brand, plus a starch filler, usually cornflour, arrowroot or ground rice. The starch keeps the mixture dry by absorbing any dampness in the air, which might cause the soda and the acid in the powder to react. The presence of the filler explains why more commercial baking powder than mixed 'bicarb' and cream of tartar would be needed to raise the same cake. A 'delayed action' or 'double action' baking powder is sold in the USA that needs heat as well as moisture to produce carbon dioxide. It is not widely known in Europe. The advantage of it is that it can be added to mixtures in advance of baking – it starts to work only once in the oven.

Preparing a cake tin

All tins should be greased before use to prevent the cake mixture from sticking or burning at the edges or bottom. Melted lard or oil are the most suitable fats. Always turn the tin upside down after greasing to allow any excess fat to drain away. Use a paint-brush to get a thin layer. Bread tins and non-stick sandwich tins need no preparation other than greasing. Tins for cakes made by the melting or creaming methods should be greased, then the base lined with greaseproof paper, cut exactly to size and the paper brushed out with more melted lard or oil. (To cut the paper accurately draw round the tin, then cut just inside the line.) For cakes made by the whisking method, a dusting of caster sugar and flour should be given after lining and greasing.

For fruit cakes, grease the tin, then line the sides and base with greaseproof paper as follows:

1. Cut 2 pieces of greaseproof paper to fit the base of the cake tin.
2. Cut another piece long enough to go right round the sides of the tin and to overlap slightly. It should be 2.5cm/1in deeper than the height of the cake tin.
3. Fold one long edge of this strip over 2.5cm/1in all along its length.
4. Cut snips at right angles to the edge and about 1cm/½in apart, all along the folded side. The snips should just reach the fold.
5. Grease the tin, place one paper base in the bottom and grease again.

6. Fit the long strip inside the tin with the folded cut edge on the bottom (the flanges wil overlap slightly) and the main uncut part lining the sides of the tin. Press them well into the corners.
7. Grease the paper and lay the second base on top of the first.
8. Brush the base again with more melted lard or oil and dust the lined tin with flour.
9. After making the cake mixture and placing in the tin, wrap the outside of the tin in newspaper.

Methods used in cake-making
RUBBING IN
The rubbing-in method gives a fairly substantial cake (such as rock cakes) with a crumbly, moist texture. The raising agent is usually bicarbonate of soda, but in rock cakes it is in the self-raising flour. The cake is delicious served sliced and spread with butter, or eaten as a warm pudding with custard.
MELTING
The melting method is used for very moist cakes like gingerbread. The fat, sugar, syrup and any other liquid ingredients are heated together to melt, then cooled slightly. The flour and other dry ingredients are sifted together and the warm sugar mixture is stirred, not beaten, into the dry mixture along with the eggs. The raising agent is always bicarbonate of soda. These cakes are perfect for the beginner – easy, reliable and delicious.
CLASSIC CREAMING
Creaming fat and sugar to a mousse-like consistency, and thereby incorporating air, is the secret of lightness in cakes like Victoria sponge, although a little chemical raising agent is usually added to ensure rising. First the butter or margarine is creamed or beaten until smooth and very light in colour, but the fat is never allowed to melt. If it did the carefully incorporated air beaten into it would escape. The sugar is then beaten in by degrees, until the mixture is pale and fluffy.

The eggs are lightly beaten and added, also by degrees, to the creamed mixture. The mixture is beaten after each addition to incorporate it thoroughly. At this point the batter can curdle, especially if the eggs are too cold, but beating in a spoonful of sifted flour taken from the recipe after each addition of eggs should prevent this. Cakes made from curdled mixtures are acceptable, but they have a less delicate, more open and coarse texture than those made from uncurdled mixture.

Plain flour, if used, should be sifted with the baking powder and salt. Self-raising flour should be sifted with salt. The flour mixture is then folded carefully into the creamed mixture with a metal spoon and with as little mixing as possible to ensure minimum air loss in the batter.
ALL-IN-ONE CREAMING
The all-in-one method is an easy version of the creaming method, because all the ingredients are beaten together at the same time, but a strong electric mixer is necessary to make these cakes really successful. Soft tub margarine gives a lighter result than butter.
CREAMING FOR FRUIT CAKES
Another version of the creaming method is suited to fruit cakes. Softened butter and sugar are creamed in a mixing bowl to incorporate air. The eggs and any other liquid are gradually beaten into the creamed mixture, with the flour added with the last few additions of egg to reduce the risk of curdling. After the mixture is well combined, the dry fruit is folded in well to distribute it throughout the cake. The mixture should have a soft, dropping consistency (it should fall reluctantly off a spoon given a slight shake, neither sticking obstinately nor running off) and be spread out evenly in the prepared tin, with a slight dip in the centre of the mixture to counteract the cake 'peaking'.

Because fruit cakes are generally large and dense and contain a high proportion of fruit, which burns easily, they are cooked extremely slowly. To prevent burning they can be placed on a folded newspaper in the oven and can be covered in several layers of greaseproof or brown paper, but not foil, which traps the steam and produces too doughy a result.

WHISKING

In the whisking method, the only raising agent is air that has been trapped in the cake batter during mixing. As the air expands in the heat of the oven, the cake rises. Cakes like Swiss roll are made by this method.

The simplest whisked sponge contains no fat. Sugar and eggs are whisked together until they are thick and light, then flour is folded in gently to keep in as much air as possible. In a lighter but more complicated whisked sponge, the eggs are separated and the yolks are whisked with the sugar and flour. The whites are whisked in another bowl, then folded into the batter. Sometimes half the sugar is whisked with the yolks, and half with the whites to give a meringue.

The sugar and eggs (or egg yolks only) are whisked in a bowl set over a pan of barely simmering water. Make sure that the bowl does not touch the water or the heat will scramble the eggs. The gentle heat from the steam speeds up the dissolving of the sugar and slightly cooks and thickens the eggs, so encouraging the mixture to hold the maximum number of air bubbles. The mixture should change colour from yellow to almost white and increase to four times its original volume. The mixture is ready when a lifted whisk will leave a ribbon-like trail. Traditionally, a balloon whisk is used, but a handheld electric one works excellently. If a powerful food mixer is used, the heat can be dispensed with, though the process is speeded up if the mixture is put into a warmed bowl.

When the flour is folded in, great care should be taken to fold rather than stir or beat, as the aim is to incorporate the flour without losing any of the beaten-in air, which alone will raise the cake. The correct movement is more of lifting the mixture and cutting into it, rather than stirring it.

Although they are light and springy, a drawback of these cakes is that they go stale quickly. Always plan to make fatless sponge on the day of serving, or freeze the cake once it is cool.

The génoise is a whisked sponge that has just-runny butter folded into it with the flour. Butter gives it flavour and richness and makes it keep a day or two longer than fatless sponges. The butter should be poured in a stream around the edge of the bowl and then folded in. If the butter is poured heavily on top of the whisked mixture, it forces out some of the air, and needs excessive mixing, with the danger of more air loss.

Whisked cakes are cooked when the surface will spring back when pressed with a finger. The cakes should be cooled for a few minutes in the tin and then turned out on to a cake rack. The baking paper should be carefully peeled off to allow the escape of steam.

CAUSES OF FAILURE IN CAKE-MAKING
Creamed cakes

Close texture	Eggs added too quickly, making the mixture curdle
Flat, dense cake	Wrong flour used or no raising agent added
Flattish cake with large bubbles on surface	a) Long delay before cake put in oven b) Oven temperature too low
Base and sides of cake wet and soggy	Cake not turned on to a wire rack to cool

Fruit cakes

Cake risen to a peak	No dip made in the cake mixture prior to baking
Hard, dark crust round base and sides	a) Cake tin not lined b) Oven too hot c) Cake overcooked
Fruit, e.g. cherries, sunk to bottom of cake	a) Not enough care taken to beat air into cake b) Cake mixture too liquid c) Too little flour d) Cherries (which can be very sticky) have not been washed, dried and dusted with flour prior to adding to the mixture

Whisked sponges

Unrisen sponge	Not whisked enough before flour added
Unrisen génoise with large bubbles on the top	Butter overfolded into the mixture
Flat sponge with very hard crust	Egg and sugar mixture too hot when flour folded in
Pockets of flour in cake	Flour underfolded into cake

Melted method cakes, e.g. gingerbreads

Slightly fizzy taste	Too much bicarbonate of soda
Greenish, orange colour	Too much bicarbonate of soda
Cake sunk in the middle	a) Oven door opened during cooking b) Cake not put in oven soon enough

General mistakes

Cake risen to high peak with the surface cracked	a) Too much raising agent b) Oven temperature too high c) Cake tin too small
Thick crust all around cake	Overcooked
Thick, crunchy crust round base and sides	Too much oil, butter or lard used to grease the tin
Cake sunk in middle	a) Not cooked for long enough b) Oven door opened before cake has set, causing cake to collapse
Hard, shiny crust	Too much sugar
Cake overflowed over sides of tin	Cake tin too small
Cake good texture but very thin and overcooked	Cake tin too big
Cake leaked out of the bottom of loose-bottomed tin	a) Tin not lined b) Wrong type of tin for particular cake
Dense, heavy texture	Cake mixed too quickly, e.g. not enough air beaten in
Cake stuck to tin	a) Tin not greased b) Tin not lined c) Silicone non-stick baking parchment not used when specified in recipe

VICTORIA SANDWICH
SERVES 6
oil for greasing
110g/4oz butter
110g/4oz caster sugar
2 eggs
110g/4oz self-raising flour, sifted
water
2 tablespoons raspberry jam
caster sugar for dusting

1. Preheat the oven to 190°C/375°F/gas mark 5.
2. Prepare 2 x 15cm/6in sandwich tins by lining the bottom of each with a disc of greaseproof paper and lightly brushing out each tin with oil.
3. Cream the butter and sugar together until light and fluffy.
4. Mix the eggs together in a separate bowl, and gradually beat into the creamed mixture a little at a time, adding 1 tablespoon of the flour if the mixture begins to curdle.
5. Fold in the flour, adding enough water to bring the mixture to a dropping consistency.
6. Divide the mixture between the prepared tins and smooth the tops with a spatula. Bake in the middle of the preheated oven for about 20 minutes, or until the cakes are well risen, golden and feel spongy to the fingertips.
7. Allow the cakes to cool for a few minutes in the tins, then turn out on to a wire rack to cool completely. Peel off the lining paper.
8. Sandwich the cakes together with the jam.
9. Dust the top of the cake with caster sugar.

LEMON CURD
MAKES 450g/1lb
2 large lemons
85g/3oz butter
225g/8oz granulated sugar
3 eggs, lightly beaten

1. Grate the zest of the lemons on the finest gauge on the grater, taking care to grate the zest only, not the pith.
2. Squeeze the juice from the lemons.

3. Put the lemon zest, juice, butter, sugar and eggs into a heavy saucepan or double boiler and heat gently, stirring all the time until the mixture is thick.
4. Strain into warmed jam jars and cover.
NOTES: This curd will keep in the refrigerator for about 3 weeks.

If the curd is boiled, no great harm is done, as the acid and sugar prevent the eggs from scrambling.

WHISKED SPONGE
oil for greasing
3 eggs
85g/3oz caster sugar
1 1/2 tablespoons warm water
85g/3oz plain flour, sifted
a pinch of salt

1. Preheat the oven to 150°C/350°F/gas mark 4. Prepare a 20cm/8in cake tin (see page 64).
2. Place the eggs and sugar in a heatproof bowl set over, not in, a saucepan of simmering water. Whisk the mixture until light, thick and fluffy. (If using an electric mixer no heat is required.)
3. Remove the bowl from the heat and continue whisking until slightly cooled. Add the water.
4. Sift the flour with the salt and, using a large metal spoon, fold into the mixture, being careful not to beat out any of the air.
5. Turn the mixture into the prepared tin and bake in the middle of the preheated oven for about 30 minutes. When the cake is ready, it will shrink slightly and the edges will look crinkled. When pressed gently it will feel firm but spongy and will sound 'creaky'.
6. Turn out on to a wire rack to cool.

BLACK STICKY GINGERBREAD
MAKES 12–16 FINGERS
butter for greasing
225g/8oz butter
225g/8oz soft dark brown sugar
225g/8oz black treacle
340g/12oz plain flour
2 teaspoons ground ginger

1 tablespoon ground cinnamon
2 eggs, beaten
290ml/1/2 pint milk
2 teaspoons bicarbonate of soda

1. Preheat the oven to 150°C/300°F/gas mark 2.
2. Grease a 30 x 20cm/12 x 8in roasting pan with butter and line the base and sides with greaseproof paper.
3. Melt the butter, sugar and treacle in a saucepan. Cool to room temperature.
4. Sift the flour with the ginger and cinnamon, then stir in the melted mixture with the beaten eggs. Warm the milk to blood heat, pour it on to the soda, stir it in and add it to the mixture. Stir well and pour the mixture into the prepared tin.
5. Bake in the preheated oven for about 1 hour. Cover the top with greaseproof paper after 45 minutes. It is cooked when a skewer inserted into the centre comes out clean.
6. When the gingerbread is cold, cut it into fingers and serve it spread with butter. This gingerbread keeps very well: in fact, it improves.

OLD-FASHIONED BOILED CHRISTMAS CAKE
This cake is not, as its name suggests, boiled instead of baked, but the fruit is boiled in water and orange juice and allowed to stand for 3 days before completing. This gives the fruit a wonderful plumpness. Instead of being decorated with marzipan and icing, the cake is finished with a glazed fruit and nut topping and a pretty ribbon.
SERVES 16
225g/8oz butter
225g/8oz sultanas
225g/8oz raisins
110g/4oz currants
55g/2oz chopped mixed peel
55g/2oz glacé cherries, halved
170g/6oz dried apricots, chopped
55g/2oz dried apples, chopped
110g/4oz dried dates, chopped
110g/4oz dried peaches, chopped
110g/4oz dried pears, chopped

225g/8oz soft dark brown sugar
grated zest and juice of 1 lemon
grated zest and juice of 1 orange
110ml/4fl oz water
110ml/4fl oz orange juice
110ml/4fl oz brandy
1/2 teaspoon freshly grated nutmeg
1 teaspoon ground cinnamon
1 teaspoon ground allspice
1/2 teaspoon ground ginger
1/4 teaspoon ground cardamom
1 tablespoon black treacle
5 eggs, beaten
310g/11oz plain flour
1 teaspoon baking powder
For the fruit topping
340g/12oz apricot jam
340g/12oz mixed dried fruit and nuts, such as pecans, brazils, almonds, apricots, red and green cherries, prunes, peaches, pears, etc.

1. Put the butter, sultanas, raisins, currants, mixed peel, cherries, apricots, apples, dates, peaches, pears, sugar, lemon and orange zest and juice, water and orange juice into a large pan. Bring slowly up to the boil. Stir with a wooden spoon, cover with a lid, and simmer for 10 minutes.
2. Remove from the heat and allow to cool slightly. Add the brandy and spices and transfer to a large bowl. When the mixture is completely cold, cover and put in a cool place (not the refrigerator) for 3 days, stirring daily.
3. Preheat the oven to 170°C/325°F/gas mark 3. Line the base and sides of a 25cm/10in round cake tin with a double thickness of greased greaseproof paper.
4. Stir the treacle into the boiled fruit mixture and beat in the eggs. Sift together the flour and baking powder and stir into the cake mixture, which will be slightly sloppy. Turn it into the prepared cake tin and bake in the preheated oven for about 4 1/2 hours, or until a skewer inserted into the centre of the cake comes out clean.
5. Leave the cake to cool in the tin.
6. When completely cold, wrap up carefully in kitchen foil until ready to decorate. It will mature well for 2–3 months.
7. To decorate the cake: put the apricot jam into a saucepan with 1 tablespoon water. Heat until boiling and then push through a sieve. Allow to cool slightly, then brush the top of the cake with the apricot glaze. Arrange the fruit and nuts all over the top of the cake in a haphazard fashion and then, using a pastry brush, glaze carefully with the apricot glaze.
8. Before serving, tie a decorative ribbon round the cake.

NOTES: The glaze will remain shiny on the cake for a few days but after a week it will begin to lose its gloss so it is better not to decorate the cake too early.

If the cake top becomes very dark during baking cover it with a double layer of damp greaseproof paper.

Causes of Failure
Cake-making. see page 67.

FRYING OFF, GRILLING, DEEP-FAT FRYING AND BATTERS
CHAPTER 9

Techniques Covered
Preparing stewing beef
Browning meat for a casserole
Making a batter
Frying pancakes

Cookery Terms
Batter: A farinaceous mixture of a thick liquid consistency. It is used to give a crisp protective coating to food that might otherwise burn or splatter when deep- or shallow-fried.
Bouillon: Broth or uncleared stock.
Crêpes: Thin French pancakes.
Mirepoix: A mixture of diced root vegetables (usually onion, carrot and celery).
Well: A hollow or dip made in a pile or bowlful of flour, exposing the tabletop or the bottom of the bowl, into which other ingredients are placed prior to mixing.

Points to Remember
Frying off:
- Fry meat in a little hot oil before adding to a casserole for colour and flavour.
- The pan must be very hot before the meat is added.
- Do not over-fill the pan when browning meat or the pan will cool down too much.
- Allow the meat to sear for 1 minute before turning over – initially the meat will stick to the pan but it will release itself when ready.
- Deglaze the pan before frying off each batch of meat.

Casseroles:
- The meat must be completely covered in liquid before slow cooking.
- Use a heavy, well-fitting lid to avoid evaporation of liquid during cooking.

Dried spices:
- Always cook the spices before adding to a recipe, this brings out the flavour.

Grilling:
- Always grill the presentation side of the food you are cooking last.
- Cook the items that will take longest first.
- Lower the grill away from the heat for gentle cooking.

Deep-fat frying:
- Delicate foods need a protective coating.
- Only the tender cuts of meat should be cooked fast.
- Some foods, e.g. potato chips, require initial cooking at a low temperature, then a second frying at a high temperature to crisp and brown.

Batters:
For a lump-free batter, add the liquid slowly, into a well in the bottom of the flour, gradually incorporating the flour from the edges.
- Allow batter to stand for 30 minutes before using to allow the starch grains to swell – this makes a lighter batter.
- Adding beer to a batter improves the texture – making it crisp and light.

Recipes
Family beef stew
French pancakes (crêpes)
Tempura

FRYING
Techniques vary depending on the texture and size of the food and the effect the cook wishes to achieve. For instance, when frying steaks or chops remember to:
- Fry in an uncovered wide pan. A lid traps the steam and the food stews or steams rather than frying crisply.
- Preheat the fat. If the fat is cool when the food is put into it, the food will not brown. It will then lack flavour, look unattractive and may even absorb some of the cool fat and become too greasy.

- Fry a little at a time. Adding too much food at one time to hot fat lowers the temperature and, again, hinders the browning.
- Fry fast until the meat is completely browned on all sides. Then turn down to medium heat to cook the inside through.

Fried food should be served as soon as possible after cooking. Juices gradually seep out and meat toughens on standing; potatoes lose their crispness, become leathery and tough-skinned; fritters deflate, and everything loses its newly fried shine.

Fish is cooked à la meunière by dusting it with flour and shallow-frying in butter until it is brown on both sides. The slight coating of flour helps to prevent sticking and adds crispness to the skin. The fish is then put on a warmed platter. Chopped fresh parsley, lemon juice, salt and pepper are added to the butter in the pan and, once sizzling, this is poured over the fish.

Stiffening
Some recipes require gentle frying without a coating of flour. When this method is used, the fat, though hot, is not fearsomely so, and the food can be gently fried to a very pale brown, or cooked without browning. This is particularly useful with kidneys and liver, which tend to burst and become grainy if fried too fast; with shellfish, which toughens if subjected to fierce heat; and with thin slices of fish (such as salmon to be served in a sorrel sauce), where the taste of butter-frying is required without a browned surface.

English breakfast frying
Eggs should be fried in clean fat. Frying them in a pan in which bacon or sausages have been cooking leads to sticking and possible breaking of the yolks. If eggs are to be fried in the same pan as other items, fry the bacon, ham, sausages, potatoes, mushrooms and bread first as this will all keep in a warm oven for a few minutes. Tip the fat into a cup. Rinse the pan, removing any stuck sediment, dry it, then pour the fat back into the pan. Using enough sizzling fat to spoon over eggs speeds up the process and prevents the edges of the whites from overcooking before the thicker parts are set.

Sausages generally have skins which, as the stuffing expands in the hot pan, can burst or split open. Avoid this by pricking them carefully all over with a thin needle (large holes like those made by the prongs of a fork provide weak points where the skin will split), and/or by

cooking slowly. Shake the pan with rapid but careful side-to-side or forward-and-backward movements; this will dislodge any pieces that are stuck with less damage than a prodding utensil. Fry the sausages slowly until evenly browned all over and firm to the touch.

Bacon rashers can be fried in an almost dry pan as they readily produce their own fat. However, they cook faster and more evenly in shallow fat.

Glazing vegetables

Vegetables are sometimes given a final shiny, slightly sweet glaze by frying them in a mixture of butter and sugar. The sugar melts and caramelizes to a pale toffee and the vegetables brown in the butter and caramel mixture. Constant shaking of the pan is necessary to prevent burning and sticking. This method is particularly successful with shallots, baby onions, mushrooms and root vegetables.

Sautéing

Sautéing is used on its own to cook foods such as chicken pieces, mushrooms or apple rings, but is most frequently used in conjunction with other forms of cooking. For example, whole small onions may be sautéed to brown them before they are added to liquid in a stew or a sauce. Sautéing is also employed after boiling to give cooked or partially cooked foods, such as potatoes, a lightly browned and buttered exterior.

Browning gives a sautéed dish its essential character. After browning, some meats, such as liver or veal escalopes, are often removed and then served with a relatively small amount of well-flavoured sauce which has been made in the same pan. Meats such as pork chops or chicken pieces may be given an initial browning and then cooked with added ingredients that will eventually form the sauce. The range of such sauces is almost endless as various as the liquids and other flavourings that can be used in making them. Stages in sautéing are as follows:
1. Fry the main ingredients together with any others, browning them in minimal fat. Remove them from the pan and keep them hot.
2. Deglaze the pan with a liquid such as stock, cream or wine.
3. Add the flavourings for the sauce.
4. If the initial browning has cooked the main ingredients sufficiently, reduce the sauce by rapid boiling and pour it over the dish. Garnish and serve immediately.
5. If the main ingredients need further cooking, simmer them in the sauce until they are tender, then proceed as above.

Stir-frying

Choose a carbon iron wok with a round base and one long wooden handle. The best size is about 35 cm/14 in. The advantage of stir-frying is that there is a large surface area all at the same temperature, so the food cooks fast and retains all its flavour, colour and texture. The trick is to stir with a Chinese ladle, strainer or spoon with one hand whilst shaking and jerking the wok with the other. When stir-frying vegetables add the firmest vegetables first, and the more tender ones a few minutes later.

Batter

Batter is a farinaceous mixture of a thick liquid consistency. It is used to give a crisp protective coating to food that might otherwise burn or splatter when deep- or shallow-fried.

Using a deep-fryer

1. If the deep-fryer is not thermostatically controlled, use a thermometer to test the temperature of the fat by dropping a crumb or cube of bread into it. If the bread browns in 60 seconds, the fat is about 182°C/360°F and suitable for gentle frying; if it browns in 40 seconds, the oil is moderately hot, about 190°C/375°F; if it browns in 20 seconds, the fat is very hot, about 195°C/385°F. If the bread browns in 10 seconds, the fat is dangerously hot and should be cooled down. Turn off the heat and fry several slices of bread in it to speed up the cooling.

2. Cook food in small amounts. Adding too many pieces at one time lowers the temperature of the fat so that the coating will not form a crisp crust. The food then absorbs fat and loses its juices in the cooking fat. This is particularly important if you are frying food that is still frozen, such as fish fingers, commercially prepared chips or Chinese spring rolls, which will of course cool the fat greatly. However, do not attempt to remedy this problem by frying in very hot fat. Comparatively cool fat is needed (about 180°C/350°F) to allow the inside to thaw and cook before the coating browns.

3. Drain the cooked fat well on absorbent paper.

4. If the food is not served right away, spread it out in a single layer on a hot baking sheet or tray and keep it uncovered in a warm oven with the door ajar to allow the free circulation of air. Covering or enclosing the food will make the crust soggy. Try not to fry far ahead of serving.

5. Add salt, or a sprinkling of caster sugar if the food is sweet, after frying. This accentuates the flavour and the dry, crisp texture.

6. After use, cool the fat and strain it through muslin or a coffee filter paper. This removes food particles which, if left in the fat, will become black and burned with repeated fryings. As soon as the fat becomes at all dark, it should be changed, as it is beginning to break down, will smoke readily and give a rancid flavour to fried food.

GRILLING

Intense heat is the secret of successful grilling. Although this method requires active attention from the cook, its advantages are that the food cooks quickly and the charred surface gives great flavour.

To produce succulent, perfectly grilled meat with a crisp brown outside and pink juicy inside, it is absolutely essential to preheat the grill to its highest setting. This may take 10 or even 20 minutes for the grill on a good domestic cooker. Under a cooler grill, the meat's surface will not brown quickly, leaving the meat tasteless and unattractive by the time it is cooked through. If the grill cannot be adequately preheated to brown meat and fish quickly, fry the steaks instead.

When grilling over an open charcoal fire, it may take 2 hours before the embers are flameless yet burn with the necessary intensity. But their fierce heat will cook a small lamb cutlet perfectly in 2 minutes and the charcoal will give it a wonderfully smoky flavour. Charcoal, when ready, glows bright red in the dark and has an ashy grey look in daylight.

Unlike braising, grilling will not tenderize meat, so only tender, choice cuts should be grilled. They should not be much thicker than 5cm/2in because of the high temperatures involved. Any thicker and the meat will remain cold and raw when the outside is black. Even so, unless the cut of meat is fairly thin, once it browns it must be moved further away from the heat source so that the interior can cook before the surface burns. Basting with the delicious pan juices or with olive oil or butter adds flavour and shine. Turning is necessary for even cooking, and should be done halfway through the estimated cooking time, when the first surface is attractively brown.

When grilling over, rather than under, heat, use a fine grill rack or wire mesh grill to support delicate cuts of fish and grease the grill rack or mesh well. Fish cuts can be wrapped in greased foil and cooked over heat, but they then cook in their own steam rather than grill in the true sense.

The following points should be remembered when grilling:

- Take food out of the refrigerator or freezer in plenty of time to bring it to room temperature before grilling. An almost frozen steak will still be cold inside when the outside is brown and sizzling. This is particularly important if the steak is to be served very rare (blue, see below).
- Do not salt food much in advance. The salt draws moisture from the food. Salt after, during or immediately before grilling.
- Brush the food with butter, oil or a mixture of the two to keep it moist and to speed the browning process. This is also essential to prevent delicate foods such as fish from sticking.
- The more well done meat or fish is, the tougher it will be to the touch and the palate.
- To avoid piercing the meat and allowing the juices to escape, turn the grilling food with tongs or spoons, not a sharp instrument.
- Serve immediately. Grilled food, even if well sealed, inevitably loses moisture, dries up and toughens if kept hot for any length of time.

Grilling steaks

All grilled meats should be well browned on the surface, but the varying degrees of 'doneness' are defined as follows:

BLUE: The inside is almost raw (but hot).

RARE: Red inside with plenty of red juices running freely.

MEDIUM RARE: As rare, but with fewer free-flowing juices and a paler centre.

MEDIUM: Pink in the centre with juices set.

WELL DONE: The centre is beige but the flesh is still juicy.

The best way to tell if meat is done is by its texture. Feel the meat by pressing firmly with a finger. Rare steak feels soft, almost raw; medium steak is firmer with some resilience to it; well-done steak feels very firm. With practice there will soon be no need to cut-and-peep.

Cooking time for steaks varies with the heat of the grill, the distance of the food from the heat, the thickness of the cut and its fat content. The density of the meat also affects the cooking time. Open-textured steak such as sirloin will cook faster than the same thickness and weight of closer-textured rump.

Grilling fish

Lay fish steaks and fillets on greased foil on the grill rack, and set close under the preheated grill. This prevents the delicate flesh from sticking to the rack and breaking up when turned.

STEWING

The term stew is so widely used that it can mean almost anything. A stew is essentially food that has been slowly and gently cooked in plenty of liquid. Most cooks envisage meat cut into smallish pieces before cooking, but the term is sometimes used for sliced, sautéed meat or poultry served in a sauce, or for a whole joint or bird poached in liquid. Many stews require

preliminary frying of the meat, and sometimes of onions, shallots, carrots or mushrooms too. This gives a richer flavour to the ingredients and adds colour and flavour to the sauce, which will be made using the browned sediment and dried-on juices sticking to the pan after frying. These are called brown stews. White stews are made without preliminary browning and are less rich, less fatty, altogether gentler and more easily digestible than brown ones.

Both brown and white stews are served in their cooking liquid, which is usually thickened to a syrupy sauce.

The principles of shallow-frying (see page 72) apply to the preliminary frying for a brown stew. If the sauce is not to taste insipid, or be pale in colour, you must start with a good even colour on both sides of each slice or all sides of each cube of meat. Good stews are made or lost in the early

stages – so take care to fry only a few pieces at a time, to keep the temperature hot enough to sizzle and to take the time to get an even colour. Deglaze the pan as often as necessary. Deglazing serves three essential purposes: it prevents the stuck sediment in the pan from burning; it allows the flavour of that sediment to be captured and incorporated into the sauce; and it cleans the pan ready for the next batch of meat.

Beef stew with suet crust is a traditional stew, classically made. But the same principles can be used to make a lamb navarin, for example. Follow the same procedure, using lean cubes of lamb instead of the beef and omitting the suet crust. Young spring vegetables such as broad beans, French beans, tiny whole carrots, peas or sprigs of cauliflower, can be added to the stew for the last 10 minutes of stewing time to give a navarin d'agneau printanier.

FAMILY BEEF STEW
SERVES 4

675g/1¹/₂lb stewing beef
dripping or oil
2 large mild onions, sliced
3 medium carrots, cubed
1 small turnip, cubed
570ml/1 pint brown stock (see page 51)
salt and freshly ground black pepper
1 bay leaf
2 parsley stalks
a pinch of chopped fresh thyme
30g/1oz pearl barley

1. Preheat the oven to 150°C/300°F/gas mark 2.
2. Remove any gristle and excess fat from the meat and cut it into 3cm/1¹/₂in cubes.
3. Melt a little of the dripping or oil in a sauté pan. Brown the beef cubes on all sides, a few at a time, and transfer to a casserole. If the bottom of the pan becomes too brown and sticky, pour in a little stock and swish it about, scraping the sediment from the bottom of the pan. Pour this into the casserole, and then heat a little more dripping or oil and continue browning the meat until all is transferred to the casserole.
4. Fry the onion, carrot and turnip in the pan until golden-brown and place them in the casserole.
5. Pour the stock into the pan and bring to the boil, scraping any remaining sediment from the bottom. Stir in the seasoning, bay leaf, parsley, thyme and barley and pour on to the meat. Bring to the boil, then simmer for 2 minutes.
6. Cover the casserole and cook in the preheated oven for 2–2¹/₂ hours. Skim off any excess fat.

NOTE: This stew is even better if kept for a day before eating – the barley swells up even more and the flavour improves.

FRENCH PANCAKES (CRÊPES)

MAKES ABOUT 12
110g/4oz plain flour
a pinch of salt
1 egg
1 egg yolk
290ml/¹/₂ pint milk, or milk
  and water mixed
1 tablespoon oil
oil for cooking
To serve
lemon wedges (see page 58)
caster sugar

1. Sift the flour with the salt into a bowl and make a well in the centre, exposing the bottom of the bowl.
2. Put the egg and egg yolk with a little of the milk into this well.
3. Using a wooden spoon or whisk, mix the egg and milk and then gradually draw in the flour from the sides as you mix.
4. When the mixture reaches the consistency of thick cream, beat well and stir in the oil.
5. Add the remaining milk; the consistency should now be that of thin cream. (Batter can also be made by placing all the ingredients together in a blender for a few seconds, but take care not to over-whizz or the mixture will be bubbly.)
6. Cover the bowl and refrigerate for about

30 minutes. This is done so that the starch cells will swell, giving a lighter result.

7. Prepare a pancake pan or frying pan by heating well and wiping with oil. Pancakes are not fried in fat – the purpose of the oil is simply to prevent sticking.

8. When the pan is ready, pour in about 1 tablespoon batter and swirl about the pan until evenly spread across the bottom.

9. Place over heat and, after 1 minute, using a palette knife and your fingers, turn the pancake over and cook again until brown. (Pancakes should be extremely thin, so if the first one is too thick, add a little extra milk to the batter. The first pancake is unlikely to be perfect, and is often discarded.)

10. Make up all the pancakes, turning them out on to a tea-towel or plate.

11. Serve with sugar and lemon wedges.

NOTES: Pancakes can be kept warm in a folded tea-towel on a plate over a saucepan of simmering water, in the oven, or in a warmer. If allowed to cool, they may be reheated by being returned to the frying pan or by warming in the oven.

Pancakes freeze well, but should be separated by pieces of greaseproof paper. They may also be refrigerated for a day or two.

TEMPURA
SERVES 4
1 small aubergine
salt
oil for deep-frying
1 medium courgette, cut into batons
110g/4oz baby sweetcorn, halved lengthways
225g/8oz scampi, seasoned with lemon
    juice and freshly ground black pepper
For the batter
225g/8oz plain flour
2 small egg yolks
340ml/12fl oz water
a pinch of salt
For the sauce

2 teaspoons sesame oil
2 tablespoons red wine vinegar
2 tablespoons soy sauce
3 tablespoons ginger syrup (from a jar of
    preserved ginger)
2 tablespoons clear honey
1 small bunch of spring onions, shredded

1. Slice the aubergine thinly, score the flesh lightly and place in a colander, sprinkling each layer with salt. Leave to degorge for 30 minutes.

2. Mix together all the ingredients for the sauce, except for the spring onions.

3. Heat oil in a deep-fryer until a crumb will sizzle vigorously in it.

4. Wash the aubergines well and pat dry on absorbent kitchen paper.

5. When the oil is hot, mix the batter ingredients together – it should not be smooth.

6. Dip the prepared aubergine, courgette, sweetcorn and scampi into the batter and deep-fry in small batches. Drain well on kitchen paper and sprinkle lightly with salt. Arrange on a large warmed serving dish.

7. Scatter the shredded spring onions on top of the sauce and hand separately.

Causes of Failure
Pale-looking casserole: Meat not browned enough.
Flavourless casserole: Meat not browned enough.
Bitter-tasting casserole: Meat burnt, pan allowed to get too hot and pan not deglazed regularly enough.
Greasy tempura: Fat not hot enough, not drained on kitchen paper immediately after cooking or sprinkled with salt to absorb excess oil.
Pancakes with holes in: Frying pan too hot.
Pancakes sticking to pan: Frying pan not proved.
Thick pancakes: Batter needs letting down to the consistency of single cream or excess batter needs to be poured out of the pan at the start of making a pancake.

BRAISING, STEAMING AND PASTRY II
CHAPTER 10

Techniques Covered
Rolling and folding a quick layered
rough puff pastry
Preparing and arranging fruit
decoratively on a tart
Suet crust pastry
Preparing and covering a pudding
basin for steaming
Braising
Steaming
Blanching lettuce leaves

❓ Cookery Terms
Braise: To bake or stew slowly on a bed of vegetables in a covered pan.
Egg wash: Beaten raw egg, sometimes with salt, used for glazing pastry to give it a shine when baked.
Glaze: To cover with a thin layer of shiny jellied meat juices (for roast turkey), melted jam
(for fruit flans) or syrup (for rum baba).
Knock up: To separate slightly the layers of raw puff pastry with the blade of a knife to
facilitate rising during cooking.

Points to Remember
Rough puff pastry: see page 86.
Suet crust pastry: see page 87.
Steaming (puddings):
- Do not fill the pudding basin to the top – allow room for the pudding to raise and expand.
- Make sure the top is well sealed to prevent water from seeping in.
- Always place in a pan of boiling water which comes halfway up the sides of the basin.
- Never allow the pan to boil dry, top up regularly.
Steaming (fish or vegetables, etc.):
- Flavour the liquid as appropriate to add to the flavour of the food.
- Do not overfill the steamer – cook food in a single layer so it steams quickly and evenly.
- This method of cooking is only suitable for quick-cooking, tender cuts of fish or meat.

Recipes

Rough puff pastry
Tarte française

Suet crust pastry
Steak and kidney pudding
Steamed trout fillets in lettuce

BRAISING

Braising, in the true sense of the word, is a method of slowly cooking meat on a mirepoix, a thick bed of finely diced mixed vegetables with the addition of strong stock. In practice, the term braising is often confused with pot-roasting, as in both methods food is cooked slowly in a pan with a tightly-fitting lid to give deliciously tender results. The main difference is that pot-roasted food is cooked with little, if any, liquid other than the fat used for browning the ingredients, and braising involves some liquid and at least some cut-up vegetables to add moisture to the pan, even if a true mirepoix is not used. A pot-roast should taste 'roasted' and be decidedly fattier than a braise, which is closer to a stew and depends more on juices and stocks than on fat for flavour.

Braising can also mean 'sweating'. This is a method of gently cooking vegetables, frequently onions and shallots, in butter or oil in a covered pan, which is shaken frequently to prevent burning and sticking. Once cooked through, softened and exuding their juices but not coloured, the vegetables are usually added to stews, sauces or soups, to which they give a subtle flavouring but no colouring. For example, to braise red cabbage, a finely chopped onion is sweated in butter until tender, then shredded cabbage, a little vinegar, sugar, apple and seasoning are added. These are left over a low heat, covered tightly, to sweat for 2–3 hours. The result is braised red cabbage, even though neither meat nor mirepoix has been included.

Occasionally the term braising is used to mean baking in a covered pan with only a little liquid. Braised celery hearts, for example, consists of quarters of celery head cooked in a little stock in a covered pan in the oven. Braised fennel is cooked with lemon juice, butter and stock.

Beef fillet and sirloin or lamb best end should be roasted or grilled, but otherwise whole joints or smaller pieces of meat can be braised with advantage. The meat should be fairly lean and any fat that melts into the stock should be skimmed off before serving. Poultry may be braised unless it is old and tough, when stewing or poaching are more suitable cooking methods as all the flesh, which will tend to be stringy and dry, is submerged in liquid.

The vegetables for the mirepoix should be browned quickly in hot fat and stirred constantly to ensure even colouring, then transferred to a heavy casserole or pan. The meat can be browned in the same fat before it is placed on top of the vegetables and stock is added. As the vegetables cook they will disintegrate, helping to thicken the stock.

Making a strong, reduced, well-flavoured stock is time-consuming, but it is one of the key factors in good braising. The best stock is one made from chopped-up beef shin bones that have been browned all over and then simmered and skimmed frequently for hours (see page 51).

As with pot roasting, meat may be marinated overnight in the refrigerator and large pieces of exceptionally lean meat may be larded to ensure that they remain moist. Dry the meat well before browning it.

The exacting and by no means easy steps for braising red meat to ideal tenderness and almost sticky juiciness are as follows:

1. Fry the mirepoix of vegetables and a few tablespoons of diced salt pork or bacon slowly in oil and butter, shaking the pan and stirring until they are evenly browned all over.
2. Brown the meat on all sides and place it on top of the vegetable bed in a heavy casserole.
3. Add stock, made from gelatinous meats such as knuckle of veal or beef shin bones, to cover the meat. If the stock is not rich and solidly set when cold, the braise will not have the correct 'melting' stickiness. Then stew, without basting, until half cooked.
4. Lift out the meat, strain the stock, and discard the mirepoix, which will by now have imparted all its flavours.

5. Return the meat to the casserole and reduce the stock by rapid boiling until it is thick and syrupy, then pour it over the meat.

6. There will no longer be enough stock to cover the meat and there is a danger, even in a covered pan, of the exposed top drying out, so turn the meat every 15 minutes and baste it with the stock.

By the end of the cooking time, when the meat is tender, the stock should be so reduced as to provide a shiny coating that will not run off the meat. It will penetrate the flesh, moistening it and giving it the slightly glutinous texture of perfectly braised meat.

STEAMING

Steaming is the cooking of food in hot vapours over boiling liquid (usually water) rather than in liquid. It occurs to some extent in braising and pot-roasting, because of the closed pans and the relatively small amounts of liquid used. In true steaming, however, the food never touches the liquid, so the loss of many vitamins is significantly reduced. Furthermore, steamed food is not browned first, so it can be cooked without fat. This makes the food more easily digestible and particularly suitable for invalids and those on low-fat diets. The method has regained great favour with nouvelle cuisine chefs because of its simplicity and purity. But excellent ingredients are essential for steaming – there is no browning, so the food must taste good without such assistance.

A variety of equipment for steaming food is available. Most common are oval or round steamers, which are like double saucepans, except that the top has holes in its base. Steam from boiling water in the lower pan rises through the holes to cook the food, while the lid on the upper pan keeps in the steam.

Another popular steaming device is a stainless steel or aluminium basket that opens and folds shut and is used with an ordinary lidded saucepan. The basket stands on its own short legs to keep it clear of the boiling water. It fits inside most saucepans and is particularly suitable for foods that do not need long cooking time as otherwise the water underneath the short legs would have to be replaced too frequently. The saucepan must have a tightly fitting lid.

Vegetables

Vegetables are the food most commonly steamed as they cook quickly and retain more of their colour and texture this way. Careful timing is essential as steamed food can be tasteless if even slightly overcooked. Today steaming times for vegetables are short, giving bright-coloured, *al dente*, palpably fresh results. Some vegetables can be steamed in their own juices. Spinach, for example, may be trimmed and put wet from washing into a covered saucepan over medium heat, and shaken occasionally until limp and cooked, but still very green. This takes about 5 minutes.

Floury potatoes that tend to break up when boiled before they are cooked are best steamed; choose potatoes that are about the same size, so that they cook in the same time.

If they are very large or different sizes, cut them into bite-sized pieces before steaming. For most other root vegetables, such as turnips, parsnips and swedes, cut them into 1cm/$\frac{1}{2}$in dice and steam them until tender before seasoning and adding butter to serve.

FISH AND POULTRY

Steaming fish is simple and quick and always produces a delicate result if the fish is not allowed to overcook. Put the fish on to a piece of muslin or cheesecloth to prevent it from sticking to the steamer bottom. Oval steamers and folding baskets are suitable for small quantities of fish, but for larger fish or cooking a number of small fish, shellfish, fish steaks or fillets, a fish kettle (usually used for poaching whole fish) may be used. Made of metal, these come in sizes to take whole fish on a perforated rack inside the kettle. Ramekins can be placed under the rack to keep it well above the boiling liquid. Whole fish can be stuffed and cooked over liquid in a covered kettle on top of the stove. Allow about 8 minutes per 450g/1lb of fish.

Delicate poultry such as chicken breasts or whole small quail may be steamed similarly.

Plate steaming is an excellent method of cooking small quantities of fish in their own juices. Put the fish fillets or steaks on a lightly buttered plate, season well and cover with another upturned buttered plate or buttered kitchen foil. Set the covered plate on top of a pan of gently boiling water or on a trivet inside a large frying pan of bubbling water and cook for 8–10 minutes, depending on the thickness of the fish.

Steamed puddings

Traditional English sweet and savoury puddings (particularly suet crust puddings) are also cooked by steaming, but here the food is cooked in a container heated by steam. This gives the suet mixture its distinctive soft, open texture. The easiest way to cook the pudding is to put its container in a saucepan with hot water that comes halfway up the sides of the container. The pan is covered and the pudding cooked over low heat to steam gently for a long time, and water is added to the pan as necessary. Take care to cover the pudding with a double thickness of kitchen foil, pleated to allow for expansion of the crust, and put a band

of folded foil under the basin with ends projecting up the sides to act as handles.

Chinese cooking traditionally involves a good deal of steaming. Fish, shellfish and tender cuts of meat, often wrapped in pastry or vegetable leaves, are quickly steamed. Food in one or more stacked rattan or metal baskets with a lid is placed over steaming liquid in a pan or wok for quick cooking.

ROUGH PUFF PASTRY

This is the quickest method of making a layered pastry. A large proportion of fat is incorporated into the dough and the pastry rolled and folded several times to create layers of pastry which will rise into light, thin leaves.

225g/8oz plain flour
a pinch of salt
140g/5oz butter
120–150ml/4–5fl oz very cold water to mix

1. Sift the flour with the salt into a chilled bowl. Cut the butter into knobs about the size of a sugar lump and add to the flour. Do not rub in but add enough water to just bind the paste together. Mix first with a knife, then with one hand. Knead very lightly.
2. Chill, wrapped, in the refrigerator for 10 minutes.
3. On a floured board, roll the pastry into a strip about 30 x 10cm/12 x 4in long. This must be done carefully: with a heavy rolling pin, press firmly on the pastry and give short, sharp rolls until the pastry has reached the required size. Take care not to over-stretch and break the surface of the pastry.
4. Fold the strip into 3 and turn so that the folded edge is to your left, like a closed book.
5. Again roll out into a strip 1cm/1/2 in thick. Fold in 3 again and chill, wrapped, in the refrigerator for 15 minutes.
6. Roll and fold the pastry as before, then chill again for 15 minutes.
7. Roll and fold again, by which time the pastry should be ready for use, with no signs of streakiness. If it is still streaky,

roll and fold once more.
8. Roll into the required shape.
9. Chill again in the refrigerator before baking.

NOTE: The aim is to create pastry layers without allowing the incorporated fat to melt. Start with everything cool, including the bowl, the ingredients, and the worktop if possible. Short, quick strokes (rather than long steady ones) allow the bubbles of air so carefully incorporated into the pastry to move about while the fat is gradually and evenly distributed in the paste. Work lightly and do not stretch the paste, or the layers you have built up will tear and allow the air and fat to escape. Chill the pastry between rollings or at any point if there is a danger of the fat breaking through the pastry, or if the pastry becomes sticky and warm. It sounds like a complicated business, but it is a lot easier done than said.

TARTE FRANÇAISE
SERVES 4

225g/8oz flour quantity rough puff pastry
  (see page 86)
beaten egg
3 tablespoons warm apricot glaze
  (see page 61)
fruit as for fruit salad, such as 2 oranges,
  a small bunch of black grapes, a small
  bunch of white grapes, a small punnet
  of strawberries, 1 banana

1. Roll out the pastry into a rectangle the size of an A4 sheet of paper.
2. Cut out a 'picture frame' 2.5cm/1in wide. Dust liberally with flour and fold into 4. Carefully set aside.
3. Roll out the remaining pastry until it is a

little larger than A4 size.

4. Preheat the oven to 220°C/425°F/gas mark 7.

5. Transfer the pastry to a baking sheet and prick it well all over with water. Using a pastry brush, dampen the edges with a fork. Place the 'picture frame', still folded, on to the pastry and unfold. Trim the edges neatly. Brush off any excess flour. Knock up the pastry and brush the frame with beaten egg (take care not to dribble the glaze down the sides or the pastry will stick together). Refrigerate for 20 minutes.

6. Bake in the preheated oven for 15 minutes or until crisp and brown.

7. Remove from the oven and leave to cool on a wire rack.

8. Use a little of the apricot glaze to brush the surface of the pastry.

9. Cut up the fruit as you would for a fruit salad and lay the pieces in rows on the pastry as neatly and closely together as possible. Be careful about colour (do not put 2 rows of white fruit next to each other, or tangerine segments next to orange segments, for example). When complete, paint carefully with the warm apricot glaze.

SUET CRUST PASTRY
As suet crust pastry is most often used for steamed puddings, instructions for lining a pudding basin are included here. Use the pastry as soon as it is made.
butter for greasing
340g/12oz self-raising flour
salt
170g/6oz shredded beef suet
very cold water to mix

1. Grease a 1.1 litre/2 pint pudding basin.
2. Sift the flour with a good pinch of salt into a large bowl. Stir in the suet and add enough water to mix, first with a knife, and then with one hand, to a soft dough.
3. On a floured surface, roll out two-thirds of

the pastry into a round about 1cm/$\frac{1}{2}$in thick. Sprinkle the pastry evenly with flour.

4. Fold the round in half and place the open curved sides towards you.

5. Shape the pastry by rolling the straight edge away from you and gently pushing the middle and pulling the sides to form a bag that, when spread out, will fit the pudding basin.

6. With a dry pastry brush, remove all excess flour and place the bag in the well-greased basin.

7. Fill the pastry bag with the desired mixture.

8. Roll out the remaining piece of pastry and use it as a lid, damping the edges and pressing them firmly together.

9. Cover the basin with buttered greaseproof paper, pleated in the centre, and a layer of pleated kitchen foil. (Pleating the paper and foil allows the pastry to expand slightly without bursting the wrappings.) Tie down firmly to prevent water or steam getting in during cooking.

NOTE: Occasionally suet crust pastry is used for other purposes than steamed puddings, in which case it should be mixed as above and then handled like any other pastry, except that it does not need to relax before cooking.

CAUSES OF FAILURE IN PASTRY-MAKING

Rough puff

Tough pastry	Too much water, over-handling, fat not cold enough.
Fat escaping	Fat has not been incorporated correctly, pastry not chilled enough, fat not cold enough.
Poor rising	Incorrectly rolled and folded, final pastry rolled too thin.
Uneven rise	Uneven pressure when rolling.

Suet crust

Grey, oily, unrisen	Water has not been boiling throughout cooking.
Tough, heavy texture	Over-handling, too much liquid.

STEAK AND KIDNEY PUDDING

SERVES 4

675g/1¹/₂lb chuck steak
225g/8oz ox kidney
plain flour
suet crust pastry made with 340g/12oz
*   self-raising flour (see page 87)*
butter for greasing
salt and freshly ground black pepper
2 teaspoons very finely chopped onion
2 teaspoons chopped fresh parsley

1. Cut the beef into cubes about 2.5cm/1in square.
2. Cut the kidney into cubes, discarding any sinews.
3. Place both beef and kidney in a large sieve. Pour over the flour and shake until the meat is lightly coated.
4. On a floured surface, roll out two-thirds of the suet pastry into a round about 1cm/¹/₂in thick. Flour the surface lightly to stop it sticking together when folded. Fold the pastry over to form a half-moon shape. Place the pastry with the straight side away from you and roll it lightly so that the straight side becomes curved and the whole rounded again. Now separate the layers, and you should have a bag, roughly the shape of a 1kg/2¹/₄lb pudding basin. Use it to line the lightly greased basin, easing the pastry where necessary to fit, and trimming off the top so that 1cm/¹/₂in sticks up over the edge.
5. Fill the lined basin with the meat, sprinkling plenty of salt, pepper, onion and parsley in between the layers.
6. Add water to come three-quarters of the way up the meat.
7. Roll the remaining third of suet pastry 5mm/¹/₄in thick, and large enough to just cover the pudding filling. Put in place, wet the edges and press them together securely.
8. Cover the pudding with a double piece of greaseproof paper, pleated down the

centre to allow room for the pastry to expand, and a similarly pleated piece of kitchen foil. Tie down with string.

9. Place in a saucepan of boiling water with a tightly closed lid, or in a steamer, for 5–6 hours, taking care to top up with boiling water occasionally so as not to boil dry.

10. Remove the paper and foil and serve the pudding from the bowl.

NOTES: Traditionally, steak and kidney puddings served from the bowl are presented wrapped in a white linen napkin.

As the filling of the pudding may, with long cooking, dry out somewhat, it is worth having a gravy boat of hot beef stock handy to moisten the meat when serving.

A delicious addition to steak and kidney pudding is a small can of smoked oysters mixed in with the meat filling.

STEAMED TROUT FILLETS IN LETTUCE
This recipe is taken from *Easy to Entertain* by Patricia Lousada.
SERVES 4
2 shallots, very finely chopped
1 tablespoon oil
170g/6oz mushrooms, finely chopped
a squeeze of lemon juice
salt and freshly ground black pepper
8 large lettuce leaves or cabbage leaves
4 large trout, pink-fleshed if possible, filleted, skinned and pinboned (see pages 55–56)

1. Sweat the shallots in the oil, stirring constantly. Add the mushrooms, lemon juice, salt and pepper. Sauté until the mushrooms give off their juices, then boil hard until all the juice has evaporated.

2. Blanch the lettuce in a large quantity of boiling salted water for 15 seconds, until just limp. Refresh in a bowl of cold water, then spread out on tea towels or absorbent kitchen paper to dry.

3. Trim the fillets and remove any bones with tweezers. By running your finger against the grain of the flesh, you can feel where they are. Pat the fillets dry and season with salt and pepper. Place a spoonful of the mushroom mixture on each fillet and roll up. Wrap in a lettuce leaf and place seam down in a steamer. Continue with the other fillets. Steam until tender (about 10 minutes).

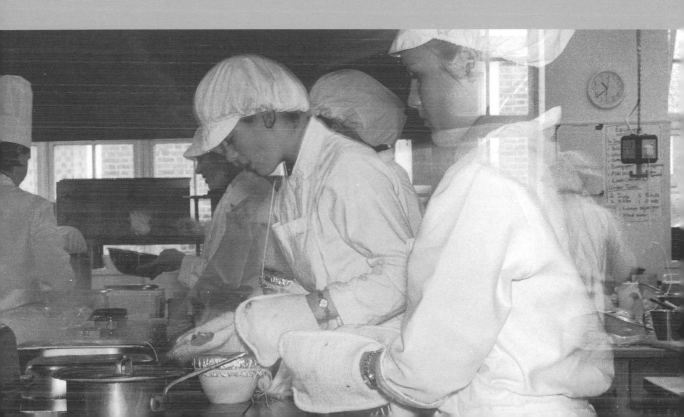

BREAD
CHAPTER 11

Techniques Covered
Handling fresh yeast
Kneading and shaping doughs
Using cream of tartar
Making a sweet, rolled and filled dough

❷ **Cookery Terms**
Knock down or **knock back:** To punch or knead out the air in risen dough so that it resumes its pre-risen bulk.
Prove: To put dough or yeasted pastry mixture to rise before baking.

Recipes
White bread
Brown soda bread
Chelsea buns

YEAST
Baker's yeast, the most usual leavening agent for bread, is a single-celled organism that belongs to the fungus family. For yeast to reproduce it needs warmth, moisture and food. Given the right conditions it can reproduce very quickly, giving off carbon dioxide as it does so. This is trapped in the dough or batter and so aerates it. The optimum temperature for yeast to reproduce is 27°C/80°F. Too much heat can kill it so care must be taken to ensure that the liquid used in making bread is lukewarm. A high concentration of sugar, fat or salt can slow down its rates of reproduction. If a dough is high in these ingredients then more yeast must be used. There are three types of yeast available: fresh, dried and easy-blend dried yeast.

Fresh yeast should be beige, crumbly-soft and sweet-smelling. It is usually thought of as the most satisfactory form of baker's yeast as it is less likely to produce 'beery' bread. Fresh yeast keeps for five days or so wrapped loosely in the refrigerator, and can be frozen for short periods, though results after freezing are very unpredictable and unreliable. If it is difficult to obtain, use dried yeast, or buy fresh yeast in a suitable quantity, divide it into 30g/1oz pieces, wrap them individually, then overwrap and freeze. Use as soon as the yeast thaws, and do not keep frozen for more than a month.

Dried yeast is bought in granular form in airtight sachets. It will remain active for about 6 months in a cool, dry place. If substituting dried for fresh yeast when following a recipe, halve the weight of yeast called for. Dried yeast takes slightly longer to work than fresh yeast, and must first be 'sponged' in liquid, partly to reconstitute it, partly to check that it is still active. To avoid any beery taste, use rather less than the amount of dried yeast called for and allow a long rising and proving time. Using too much yeast generally means too fast a rise, resulting in bread with a coarse texture that goes stale quickly.

Easy-blend dried yeast is mixed directly with the flour, not reconstituted in liquid first. Sold in small airtight packages, it is usually included in bought bread mixtures. One 7g/1/4oz package usually equals 15g/1/2oz conventional dried yeast or 30g/1oz fresh yeast.

STAGES IN BREAD-MAKING

It is important to create the right conditions for the yeast to grow so that the dough will be elastic and accommodate the maximum carbon dioxide.

1. MIXING

If the yeast is fresh, first cream it in a warm, not hot, cup with about 1 teaspoonful caster sugar until smooth, then with a spoonful of lukewarm water. Dried yeast should be mixed with a little sweetened lukewarm water and left in a warm place for about 15 minutes. Once the yeast liquid is frothy, or 'sponges', add it to the flour, and mix in any remaining ingredients specified. If it does not froth, the yeast is dead and should not be used. Some recipes, usually those enriched with fat and sugar, require the yeast mixture and all the liquid to be beaten with a small proportion of the flour to a yeasty batter, called the starter, and left in a warm place until it 'sponges'. Then the remaining flour is added and the mixing completed. This method used to be common to all breads. The process takes longer but is said by old-fashioned bakers to produce the lightest, most even-textured bread.

2. KNEADING

Kneading, or manipulating, the dough, is the next stage. It is necessary in order to distribute the yeast cells evenly and promote the dough's elasticity. The length of time for kneading varies according to the type of flour and the skill of the kneader, but the dough must lose its stickiness and become smooth, elastic and shiny – this usually takes about 15 minutes.

Techniques vary, but the most common is to push the lump of dough down and away with the heel of the hand, then to pull it back with the fingers, slap it on the worktop and repeat the process, turning the dough slightly with each movement. Table-top electric mixers with dough hooks or robust food processors can also be used for kneading. Kneading in a machine takes less time than kneading by hand, but follow the manufacturer's instructions closely.

3. RISING

Once kneaded, the dough is formed into a ball and put into a lightly oiled, warmed – not hot – bowl, and turned to coat it evenly with grease to prevent hardening and cracking. The bowl is covered with a piece of clingfilm or a damp cloth, put in a warm (32°C/90°F) draught-free place and left until about 1½ times its original size. The dough should spring back when pressed lightly with a floured finger. The longer the rising takes the better. Too rapidly risen or over-risen bread has a coarse texture and a beery smell.

4. KNOCKING BACK

Knocking back is the next process. The risen dough is knocked down, or punched with the knuckles to push out air that may have formed large, unevenly shaped holes. Punched to its original size, it is then kneaded briefly to make it pliable. Extra sugar or dried fruit is usually added at this point, before the dough is shaped and put into a loaf tin or on to a baking sheet.

5. PROVING

Proving is the second rising of the dough. When this is completed, the loaf will have doubled in bulk and should look the size and shape you hope the finished bread will be. Proving can be done in a slightly warmer place, about 38°C/100°F, for a shorter time, about 20 minutes, because the previous rising and further kneading will have made the dough even more elastic and it will rise more easily. With a second rising, the bread will be lighter when baked.

6. BAKING

The bread will continue to rise in the oven for a short time partly because of the rising steam in the loaf and partly because the yeast keeps working until the dough reaches 60°C/140°F. Then the heat of the oven will cook the dough into a rigid shape. Called 'oven spring', this final rising is likely to push the top crust away from the body of the loaf. To avoid too much oven spring, bread is baked at a fairly high temperature to kill the yeast quickly.

The baked bread should be golden-brown and have shrunk slightly from the sides of the tin. To make sure that the bread is done, it should be turned out on to a cloth and tapped on the underside. If it sounds hollow, it is done. If not, it should be returned to the oven, on its side, without the tin. Bread is cooled on a wire rack. After 2 hours, it will slice easily. Once stone-cold it may be stored in a bread tin or a plastic bag. A lukewarm loaf stored in an airtight container will become soggy, if not mouldy.

Soda bread

Soda bread has bicarbonate of soda as a raising agent. However, in order to activate the soda an acid must be included in the ingredients. This is usually cream of tartar, which must be sifted with the bicarbonate of soda and the other dry ingredients to incorporate it thoroughly. When liquid is added to the dough, the alkali (bicarbonate of soda) and acid (cream of tartar) enter a chemical reaction and form carbonic acid gas. As soon as this is liberated the dough must go into the oven or the bread will not work and the flavour will be impaired. In some recipes cream of tartar is replaced by sour milk or buttermilk. These doughs are the exact opposite of yeast doughs. High-speed mixing and quick light handling are required, rather than careful mixing and vigorous kneading.

WHITE BREAD

You will need a 1kg/2¼lb bread tin. If it is old and used, you may not need to grease or flour it, but if it is new and not non-stick, brush it out very lightly with flavourless oil and dust with flour.

15g/½oz fresh yeast
scant 290ml/½ pint lukewarm milk
1 teaspoon caster sugar
450g/1lb strong plain flour
2 teaspoons salt
30g/1oz butter
1 egg, lightly beaten
beaten egg to glaze

1. Dissolve the yeast with a little of the milk and the sugar in a teacup.
2. Sift the flour with the salt into a warmed large mixing bowl and rub in the butter as you would for pastry.
3. Pour in the yeast mixture, the remaining milk and the beaten egg and mix to a softish dough.
4. Add a small amount of flour if the dough is too sticky. When the dough will leave the sides of the bowl, press it into a ball and tip it out on to a floured board.
5. Knead until it is elastic, smooth and shiny (about 15 minutes).
6. Put the dough back into the bowl and cover it with a piece of lightly greased clingfilm.
7. Put it in a warm, draught-free place and leave it to rise until it has doubled in size (at least 1 hour). Bread that rises too quickly has a yeasty, unpleasant taste; the slower the rising the better – overnight in a cool larder is better than 30 minutes over the boiler!
8. Knock down and knead for a further 10 minutes or so.
9. Shape the dough into an oblong and put it into a 1kg/2¼lb loaf tin.
10. Cover again with oiled clingfilm and

prove (allow to rise again) until it is the size and shape of a loaf. Brush with beaten egg.

11. Preheat the oven to 220°C/425°F/gas mark 7. Bake the loaf in the oven for 10 minutes, then turn the oven temperature down to 190°C/375°F/gas mark 5 and bake for a further 25 minutes, or until it is golden and firm.

12. Turn the loaf out on to a wire rack to cool. It should sound hollow when tapped on the underside. If it does not, or feels squashy and heavy, return it to the oven, without the tin, for a further 10 minutes.

NOTE: If using dried or easy-blend yeast, see pages 90–91.

BROWN SODA BREAD

Many soda bread recipes call for buttermilk, but we have found that ordinary milk works well too.

MAKES 1 KG/2LB LOAF

900g/2lb wholemeal flour, or 675g/1 1/2lb wholemeal flour and 225g/8oz plain white flour
2 teaspoons salt
2 teaspoons bicarbonate of soda
4 teaspoons cream of tartar
2 teaspoons sugar
45g/1 1/2oz butter
570–860ml/1–1 1/2 pints milk (if using all wholemeal flour, the recipe will need more liquid than if made with a mixture of 2 flours)

1. Preheat the oven to 190°C/375°F/gas mark 5.
2. Sift the dry ingredients into a warmed large mixing bowl.
3. Rub in the butter and mix to a soft dough with the milk.
4. Shape with a minimum of kneading into a large circle about 5cm/2in thick. Dust lightly with flour. With the handle of a wooden spoon, make a cross on the top of the loaf. The dent should be 2cm/3/4 in deep

5. Bake in the preheated oven on a greased baking sheet for 25–30 minutes. Allow to cool on a wire rack.

CHELSEA BUNS

MAKES 12

15g/1/2oz fresh yeast
85g/3oz caster sugar
450g/1lb strong plain flour
1 teaspoon salt
85g/3oz butter
1 egg
225ml/7 1/2 fl oz warm milk
1/2 teaspoon ground mixed spice
55g/2oz sultanas
55g/2oz currants
sugar for sprinkle
apricot glaze (see page 61)

1. Cream the yeast with 1 teaspoon of the sugar.
2. Sift the flour with the salt into a warmed dry mixing bowl. Rub in half the butter and stir in half the sugar.
3. Beat the egg and add to the yeast mixture with the lukewarm milk.
4. Make a well in the centre of the flour and pour in the liquid. Using first a knife and then your hand, gradually draw the flour in from the sides of the bowl and knead until smooth.
5. Cover the bowl with lightly oiled clingfilm and leave to rise in a warm place until doubled in size (about 1 hour).
6. Knock the dough down and knead again on a floured board. Roll into a 23cm/9in square. Sprinkle over the dried fruit.
7. Mix the remaining butter with the remaining sugar and the mixed spice and spread over the dough.
8. Preheat the oven to 200°C/400°F/gas mark 6.
9. Roll the dough up like a Swiss roll and cut into 2.5cm/1in slices.
10. Arrange the buns cut side up on the baking sheet and leave in a warm place to

prove (rise again) for 15 minutes.

11. Sprinkle with sugar. Bake in the preheated oven for 20–25 minutes. Brush with apricot glaze.

12. Leave the buns to cool on a wire rack before separating.

NOTE: If using dried or easy-blend yeast, see pages 90–91.

CAUSES OF FAILURE IN BREAD-MAKING

Close texture:

Stale yeast

Insufficient yeast

Too much salt or sugar

Insufficient kneading

Too much/too little liquid

Second rising too short

Dough left to rise in too warm a place

Oven too cool

Poor rising of dough:

Stale yeast

Too much salt or sugar

Mixture too dry

Rising time too short

Uneven texture and holes:

Too much liquid

Too much salt

Insufficient kneading

Too long/short risings

Dough left uncovered during rising

Oven too cool

Not knocked back enough

Coarse texture:

Too much/too little salt

Too much/too little liquid

Insufficient kneading

Too long/short rising

Dough left uncovered

Wrinkled top crust:

Second rising too long

Dough not covered

Insufficient kneading

Not knocked back enough

Sour or yeasty flavour:

Stale yeast

Too much yeast

Yeast creamed with too much sugar

Second rising too long – overproved

Cracked crust:

Second rising too short

Tin too small for mixture

Oven too cool

If the oven is too cool the bread will be pale, dry and hard, with an uneven texture. If the oven is too hot the crust will be too dark or burnt.

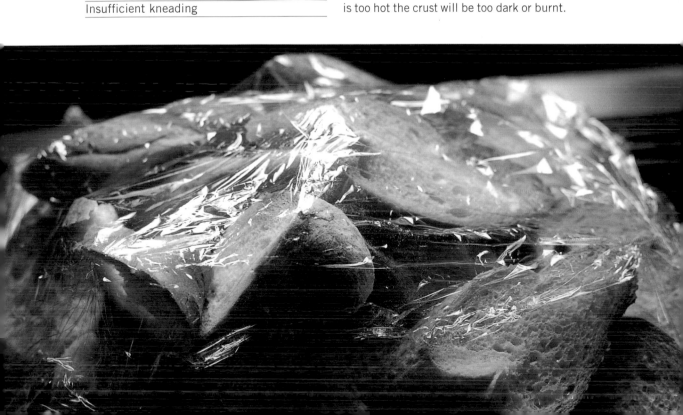

STRUCTURE OF MEAT AND CARVING
CHAPTER 12

Techniques Covered
Structure of meat
Carving classic joints

Recipes
Liver and bacon
Chicken liver pâte

❷ Cookery Term
Piquer: To insert a flavouring ingredient into meats, e.g. cloves into a baked ham or garlic slivers into a lamb joint.

MEAT

Because tenderness is rated highly today, the most expensive cuts of meat are those from the parts of the animal's body that have had little or no exercise. For example, the leg, neck and shoulder cuts of beef are tougher (and therefore cheaper) than those taken from the rump or loin.

But apart from the age of the animal, there are other factors that affect tenderness. Meat must not be cooked while the muscle fibres are taut due to rigor mortis, which can last, depending on the temperature at which the carcase is stored, for a day or two. The state of the animal prior to slaughter can also affect the tenderness of the meat; for example, if it is relaxed and peaceful the meat is likely to be more tender. Injections of certain enzymes (proteins that produce changes in the meat without themselves being changed) given to the animal before slaughter will produce the same result artificially.

But the most crucial factor affecting tenderness is the length of time that meat is stored before cooking. If hung in temperatures of 2°C/35°F it will, due to enzyme activity, become increasingly tender. Temperatures should not be higher than this, because although the enzyme activity would be greater, the risk of spoilage due to bacterial action would become high. For beef, 7 days is the minimum hanging time, while 3 weeks or a month are more desirable. However, with the commercial demands for quick turnover, the weight-loss during storage and the expense of storing, good hanging is rare these days. Some enzyme activity continues if the meat is frozen, and the formation, and subsequent melting, of ice-crystals (which, in expanding, bruise the fibres of the meat) mean that freezing meat can be said to tenderize it. However, the inevitable loss of juices from the meat (and subsequent risk of dryness after cooking) is a disadvantage that outweighs the minimal tenderizing effect.

Hanging is most important in beef, as the animals are comparatively old, perhaps 2 or 3 years, when killed. It is less important for carcases of young animals, such as calves and lambs, as their meat is relatively tender anyway.

Because, inevitably, some bacterial action (as well as enzyme action) must take place during hanging, the flavour of well-hung meat is stronger, or gamier, than that of under-hung meat. The colour will also deepen and become duller with hanging. But the prime reason for hanging meat is to tenderize it, rather than to increase or change its flavour. This is not so with game, including venison, which is hung as much to produce a game flavour as to tenderize the meat.

The last, and probably most important, factor that affects the ultimate tenderness of meat is the method of cooking. Half-cooked or rare meat will be tender simply because its fibres have not been changed by heat, and will still retain the softness of raw meat. But as the heat penetrates the whole piece of meat the fibres set rigidly and the juices cease to run. Once the whole piece of meat is heated thoroughly, all the softness of raw meat is lost and it is at its toughest. This explains the natural reluctance of chefs to serve well-done steaks – it is almost impossible to produce a tender well-done grilled steak.

But, paradoxically, further cooking (though not fast grilling or frying) will tenderize that tough steak. This is seen in stewing, when long, slow cooking gradually softens the flesh. A joint from an older animal, which has used its muscles exensively during its lifetime and is coarse-grained and fibrous, can be made particularly tender by prolonged gentle cooking. This is because much of the connective tissue present in such a joint, if subjected to a steady temperature of, say, 100°C/200°F, will convert to gelatine, producing a soft, almost sticky tenderness.

Joints with finer graining and little connective tissue, such as rump or sirloin, will never become gelatinous, and are consequently seldom cooked other than by roasting or grilling, when their inherent tenderness (from a life of inaction) is relied on. But they will never be as tender as the slow-cooked shin or oxtail, which can be cut with a spoon.

It does not matter that few people have any idea which part of the animal their meat comes from. But it is useful to know, if not how to do the butcher's job, at least which cuts are likely to be tender, expensive, good for stewing, or not worth having, and what to look for in a piece of meat.

CARVING MEAT

The most important factors in good carving are a really sharp knife, a fork with a safety guard, and a board or flat plate unencumbered by vegetables and garnishes. Common sense usually dictates how joints are to be tackled. Meat off the bone is simple: just cut in slices of whatever thickness you prefer, across the grain of the meat. Pork, beef and veal are traditionally carved in thinner slices than lamb.

Legs

The legs of pork, lamb, bacon (gammon or ham), veal and venison are carved similarly. Put the leg meaty side up on the board or plate and grasp the knuckle bone with one hand, or pierce the joint firmly with a carving fork. Cut a small shallow 'V' or scoop out the middle of the top of the meat. Carve slices of meat from both sides of the 'V'. Then turn the leg over and take horizontal slices from the other side.

Legs can also be cut in diagonal slices from the knuckle end. This is more common with hams, but both methods are used for all legs.

Loins

Loins and best end of pork, veal and lamb are often roasted on the bone to prevent shrinkage, but to carve them it is easier to remove the meat off the rib cage and slice to the desired thickness. To carve a loin of pork, the crackling can be removed in one piece. The meat is then sliced and the crackling can be cut, with scissors, in the same number of pieces as there are slices of meat. If boned, the meat is cut similarly, but in thinner slices, about 5mm/¼in thick. Beef strip loin (boned sirloin) is cut in the same way, thinly in Britain, thickly in America.

Sirloin of beef on the bone is tackled from the top and bottom, the slices cut as thinly as possible on the top, the undercut of fillet slices being carved more thickly. Each diner should be given a slice or two from both top and bottom.

Saddle of lamb

The chump end of the saddle is cut in thin angles across the grain of the meat, at right angles to the backbone. But the main part of the saddle, lying each side of the backbone, is cut in thin strips or narrow slices down the length of the saddle. This can be done on the bone, but it is easier if you lift the whole side of the saddle off in one piece and cut into long slices.

Crown roast and guard of honour

Remove the string and split into cutlets.

Shoulder of lamb

A shoulder is simple to carve as long as you know where the bones are. Place it fatty side up and cut like a cake on the side opposite to the bone.

Small forerib of beef

A single forerib of beef is cooked on the bone and then cut off the bone in one piece.

Instead of slicing into thin horizontal slices it can be cut into shorter fatter vertical slices.

Large forerib of beef

Place the roast on its side and make a 5cm/2in cut along the length of the rib. Stand the meat up, rib side down. Carve several slices and lift off and place on a warm serving dish. Turn the rib back on its side and make a second 5cm/2in cut along the length of the rib. Carve.

LIVER AND BACON

SERVES 4

55g/2oz butter
1 onion, thinly sliced
6 rashers of rindless bacon
450g/1lb calves' or lambs' liver, skinned and sliced
seasoned plain flour
290ml/½ pint brown stock (see page 51)
2 tablespoons sherry
To garnish
1 small bunch of watercress

1. Heat half the butter in a frying pan and fry the onion slowly until soft and brown. Tip the onion into a saucer.
2. Preheat the grill. Grill the bacon under it until crisp and brown but not brittle. Turn off the grill and leave the bacon under it to keep warm.
3. Remove any large tubes from the liver. Dip the slices in seasoned flour and keep well separated on a plate.
4. Heat the remaining butter in the frying pan and fry the liver slices, a few at a time, adding more butter if necessary. Note that liver is easily spoiled by overcooking. Arrange the slices on a warmed shallow platter and keep warm.
5. Put the onion, and any of its fat, back into the pan and add a sprinkling of the seasoned flour – just enough to absorb the fat. Cook for 1 minute. Pour in the stock and stir well as it comes to the boil. Add the sherry.

6. Boil the sauce rapidly to reduce in quantity and thicken. This will also give a richer appearance and concentrate the flavour. Check the seasoning.

7. Pour the sauce over the liver, top with the bacon and garnish with watercress. Serve immediately as liver toughens on standing.

CHICKEN LIVER PÂTÉ

SERVES 4

225g/8oz butter
1 large onion, very finely chopped
1 large clove of garlic, crushed
450g/1lb chicken livers, or 225g/8oz duck livers and 225g/8oz chicken livers
1 tablespoon brandy
salt and freshly ground black pepper
85g/3oz clarified butter (see page 192), if the pâté is to be stored

1. Melt half the butter in a large, heavy frying pan and gently fry the onion until soft and transparent.

2. Add the garlic and continue cooking for 1 further minute.

3. Discard any discoloured pieces of liver as they will be brittle. Rinse under water.

4. Add the livers to the pan and fry, turning to brown them lightly on all sides, until cooked. Flame the brandy and add to the livers.

5. When the flames subside, add salt and plenty of pepper.

6. Mince the mixture or liquidize in a blender or food processor with the remaining butter. Put it into an earthenware dish or pot.

7. If the pâté is to be kept for more than 3 days, cover the top with a layer of clarified butter.

NOTE: If making large quantities of chicken liver pâté simply bake all the ingredients together under foil or a lid in the oven preheated to 190°C/375°F/gas mark 5 for 40 minutes. Cool for 15 minutes, then proceed from step 6.

Causes of Failure
Tough liver: Overcooked.
Separated or curdled chicken liver pâté: The cooked liver and melted butter were at very different temperatures.

PRESSURE COOKING, MICROWAVING AND BARBECUING
CHAPTER 13

Techniques Covered
Pressure-cooking:
Suet crust pudding
Dried pulses
Vegetables
Microwaving:
Baked custard and caramel
Barbecuing

❷ Cookery Terms
Caramel: Sugar cooked to a toffee.
Marinate: To soak meat, fish or vegetables before cooking in acidulated liquid containing flavourings and herbs. This gives flavour and tenderizes the meat.
Papillote: A paper wrapping in which fish or meat is cooked to contain the aroma and flavour. The dish is brought to the table still wrapped up. Foil is sometimes used, but as it does not puff up dramatically, it is less satisfactory.

Recipes
Sussex pond pudding
Microwave crème caramel

PRESSURE-COOKING
There are many advantages to using a pressure cooker – it is quick and thus economical on fuel and it preserves many vitamins and minerals with a minimum loss of colour and flavour. It is versatile and can be used for many ingredients. Unfortunately for manufacturers, the pressure cooker has been replaced in many instances by the microwave oven but for jam making, cooking pulses, steaming puddings and making soups it remains a useful piece of kitchen equipment.

The basic principle of pressure cooking is that the ingredients and liquid are cooked in an enclosed pressure-tight vessel. The steam, which escapes freely from a conventional saucepan, is contained thus raising the pressure and the cooking temperature. Food is cooked quickly in a pressure cooker both because of the high temperature and because the steam is forced through the food. The steam incidentally also acts as a good tenderizer and generally dishes are cooked in about a third of the conventional cooking time.

Before using a pressure cooker check that the rubber seals and safety valves are in good working order. Put the ingredients required in the cooker as though using a conventional saucepan (see safety notes and advice below). When you are ready to bring it up to pressure cover tightly with the lid and increase the heat. When it reaches the required pressure the valves will close and you will hear a 'pssht' sound. At that point control the temperature as per the manufacturer's instructions and cook for as long as is indicated in the recipe. Allow the pressure to release before opening the pan. The pressure can be released slowly by allowing the pan to cool naturally or quickly by using an automatic vent or by placing the cooker in a basin of cold water.

There are up to 3 settings for a pressure cooker.

Low/5lbs pressure	109°C/228°F	Steamed puddings containing raising agents and bottling fruits
Medium/10lbs pressure	115°C/240°F	Softening fruits for jam
High/15lbs pressure	121°C/250°F	Everyday cooking

Safety features are built into pressure cookers to ensure that they do not explode. For example, the automatic air vent will melt and thus open by itself if it gets too hot. Nevertheless it is always wise to take precautions so here are some notes of advice about both safety and methods of cooking.

- A minimum of 290ml/½ pint of liquid (which must produce steam when boiled e.g. stock, water, milk, wine, NOT oil or melted fat), for each 15 minutes of cooking time is required.
- A steamed pudding must be allowed 10–20 minutes of conventional steaming before being put under pressure or the raising agent will be lost and the pudding will be heavy.
- Never allow a pressure cooker to boil dry.
- Never force open a pressure cooker.
- Never fill a pressure cooker too full – the general rule is
    ⅓ full of cereals, pulses, beetroot and anything that 'boils up' when cooking such as jam
    ½ full of soups, stews, rice, etc.
    ⅔ full of solid foods, vegetables, joints, etc.
- Thicken stews and sauces after pressure cooking – if the sauce is too thick it may 'catch' on the bottom of the cooker and burn.
- Use the pressure cooker as a conventional saucepan if you want to brown meat or vegetables in advance. Allow the cooker to cool slightly before adding the liquid.
- Use a trivet in the base of the cooker for foods that need to be steamed – such as a steamed pudding.

DRIED PULSES
Dried peas and beans (lentils, split peas, chickpeas, green peas, black-eyed peas, haricot beans, lima beans, butter beans, brown beans, red kidney beans, etc.) are generally cheaper than their fresh or canned equivalents, are easy to cook and are very nutritious. They should be bought from grocers with a good turnover, and as a rule small butter beans are better than large ones.

Most pulses need soaking until softened and swollen before cooking. Soaking can take as much as 12 hours (butter beans) or as little as 20 minutes (lentils). Do not soak for more than 12 hours in case the beans start germinating or fermenting. If there is no time for preliminary soaking, unsoaked pulses may be cooked either in a pressure cooker or very slowly in a saucepan; but remember that enough water must be used to allow the beans first to swell and then to cook. Preliminary soaking is less hazardous.

To cook the pulses, cover them with fresh cold water, bring to the boil and then simmer for 5 minutes. Change the water and cook until tender. Boiling times vary according to the age and size of the pulses: new season's pulses will cook faster. Small lentils may take as little as 15 minutes and large haricot beans or chickpeas can take as long as 2 hours. Pressure-cooking will reduce cooking time considerably.

NOTE: Red kidney beans must be boiled fast for at least 15 minutes to destroy dangerous toxins.

MICROWAVE COOKING

In conventional oven cooking the air is heated and the heat is passed slowly into the centre of the food by conduction. In microwaving the microwaves cause the moisture molecules in the food to vibrate, causing friction which results in heat. The heat that is generated in the food begins to cook it from the inside. Microwaves only penetrate about 5cm/2in into the food. The centre of large pieces of food is cooked by the conduction of the heat produced near the food's surface. The microwaves are reflected off the metal cavity of the oven and form criss-cross patterns. The food absorbs waves from all directions. The waves pass through china, glass, paper, etc., all of which make suitable microwave containers. Metal must not be used for microwaving as the waves are reflected and bounce off.

Microwave ovens can cook all foods but with varying results. They are very useful for cooking vegetables that would normally be boiled, such as peas and asparagus, saving on washing up and preserving vitamins and minerals, but not so good for those that would naturally be baked – a microwave-'baked' jacket potato tastes boiled.

A microwave is excellent for reheating, melting butter and defrosting food in small quantities. However, it is less suitable for defrosting large joints of meat or poultry: as the food begins to thaw, the microwaves are attracted to the defrosted water molecules and keep causing vibration/friction in the same place, while other parts remain frozen. The joint or bird should be removed from the oven and left to stand every so often so that the heat can be conducted to the centre. The speed at which a microwave cooks means that food benefiting from long cooking, such as roast beef, simply does not have the depth of flavour that a conventionally cooked piece has. On the other hand, it is good for cooking fish, which it will steam or poach beautifully.

There is no need to preheat a microwave oven but the colder the food is the longer it will take to cook. There is only a set amount of energy coming into the oven so when more than one item of food is put in, the energy is divided between them. Thus five potatoes will take considerably longer to cook than one. The shape of the food should also be taken into account – the more even the shape the more evenly it will cook. Thinner areas of food can be covered to prevent further cooking. Very dense foods, such as shepherd's pie, are more difficult to reheat than those with a light, open texture, such as a sponge pudding.

Do not cover food to be microwaved with tin foil, which reflects the waves; instead use clingfilm, which should be pierced to prevent it from bursting. As a general rule moist food should be pricked.

At Leith's we have decided that a microwave is most useful for:

- Melting butter
- Softening butter for cake making (be careful not to oversoften and melt)
- Cooking vegetables in a minimum of water
- Cooking small pieces of fish
- Cooking chestnuts (pierce the tops and place on absorbent kitchen paper, cook on High for 2 minutes and peel while warm)
- Reheating plated meals and cups of coffee
- Making caramel (make it in a dish. See page 104, Microwave Crème Caramel)
  Do not use the following utensils in the microwave:
- Metal containers, which reflect the waves
- Packets with a gold line, which will get so hot that the paper will burst into flames
- Anything containing glue
- Pottery, which often has a metallic glaze
- Melamine or similar, which will absorb the waves
- Crystal glass, which contains lead
- Thin-stemmed glasses, which may break
- Jagged pieces of tin foil, which may cause arcing. If foil is used to prevent cooking, make sure it has smooth edges.

BARBECUING

This is a fashionable way of entertaining over the summer months. It originated in America where the Spanish saw the Mexican Indians smoking dry fish and cooking meat on a frame called a *barbacoa*.

Cooking over wood and charcoal is an ancient form of cooking which imparts a smoky flavour to food. The secret lies in a good fire, controlling the heat and distributing it evenly.

You can use wood but briquets give more uniform heat and are longer-lasting. A barbecue can be very simple or highly elaborate, e.g. American-style gas-fired barbecues.

- Tongs are essential.
- Only start to cook when the fire has burned down and the coals are white.
- Marinating meat and fish gives extra depth of flavour.
- Wrapping food in leaves or cooking *en papillote* protects delicate flavours and protects the food from the fierce heat.

SUSSEX POND PUDDING

This recipe has been taken from Jane Grigson's *English Food*.

SERVES 6

225g/8oz self-raising flour
110g/4oz shredded beef suet
150ml/¼ pint milk and water, half and half
110g/4oz slightly salted butter
110g/4oz demerara sugar
2 large lemons or 2 limes, very well washed

1. Mix the flour and suet together in a bowl. Make into a dough with milk and water. The dough should be soft, but not too soft to roll out into a large circle. Cut a quarter out of this circle, to be used later as the lid of the pudding.
2. Butter a 1.4 litre/2½ pint pudding basin lavishly. Drop the three-quarter circle of pastry into it and press the cut sides together to make a perfect join. Put half the remaining butter, cut up, into the pastry, with half the sugar.
3. Prick the lemons or limes all over with a larding needle, so that the juices will be able to escape, then put the fruit on to the butter and sugar. Add the remaining butter, again cut into pieces, and sugar.
4. Roll out the pastry set aside to make the lid. Lay it on top of the filling, and press the edges together so that the pudding is

sealed completely. Cover the basin with pleated kitchen foil. Tie it in place with string, and make a string handle over the top so that the pudding can be lifted easily.

5. Put a large saucepan of water on to boil, and lower the pudding into it; the water must be boiling, and it should come halfway or a little further up the basin. Cover and leave to steam for 3–4 hours. If the water gets too low, replenish with boiling water.
6. To serve: put a deep dish over the basin after removing the foil lid, and quickly turn the whole thing upside down: it is a good idea to ease the pudding from the sides of the basin with a knife first. Serve immediately. The buttery juices will flow out of the pudding to form a 'pond'.

NOTE: To pressure-cook:

1. Pre-steam the pudding for 10 minutes, i.e. cook in the pressure-cooker without securing the pressure-cooking lid.
2. Pressure-cook for 30 minutes at 5lb of pressure.
3. Release steam slowly.

MICROWAVE CRÈME CARAMEL

SERVES 4

For the caramel
110g/4oz granulated sugar
2 tablespoons water

For the custard
570ml/1 pint milk
5 eggs
2 tablespoons sugar
2–3 drops vanilla essence

1. Make the caramel: put the sugar and water into a 1litre/2 pint capacity Pyrex dish.
2. Cover with clingfilm and pierce several times. Microwave on high for 2–3 minutes to dissolve the sugar, then microwave for a further 6–7 minutes until the caramel is an even medium-brown colour.
3. With the clingfilm in place, swirl the caramel around the dish to coat the sides. Leave to cool.
4. Scald the milk in a Pyrex jug covered with clingfilm for 3 minutes on high power. Stir the eggs with the sugar.
5. Pour the milk slowly on to the eggs, stirring. Add the vanilla essence.
6. Strain the custard on to the cold caramel. Cover with clingfilm and pierce the film in several places.
7. Microwave on low power for 4 minutes. Leave to stand for 2 minutes. Microwave for a further 4–5 minutes on low power. Allow to cool to room temperature.
8. Remove the clingfilm serve, or refrigerate, covered, until required.

Causes of Failure
Pressure-cooking: Steamed pudding exploding – basin filled too full.
Microwave: Tough crème caramel – overcooked.
Barbecue: Burnt food and flames leaping everywhere – coals not yet ready for cooking.

ICE CREAMS, SORBETS AND PASTRY III
CHAPTER 14

Techniques Covered
Sugar syrups
Ice cream
Sorbets
Choux pastry

❓ Cookery Terms
Needleshreds: Fine, evenly cut shreds of citrus zest (French julienne) generally used as a garnish.

Panade: Very thick mixture used as a base for soufflés or fish cakes, etc., usually made from milk, butter and flour.

Quenelle: A 3-sided oval shape formed using 2 identical spoons – usually used for mousses, pâtés, ice creams and sorbets.

Soft ball: The term used to describe sugar syrup reduced by boiling to sufficient thickness to form soft balls when dropped into cold water and rubbed between wet finger and thumb.

To the thread: Of sugar boiling. Term used to denote degree of thickness achieved when reducing syrup, i.e. the syrup will form threads if tested between wet finger and thumb. Short thread: about 1cm/1/2in long; long thread: 5cm/2in or more.

Recipes

Coffee ice cream	Choux pastry
Lemon sorbet	Coffee éclairs
Brandy snap cups/brandy snaps	Apricot choux ring

ICE CREAMS AND SORBETS

Ice cream is a foam stabilized by freezing much of the liquid (even in frozen ice cream some of the liquid is left unfrozen). Ice cream contains tiny ice crystals composed of pure water, solid globules of milk fat and tiny air cells. The liquid in ice cream prevents the formation of a solid block. The ice crystals stabilize the foam by trapping air and fat in its structure and if ice creams contain a good proportion of fat they freeze to a smooth creaminess without too much trouble. If they consist of mostly sugar and water or milk they need frequent beating during the freezing process to prevent too large ice crystals from forming. In any event the more a mixture is beaten and churned during freezing the more air will be incorporated and the creamier in texture it will be. The tiny air cells are very important as they break up the solid liquid to make a lighter, softer texture. Ice cream without air would be difficult to serve, scoop or eat.

The recipe for ice cream assumes that you do not have an ice-cream maker – if you do, however, simply follow the manufacturer's instructions. Light, sweet wines go with most ice creams, particularly Italian Muscato with fruit ices. Also, try sweet sparkling wine or champagne.

SUGAR SYRUPS
Making a sugar syrup
Dissolve sugar slowly in water then boil as required. The addition of dissolved sugar molecules means that boiling point is above that of water (over 100°C).

The more concentrated a solution the higher the boiling point. In other words 'the boil point' is an indication of how concentrated a liquid is, e.g. a syrup that boils at 113°C/235°F is about 85 per cent sugar.

Generally the more water a syrup contains the softer the final result will be. The longer a syrup is boiled, the more concentrated it becomes.

Pure sugar liquefies at 160°C/320°F and begins to caramelize at 168°C/335°F. For each 500 feet above sea level, subtract 1°F from every boiling point listed.
NOTE: Use a sugar thermometer or test between wet finger and thumb. Take the syrup off the heat (so it doesn't move on to a further stage while you are testing), put a little syrup on a teaspoon and allow it to cool a little. Take some of the syrup between your index finger and thumb and rub it. Before the syrup reaches short thread it will feel like vaseline. After this stage if you separate your fingers quickly it will hold a 'thread' about 1cm/1/2in long for a short time – this stage is called short thread. The next stage would be when this thread can be increased to about 2.5cm/1in – hence being called long thread. In the final stages before caramelization the thread will become hard and brittle, which is called hard crack.

Crystallization
A sugar syrup can crystallize at almost any time. The sugar is dissolved before boiling so that the liquid sugar cooks uniformly.

The syrup can crystallize when it has reached the correct cooking temperature. This happens because the amount of sugar that can be dissolved in water is limited. If that limit has been reached it is said to be 'saturated'. The molecules of sugar and water are balanced. If the molecules are 'crowded' the slightest bit, they will be attracted to each other rather than to the water and will clump together forming crystals. This can also occur through stirring or if any dirt or undissolved sugar gets mixed into the syrup. The dirt acts as a seed or nucleus, an initial surface to which the sugar molecules can attach themselves and form crystals.

To prevent crystallization the syrup can be doctored by adding a small amount of acid, usually in the form of powdered cream of tartar which has the advantage of not diluting the syrup.

In the presence of acid and heat the sugar (sucrose) is 'inverted' or broken down to its two components: glucose and fructose. Invert sugar complicates matters for the sucrose molecules by getting in the way during crystallization. They slow the process down and thus give the cook more time either to cool the syrup into a clear candy or to get more crystals into the sugar for a rocky granular fudge.

Corn syrup or glucose also inhibits crystallization: the assorted chains of glucose units form a tangle that impedes the motion of sugar and water molecules and makes it more difficult for the sucrose to find a crystal on which to fit. This is useful if you want to prevent crystallization altogether. Both hard sweets and fine crystalline sweets like fudge are made with corn syrup or glucose (powdered or liquid form).

SUGAR SYRUP

MAKES 570ml/1 pint
285g/10oz granulated sugar
570ml/1 pint water
thinly pared zest of 1 lemon

1. Put the sugar, water and lemon zest into a saucepan and heat slowly until the sugar has completely dissolved.
2. Bring to the boil and cook to the required consistency (see below). Allow to cool.
3. Strain. Keep covered in a cool place until needed.
NOTE: Sugar syrup will keep unrefrigerated for about 5 days, and for several weeks if kept chilled.

STAGES IN SUGAR SYRUP CONCENTRATION

Type of sugar syrup	Boiling point	Uses
Vaseline	107°C/220–221°F	Syrup and sorbets
Short thread	108°C/225–226°F	Syrup and mousse-based ice creams
Long thread	110°C/230–235°F	Syrup
Soft ball	115°C/235–240°F	Fondant, fudge
Firm ball	120°C/248–250°F	Italian meringue
Hard ball	124°C/255–265°F	Marshmallows
Soft crack	138°C/270–290°F	Soft toffee
Hard crack	155°C/300–310°F	Hard toffee and some nougat
	160°C/318°F	Nougat
Spun sugar	152°C/305–308°F	Spun sugar

CHOUX PASTRY

Like Yorkshire pudding batter, this pastry contains water and eggs and depends on the rising of the steam within it to produce a puffy, hollow pastry case. It is easy to make if the recipe is followed closely. The following points are particularly important:

- Measure ingredients exactly. Proportions are important with choux.
- Do not allow the water to boil until the butter has melted, but when it has, bring it immediately to a full rolling boil. Boiling the water too soon will cause too much evaporation.
- Have the sifted flour ready in a bowl so that the minute the rolling ball is achieved, you can tip in the flour, all in one go.
- Beat fast and vigorously to get rid of lumps before they cook hard.
- Do not over-beat. Stop once the mixture is leaving the sides of the pan.
- Cool slightly before adding egg, otherwise it will scramble.
- Do not beat in more egg than is necessary to achieve a dropping consistency. If the mixture is too stiff, the pastry will be stodgy. If it is too thin, it will rise unevenly into shapeless lumps.
- Bake until it is a good, even brown, otherwise the inside of the pastry will be uncooked.
- If the pastry is to be served cold, split the buns/rings, or poke a hole in each of them with a skewer, to allow the steam inside to escape. If steam remains trapped inside, the pastry will be soggy and a little heavy. Opened-up pastry or small buns with holes in them can be returned to the oven, hole uppermost, to dry out further.
- Serve the pastry on the day it is made (or store frozen), as it stales rapidly and does not keep well in a tin.

COFFEE ICE CREAM

This ice cream is made with a custard base.

SERVES 4–6

4 egg yolks
85g/3oz caster sugar
a pinch of salt
425ml/³/4 pint single cream
5 teaspoons instant coffee powder

1. Mix the egg yolks with the sugar and salt.
2. Place the cream and coffee in a saucepan and heat gently until the coffee dissolves.
3. Add the cream to the egg-yolk mixture, stirring all the time.
4. Pour the mixture into the top of a double saucepan or into a heatproof bowl set over, not in, a saucepan of simmering water.
5. Stir continuously until thick and creamy.
6. Strain into a bowl and allow to cool, whisking occasionally.
7. Chill, then pour into an ice tray and freeze.
8. When the ice cream is half-frozen, whisk again and return to the freezer.

LEMON SORBET

SERVES 4

thinly pared zest and juice of 3 lemons
140g/5oz granulated sugar
570ml/1 pint water
¹/2 egg white

1. Place the lemon zest, sugar and water in a heavy saucepan. Dissolve the sugar over a low heat and, when completely dissolved, boil rapidly to the short thread stage (when a little syrup is put between wet finger and thumb and the fingers opened, it should form a sticky thread 2.5cm/1in long).
2. Remove from the heat and allow to cool completely. When the syrup is cold, add

the lemon juice and strain.
3. Freeze for 30 minutes, or until beginning
   to solidify.
4. Whisk the egg white until stiff and fold
   into the mixture.
5. Return to the freezer until firm.
NOTE: If you have a food processor, allow the
lemon syrup to freeze and then whisk until
soft. Pour in the egg white, through the funnel,
whisking all the time. Freeze until firm.

BRANDY SNAP CUPS
MAKES 8
110g/4oz caster sugar
110g/4oz butter
4 tablespoons golden syrup
110g/4oz plain flour
juice of 1/2 lemon
a large pinch of ground ginger
To serve
whipped cream or ice cream

1. Preheat the oven to 190°C/375°F/gas
   mark 5. Grease a baking sheet, a palette
   knife and one end of a wide rolling pin or
   a narrow jam jar or bottle.
2. Melt the sugar, butter and syrup together
   in a saucepan. Remove from the heat.
3. Sift in the flour, stirring well. Add the
   lemon juice and ginger.
4. Place teaspoonfuls of the mixture on the
   prepared baking sheet about 15cm/6in
   apart. Bake in the preheated oven for 5–7
   minutes until golden-brown and still soft.
   Watch carefully as they burn easily.
   Remove from the oven.
5. When cool enough to handle, lever each
   biscuit off the baking sheet with a greased
   palette knife.
6. Working quickly, shape around the end of
   the rolling pin or greased jam jar to form a
   cup-shaped mould.
7. When the biscuits have been shaped, remove
   them and leave to cool on a wire rack.
8. Serve filled with whipped cream or
   ice cream.

NOTES: If the brandy snaps are not to be
served immediately, once cool they must be
put into an airtight container for storage, or
they will become soggy. Similarly, brandy
snaps should not be filled with moist mixtures
like whipped cream or ice cream until shortly
before serving, or they will quickly lose their
crispness. Do not bake too many snaps at one
time as once they become cold, they are too
brittle to shape. They can be made pliable
again if returned to the oven.

BRANDY SNAPS
The mixture for these is exactly the same as
for brandy snap cups (above) but the
biscuits are shaped round a thick wooden
spoon handle and not over the end of a
rolling pin or jam jar. They are filled with
whipped cream from a piping bag fitted with
a medium nozzle.
   Miniature brandy snaps (served as petits
fours after dinner) are shaped over a skewer.
They are not generally filled.

CHOUX PASTRY

85g/3oz butter
200ml/7fl oz water
105g/3³/₄oz plain flour, well sifted
a pinch of salt
3 eggs

1. Put the butter and water into a heavy saucepan. Bring slowly to the boil so that by the time the water boils the butter is completely melted.
2. Immediately the mixture is boiling really fast, tip in all the flour with the salt and remove the pan from the heat.
3. Working as fast as you can, beat the mixture hard with the wooden spoon: it will soon become thick and smooth and leave the sides of the pan.
4. Stand the bottom of the saucepan in a bowl or sink of cold water to speed up the cooling process.

5. When the mixture is cool, beat in the eggs, a little at a time, until it is soft, shiny and smooth. If the eggs are large, it may not be necessary to add all of them. The mixture should be of a dropping consistency – not too runny. ('Dropping consistency' means that the mixture will fall off a spoon rather reluctantly and all in a blob; if it runs off, it is too wet, and if it will not fall even when the spoon is jerked slightly, it is too thick).

COFFEE ÉCLAIRS

MAKES 20–25
1 quantity choux pastry (see above)
For the filling and topping
425ml/³/₄ pint double cream, lightly whipped and sweetened with 1 tablespoon sifted icing sugar
225g/8oz icing sugar
2 tablespoons very strong hot black coffee

1. Preheat the oven to 200°C/400°F/gas mark 6.
2. Using a piping bag fitted with a 1cm/¹/₂in plain nozzle, pipe 5cm/2in lengths of choux pastry on to the baking sheets (keep them well separated as choux pastry puffs up during baking). Bake in the preheated oven for 25–30 minutes until crisp and pale brown.
3. Using a skewer, make a hole the size of a pea in each éclair and return to the oven for 5 minutes to allow the insides to dry out. Leave to cool completely on a wire rack.
4. Put the sweetened cream into a piping bag fitted with a medium plain nozzle. Pipe the cream into the éclairs through the holes made by the skewer, until well filled.
5. Mix the icing sugar and very hot coffee together and beat with a wooden spoon until smooth. The mixture should be just runny.
6. Dip each eclair upside down into the icing so that the top becomes neatly coated.
7. Set aside to dry. Alternatively, the icing can be carefully spooned along the top ridge of each éclair.

NOTE: The éclairs may be split lengthways when cooked, allowed to dry out, and filled with cream or crème pâtissière when cold. The tops are then replaced and the icing spooned over but they are then messier to eat in the fingers.

APRICOT CHOUX RING

SERVES 6

225g/8oz fresh apricots
150ml/¼ pint sugar syrup (see page 108)
1 quantity choux pastry (see page 111)
2 tablespoons apricot jam
140g/5oz icing sugar, sifted
290ml/½ pint double cream, whipped
30g/1oz almonds, toasted

1. Preheat the oven to 200°C/400°F/gas mark 6.
2. Wash and halve the apricots and remove the stones. Poach in the sugar syrup until just tender (about 15 minutes). Drain well and leave to cool.
3. Put the choux pastry into a piping bag fitted with a large plain nozzle and pipe into a circle about 15cm/6in in diameter on a baking tray. Bake in the preheated oven for about 30 minutes until brown and crisp.
4. Split horizontally with a bread knife. Scoop out any uncooked pastry and discard. Leave the choux ring on a wire rack to cool completely.
5. Heat the jam and spread it on the base of the choux ring.
6. Mix 30g/1oz of the icing sugar with the cream and fold in the apricots.
7. Spoon the mixture on to the base and press the lid on firmly.
8. Mix the remaining icing sugar with a little boiling water until just runny. Coat the top of the choux ring with the icing and, while still wet, sprinkle with browned almonds.

Causes of Failure

Choux pastry	Flat, cracked appearance	Panada beaten too much when flour was added.
Ice creams	Buttery taste	Over-churned, cream has split.
	Ice crystals	Under-churned, ice crystals need to be whizzed to make a smooth ice cream; or not enough sugar in mixture (same for sorbets)
	Will not freeze	Too much sugar or alcohol in mixture (same for sorbets)
	No flavour	Unfrozen mixture needs to be over-seasoned because frozen food loses a lot of flavour.

COOKING WITH LEFTOVERS
CHAPTER 15

Techniques Covered
Creative leftovers
Instant cooking

❓ Cookery Terms
Paner: To egg and crumb ingredients before frying.
Rechauffée: A reheated dish made with previously cooked food.
Revenir: To fry meat or vegetables quickly in hot fat in order to warm them through.

Recipes
Salmon fish cakes
Parsley sauce
Warm red salsa
Bubble and squeak
Trifle

CREATIVE LEFTOVERS AND INSTANT COOKING
When not cooking for a special occasion most of us spend time foraging in the refrigerator or store cupboard looking for inspiration. Some types of dishes are particularly suitable for leftover cooking such as:
Soups: leftover vegetables
Soufflés: cheeses
Flans: vegetables
Pies: cooked meats
Stir-fries: cooked meats
Warm salads: cooked chicken, turkey, etc.
Gougères: cooked game, chicken, fish
Stuffed pancakes: fish, meat, vegetables
Risottos: fish, meat, vegetables
Pilaffs: fish, meat, vegetables
Rice, noodle and pasta salads: fish, meat, chicken
Pasties: cooked meat

Ice creams: 'tired' fruit
The important thing when cooking with leftovers is not to be tempted to use too many different ingredients in one recipe. There are a number of store cupboard ingredients that can make leftover cooking more exciting and instant cooking easier:
Good-quality oils such as walnut, hazelnut, extra virgin olive
Fresh herbs (these keep well, stalks down, in the refrigerator)
Soy sauce
Stem ginger
Pinenuts
Chinese noodles
Sesame seeds
Pasta, different types
Cheeses, including Parmesan
Chestnut purée, sweetened and unsweetened
Fruit cordials such as elderflower, etc.
Rice, all types – basmati, organic, etc.
Dried milk
Boxed juices
Worcestershire sauce
Sundried tomatoes
Olives
Capers
Hoisin sauce
Vinegar, including balsamic
Canned tomatoes
Passata (sieved tomatoes)
Canned beans
Dried mushrooms

Dried beans and lentils
Good-quality canned fruits, such as figs
Alcohol – red and dry white wine, sherry,
    port, brandy, liqueurs such as Cassis,
    Cointreau, Kirsch

Sometimes it is not necessary to be
particularly creative. If you have some
delicious cold meat all you need do is to
cheer up the dinner with an instant chutney
made from chopped fruit, chopped mint,
stem ginger, balsamic vinegar and olive oil. If
you have some pasta but no time to make a
sauce, use passata mixed with a little stem
ginger syrup to make a tomato and ginger
sauce. A fruit salad can be made more
sophisticated by adding alcohol or a cordial
such as elderflower.

THREE-FRUIT MARMALADE
MAKES 2.7kg/6lb
900g/2lb oranges
3 lemons
1 grapefruit
2.7kg/6lb warmed preserving sugar

1. Scrub the fruit well and put into a preserving
   pan or large saucepan with 3.3 litres/6 pints
   of water. Bring to the boil, then simmer until
   the fruit is tender. Test by piercing the skin
   with the handle of a wooden spoon. This
   will take about 1½ hours and the water will
   have reduced in quantity.
2. Leave the water in the pan and remove
   the fruit, allow to cool and cut in half.
   Scoop out the pips and tie them in a
   piece of muslin, leaving a long piece of
   string that can be tied to the pan handle.
3. Cut the fruit halves into strips or
   alternatively chop them, in batches, in a
   blender. Put back into the pan of water
   and add the sugar. Warm gently and stir
   until the sugar dissolves.
4. Bring to the boil and boil rapidly until
   setting point is reached.
5. Leave for 15 minutes until the peel has
   settled. Stir the marmalade and discard

the pips.
6. Fill the warmed sterilized jars and seal.
   Leave for 24 hours. Label and store in a
   cool, dark, dry place.

APPLE AND SAGE JELLY
MAKES 1.8kg/4lb
2kg/4½lb cooking apples
1.1 litre/2 pints water
150ml/¼ pint cider vinegar
450g/1lb warmed preserving sugar to each
    570ml/1 pint juice
55g/2oz fresh sage leaves, finely chopped

1. Wash the apples and cut them into thick
   pieces without peeling or coring.
2. Put the apples and water into a saucepan,
   bring to the boil, cover and simmer for
   about 1 hour. Add the vinegar and boil for
   a further 5 minutes.
3. Meanwhile, scald a jelly bag twice with
   boiling water.
4. Hang the jelly bag from the legs of an
   upturned stool and place a bowl
   underneath it.
5. Pour the apple pulp and juice into the
   jelly bag and allow to drip steadily for
   about 1 hour or until the bag has stopped
   dripping. Do not squeeze the bag.
6. Measure the juice and pour into the
   preserving pan. Add 450g/1lb sugar to
   every 570ml/1 pint of juice.
7. Bring to the boil slowly, ensuring that the
   sugar has dissolved before the juice has
   boiled, and stirring constantly.
8. Boil briskly, uncovered, for about 10
   minutes, skimming frequently. Test for
   setting point. When this has been
   reached, allow the jelly to cool slightly
   and stir in the sage.
9. Pour into the warmed jam jars and cover.

SPICED FRUIT PICKLE
MAKES 1.3kg/3lb
900g/2lb mixed fresh fruit, such as plums,
apricots, peaches, rhubarb

455g/1lb granulated sugar
425ml/ 3/4 pint cider vinegar
grated zest and juice of 1 orange
1 teaspoon ground ginger
4 teaspoons mustard seeds
6 cloves
1 cinnamon stick

1. Prepare the fruit by removing the stones
   and cutting the flesh into 1cm/ 1/2 in
   pieces. Do not peel.
2. Dissolve the sugar in the vinegar and add
   the orange zest and juice, ginger, mustard
   seeds, cloves and cinnamon stick.
3. Add the fruit and bring to the boil.
   Simmer carefully for 15 minutes.
4. Strain the fruit and reduce the liquid by
   boiling until syrupy. Mix it with the fruit.
5. Pour the pickle into sterilized jam jars and
   seal with jam seals.

NOTE: This can be used straight away but is
better if left to mature for at least a month.
Store in a cool, dry, dark place.

SALMON FISH CAKES

Other fish such as cod or smoked haddock
can also be used.

SERVES 4

450g/1lb cooked salmon, flaked
340g/12oz mashed potatoes (see page 30)
salt and freshly ground black pepper
30g/1oz butter, melted
1 tablespoon chopped fresh parsley
2 eggs, beaten
dried white breadcrumbs
6 tablespoons oil for frying
To serve
290ml/ 1/2 pint parsley sauce (see page 117)
Lemon wedges (see page 58)

1. Mix the salmon and potato together.
   Season well with salt and pepper.
2. Add the melted butter, parsley and
   enough beaten egg to bind the mixture
   until soft but not sloppy. Allow to cool.
3. Flour your hands and shape the mixture
   into 8 flat cakes 2.5cm/1in thick. Brush

with beaten egg and coat with breadcrumbs.

4. Heat the oil in a frying pan and fry until the fish cakes are brown on both sides. Serve with parsley sauce and lemon wedges.

NOTE: Fishcakes are also delicious served with salsa (see below).

PARSLEY SAUCE

290ml / 1/2 pint creamy milk
1 slice of onion
a good handful of fresh parsley
4 black peppercorns
a bay leaf
20g / 3/4 oz butter
20g / 3/4 oz plain flour
salt and freshly ground black pepper

1. Put the milk, onion, parsley stalks (but not leaves), peppercorns and bay leaf into a saucepan and slowly bring to simmering point.
2. Remove from the heat and leave for the flavour to infuse for about 10 minutes.
3. Melt the butter in a heavy saucepan, stir in the flour and cook, stirring, for 1 minute.
4. Remove from the heat. Strain in the infused milk and mix well.
5. Return the sauce to the heat and stir continuously until boiling, then simmer for 2–3 minutes. Season to taste with salt and pepper.
6. Chop the parsley leaves very finely and stir into the hot sauce. Serve immediately.

WARM RED SALSA

SERVES 8
2 red peppers
2 large tomatoes, pcclcd, deseeded and finely diced
1 tablespoon chopped fresh basil
1 tablespoon olive oil
juice of 1/2 lemon
juice of 1/2 orange
salt and freshly ground black pepper

1. Preheat the oven to 180°C/350°F/gas mark 4.
2. Place the peppers on a baking sheet and roast in the preheated oven for about 30 minutes, or until the peppers are soft and the skins will come off easily.
3. Leave the peppers until cold, then cut them in half and remove and discard the seeds, membrane and skin. Dice the flesh finely and mix with the remaining ingredients. Season to taste with salt and pepper.
4. Just before serving, heat through very gently until just warm.

BUBBLE AND SQUEAK
SERVES 4

450g/1lb mashed potatoes (see page 30)
450g/1lb cooked vegetables, such as cabbage, onion, leeks or Brussels sprouts
salt and freshly ground black pepper
55g/2oz good dripping or butter

1. Mix the potato with the other vegetables. Season to taste with salt and pepper.
2. Melt the dripping or butter in a heavy frying pan.
3. Put in the vegetable mixture, pressing it down flat on the hot fat. Cook slowly to heat through and allow a crust to form on the bottom of the mixture.
4. Now flip the cake over on to a plate and return it to the pan to brown the second side.
5. Slide on to a warmed serving dish and serve immediately.

NOTE: Bubble and squeak is really a leftover fry-up and it does not matter if the cake is neat and even or crumbly and broken. But if you prefer it to be round and neat so that you can cut it into slices, a beaten egg added to the mixture will ensure that the ingredients hold together.

TRIFLE
SERVES 6

1 Victoria sandwich cake (see page 69),
preferably stale
very good-quality raspberry jam
4 tablespoons sherry
2 tablespoons brandy
290ml/1/2 pint milk
5 egg yolks
2 tablespoons caster sugar
2 drops vanilla essence
290ml/1/2 pint double cream
30g/1oz split blanched almonds, toasted
a few ratafia biscuits (optional)

1. Cut the sponge cake into thick pieces. Sandwich the pieces together sparingly with jam. Pile them into a large glass serving dish.
2. Pour over the sherry and brandy and leave to soak while you prepare the custard.
3. Put the milk into a saucepan and scald by bringing to just below boiling point.
4. In a large bowl, lightly beat the yolks and sugar with a wooden spoon. Pour the scalding milk on to them, stirring.
5. Return the mixture to the pan and reheat carefully, stirring all the time, until the mixture is thick enough to coat the back of the spoon. Care must be taken not to boil the custard, or it will curdle. Add the vanilla essence.
6. Strain on to the cake and leave to get completely cold.
7. Whip the cream until fairly stiff and spread or pipe over the trifle.
8. Decorate with the almonds and the ratafia biscuits, if using.

Causes of Failure
Jam/jelly not setting: Over-ripe produce used; low pectin levels/not enough pectin in fruit to achieve setting point; or not boiled far enough.
Very firm jam/jelly: Over-boiled.
Mould appearing in jar: Jars not sterilized properly or not enough sugar in jam.
Fruit rising to top of jar: Jam not left to stand for 15 minutes off the heat before filling jars.

WINTER BUFFET AND WINE I
CHAPTER 16

Techniques Covered
Planning a buffet party
Introduction to wine

Recipes
Aubergine and chestnut pie
Venison casserole
Leith's Good Food's Dauphinoise potatoes
Sauté of winter vegetables
Black cherry clafoutis

PLANNING A BUFFET PARTY

If you are going to be cooking for a buffet party, here are a few hints that may be helpful when planning your menu and arranging your food.

- The larger the choice of dishes, the more generous you have to be, and therefore if you are cooking for a small number the increased costs can be significant.
- Think about ease of both serving and eating – if there are not many places for guests to sit down it should be a fork buffet.
- Think about what the food will look like once people have started to fill their plates. We decorate the underplates with fresh flowers or bunches of herbs and leave the dishes themselves very simply garnished. Do not put too many flowers on the table – let the food speak for itself.
- Have more than one service point with only about 16 sets of knives, forks and plates in any one pile – the crockery must not dominate the table. If you are cooking for 100 people, you will need at least 4 service points.
- Think carefully about the appearance of the food – it should be a good mixture of colours.
- Try to make the table look attractive by using height. Place the food on cake stands and put boxes under the tablecloths.
- Don't decorate the front of the tablecloth with garlands of flowers – they'll get crushed and look untidy.
- Always think about what the buffet will look like at the end of the meal.
- If possible change the tablecloth in between courses – if not, then certainly after coffee.
- Use linen napkins to hide spills.
- Never underestimate the number of helpers you'll need – people helping themselves often have eyes bigger than their stomachs. For 100 people you will need 4 people serving the food.
- Make sure that there is easy access to all service points and that there is a choice of all the dishes beside each pile of plates.
- It is possible to buy (from disposable products suppliers) little plastic holders so that the wine glasses can be attached to plates.
- Don't use linen napkins – they are too cumbersome at a buffet.
- Precut and slice most of the food but for the sake of appearance leave some whole.
- Never put out all the food – keep some back so that the last shall be first. Always hide the vegetarian dishes – you could run out and genuine vegetarians would not be able to have any.
- Try to avoid individual dishes as they dictate how many people can have how much of a certain dish – you may well calculate tastes incorrectly.
- If people have to queue you'll find that only about two-thirds of the guests will come back for puddings, and only about half will come back again for coffee. Obviously you have to cater for full take-up but don't be over-generous.

AUBERGINE AND CHESTNUT PIE

This wonderful moist layered pie would make a perfect dish for any vegetarian's Christmas day.

For the aubergine layer

1 medium aubergine, cut into cubes
85ml/3fl oz olive oil
3 tomatoes, roughly chopped
2 tablespoons tomato purée
1 clove garlic, crushed
1 tablespoon chopped fresh basil
1 tablespoon chopped fresh marjoram
salt and freshly ground black pepper
For the nut layer
1 small onion, finely chopped
2 sticks celery, finely chopped
100ml/4fl oz water
110g/4oz walnuts, roughly chopped
110g/4oz unsweetened chestnut purée
55g/2oz peeled and cooked chestnuts, roughly chopped
30g/1oz fresh wholemeal bread cubes

Salt and freshly ground black pepper
For the courgette layer
225g/8oz courgettes, sliced
1 small bunch chives, finely-chopped
1 tablespoon single cream
salt and freshly ground black pepper
To finish
3 tablespoons oil
7 sheets filo pastry
1 tablespoon sesame seeds

1. Put the aubergines into a colander. Sprinkle with salt and leave to stand for 20 minutes.
2. Preheat the oven to 200°C/400°F/gas mark 6.
3. Rinse the aubergines and pat dry. Fry them in three-quarters of the oil until beginning to soften, add the tomatoes, tomato purée, garlic, basil and marjoram. Season with salt and pepper and cook gently until tender.
4. Make the nut layer. Cook the onion and celery in the oil until soft. Add the water, walnuts, chestnut purée, chestnuts, bread cubes, salt and pepper. Cook for 2–3 minutes.
5. Sauté the courgettes in the remaining oil. When tender add the chives, cream, salt and pepper.
6. Layer the fillings up in a large dish, starting with the aubergines and finishing with the courgettes.
7. Cover the pie with 7 layers of filo pastry, brushing each layer with oil. Brush the top with oil and sprinkle with the sesame seeds.
8. Bake for 20 minutes or until the top is golden brown.

NOTE: To get 55g/2oz of peeled cooked chestnuts you will need to buy about 170g/6oz of fresh chestnuts. To cook them, make a slit in the skin of each chestnut, and put them into a pan of cold water. Bring to the boil, simmer for 10 minutes, and then take off the heat. Remove 1 or 2 nuts at a time and peel – the skins come off quite easily if the chestnuts are hot but not overcooked.

VENISON CASSEROLE

SERVES 4

675g/1 1/2lb venison
For the marinade
5 tablespoons sunflower oil
1 onion, sliced
1 carrot, sliced
1 stick celery, sliced
1 clove garlic, crushed
6 juniper berries
1 slice of lemon
1 bay leaf
290ml/1/2 pint red wine
2 tablespoons red wine vinegar
6 black peppercorns
For the casserole
1 tablespoon sunflower oil
30g/1oz butter
110g/4oz onions, peeled
1 clove garlic, crushed
110g/4oz button mushrooms
2 teaspoons plain flour
150ml/1/4 pint brown stock (see page 51)
1 tablespoon cranberry jelly
salt and freshly ground black pepper
55g/2oz fresh cranberries
15g/1/2oz sugar
110g/4oz cooked whole chestnuts
To garnish
chopped fresh parsley

1. Cut the venison into 5cm/2in cubes, trimming away any tough membrane or sinew.
2. Mix the ingredients for the marinade together in a bowl and add the venison. Mix well, cover and leave in a cool place or in the refrigerator overnight.
3. Preheat the oven to 170°C/325°F/gas mark 3.
4. Lift out the venison cubes and pat dry with absorbent kitchen paper. Strain the

marinade, reserving the liquid for cooking.

5. Heat half the oil in a heavy saucepan and brown the venison cubes a few at a time. Place them in a casserole. If the bottom of the pan becomes brown or too dry, pour in a little of the strained marinade, swish it about, scraping off the sediment stuck to the bottom, and pour over the venison cubes. Then heat a little more oil and continue browning the meat.

6. When all the venison has been browned, repeat the déglaçage (boiling up with a little marinade and scraping the bottom of the pan).

7. Now melt the butter in a saucepan and fry the onions and garlic until the onions are pale brown all over. Add the mushrooms and continue cooking for 2 minutes.

8. Stir in the flour and cook for 1 minute. Remove from the heat, add the remaining marinade and the brown stock, return to the heat and stir until boiling, again scraping the bottom of the pan. When boiling, pour over the venison.

9. Add the cranberry jelly. Season with salt and pepper.

10. Cover the casserole and cook in the heated oven for about 2 hours or until the venison is very tender.

11. Meanwhile, cook the cranberries briefly with the sugar in 2–3 tablespoons water until just soft but not crushed. Strain off the liquor. Lift the venison, mushrooms and onions with a slotted spoon into a serving dish.

12. Boil the sauce fast until reduced to a shiny, almost syrupy consistency. Add the chestnuts and cranberries and simmer gently for 5 minutes.

13. Pour the sauce over the venison and serve garnished with chopped parsley.

LEITH'S GOOD FOOD'S DAUPHINOISE POTATOES
SERVES 4–6

1 onion, thinly sliced
1 clove garlic, crushed (optional)
15g/1/2 oz butter
900g/2lb old floury potatoes, peeled and thinly sliced
425ml/3/4 pint mixed single and double cream
150ml/1/4 pint soured cream, thinned down to double cream consistency with milk
salt and freshly ground black pepper

1. Preheat the oven to 170°C/325°F/gas mark 3.

2. Cook the onions and garlic in the butter until soft but not brown.

3. Layer up the potatoes and creams with the onions and seasoning in a lightly buttered dish, and bake in the preheated oven for 1½ hours, or until tender.

SAUTÉ OF WINTER VEGETABLES
SERVES 6

900g/2lb weight of mixed winter vegetables, for example:
sweet potatoes
parsnips
carrots
pumpkin
button onions
leeks
turnips
swedes
celeriac
30g/1oz butter
salt and freshly ground black pepper
2 tablespoons sugar
2 tablespoons lemon juice
1 tablespoon chopped fresh parsley

1. Peel the vegetables and cut into largish (double bite-size) irregular chunks.

2. Cook them in boiling water for about 5 minutes, drain and refresh in running cold water.

3. Melt the butter in a large sauté pan and add the vegetables. Season with salt and pepper.

4. Sauté over a very low heat, turning the

vegetables occasionally, for about 20 minutes. Do not allow them to burn.

5. When the vegetables are soft and beginning to colour, add the sugar and lemon juice. Turn the heat up to caramelize them slightly. Season with more salt and pepper and sprinkle with chopped parsley. Serve immediately.

NOTE: If cooking a large quantity of vegetables it is possible to finish them off in the oven. Preheat the oven to 200°C/400°F/gas mark 6. Melt the butter in a roasting tin and add the blanched vegetables. Cook them at the top of the preheated oven for 45 minutes to 1 hour, turning them occasionally. Add the sugar, lemon juice and seasonings and bake for an extra 5 minutes. Sprinkle with parsley.

BLACK CHERRY CLAFOUTIS

This recipe has been adapted from a recipe by Raymond Blanc in *Cooking for Friends*. It should be prepared an hour in advance and served warm.

SERVES 4

4 tablespoons Kirsch
450g/1lb canned black cherries, drained
100ml/3 1/2 fl oz milk
150ml/1/4 pint whipping cream
1/2 vanilla pod
4 eggs
140g/5oz caster sugar
20g/3/4 oz plain flour
a pinch of salt
butter and caster sugar for greasing
  and sprinkling

Leiths School
Of
Food And Wine

1. Preheat the oven to 200°C/400°F/gas mark 6.
2. Sprinkle the Kirsch over the cherries. Leave to macerate.
3. Put the milk, cream and vanilla pod into a small saucepan. Bring to the boil, then turn off the heat and leave to infuse.
4. Place the eggs and sugar in a mixing bowl. Whisk until creamy. Add the flour and salt and whisk until smooth. Strain in the infused milk and cream, and beat until well mixed.
5. Generously butter an ovenproof dish about 25 x 23 x 5cm/10 x 9 x 2in and sprinkle with caster sugar.
6. Add the cherries and pour over the batter.
7. Bake in the preheated oven for 25 minutes. Remove and allow to cool before serving sprinkled with a little extra caster sugar.

WINE 1

by Philippa Carr M.W.

Wine is made all over the world, in countries as far flung as China and Canada, but what connects all these places is their suitability to the vine's cultivation. *Vitis Vinifera*, the species of vine responsible for the world's quality wines, is very adaptable to widely differing conditions – just compare the climate round Lake Ontario to that in Spain's La Mancha region – but wherever it is grown it needs to be controlled.

Decisions in the vineyard

Imagine you have just moved into a new house and the garden is a barren builder's yard. What do you do? You will probably sit down with the seed catalogues and dream through the winter of the riot of colour to come. Planning a vineyard is very similar – you start with what you want to achieve in the glass, and work backwards. The gardener may hanker after an abundant herbaceous border, the vigneron might want to make lightly oaked Chardonnay. Firstly, is there a market for these wines? Chardonnay may be everywhere, almost synonymous with 'dry white', but the world needs more, and at the price the winemaker can afford to produce it. Are the conditions suitable in his vineyard? Chardonnay, as it happens, is a very accommodating variety, but many grapes are not, so the vineyard owner needs to consider the climate and soil type, the drainage and the elevation before planting.

In many European countries what you can plant, where and how is governed by law, enshrining in legislation generations of local practice. In France, how you grow grapes and make wine is strictly controlled under the Appellation Contrôlée system. It starts with the importance of place – or the vineyard site itself: the closer you can define the vineyard area and therefore the factors affecting the local growing conditions, in theory, the finer the wine. Crucial to quality in Europe is the ripeness of grapes, so that most favoured sites have traditionally produced the finest quality grapes and wines.

What makes quality? In the vineyard it is a combination of climate, soil, grape variety, how the grapes are grown, all of which add up to the quality of the grapes at harvest. Any cook worth her salt will tell you that you can not make a good dish from poor ingredients – the same applies to wine. Get it right in the vineyard and you are ready to make good wine.

Wine making

Making wine is like making bread – both use fermentation. Put simply, in wine making the sugar comes from the grapes, yeasts are found in the bloom on the grape skin; put the two together in a warm place and you get alcohol and carbon dioxide. If you want good wine, though, you will need more control and today technology has utterly transformed the quality and style of the bulk of medium-priced wines on our supermarket shelves.

The major difference between making white wines and red is obvious – colour. Red wines exploit the colour in the skins which white wines do not need.

White wines use the free-run juice from the first gentle pressing of the grapes after which the grapes are fermented at a coolish temperature (around 15°–18°C). Nowadays this is often in huge stainless steel vats which, though expensive, have two overwhelming advantages – easy to keep clean and easy to control the fermentation temperature. Wood can be used at some stage: new oak barrels are a huge outlay for a winery but oak does add complexity to the wine and has a particular affinity to Chardonnay.

Red grapes go into a crusher and then the juice is fermented with the skins, pips and sometimes the stalks for, perhaps, a fortnight, depending on how full-bodied you want the wine, and at a higher temperature than whites to extract more colour from the skins.

Sweet wines are usually made by stopping the fermentation before all the sugar in the grapes has been converted to alcohol, thus leaving sweetness in the wine. This can be done by chilling the wine then centrifuging out the yeasts or adding sulphur dioxide to kill the yeasts (not a method favoured widely today). Wines like fine Sauternes are made from grapes affected by noble rot (*pourriture noble*) – full of sugar but dehydrated so the yeasts cannot possibly convert all the sugar before they are knocked out by the alcohol and you are left with an intensely luscious wine. An Australian Liqueur Muscat is made by fortifying the wine with spirit when fermentation is still incomplete – sugar remains but the yeasts cannot survive, so again, you have a sweet wine.

Sparkling wines need bubbles of carbon dioxide and how they get into the bottle is a good guide to the quality of the wine and how long the bubbles will stay in the glass. The best techniques harness the carbon dioxide naturally produced by fermentation.

Firstly, the Bicycle Pump method – pumping gas into the finished wine does not achieve long-lasting quality results. Secondly, fermentation in a tank by adding yeast and sugar. The carbon dioxide dissolves into the wine and is only realized when the bottle is opened. A perfectly good method when, and only when, the base wine is good.

The traditional method, as usual in Champagne and other quality sparkling wines, for example, Cava, Saumur and top of the range examples from Australia, California, South Africa and New Zealand, was invented by a monk called Dom Perignon. The technique involves a second fermentation in the same bottle you will see on the shelf. The problem, solved by a doughty lady called Veuve Cliquot, was to get rid of the sediment, the dead yeasts, from the bottle. Visitors to a Champagne cellar will see in action the technique she invented called 'rémuage', or riddling – tipping and turning the bottle so the sediment spirals through the wine on to the cork. The plug of sediment is frozen, disposed of, and the bottle topped up and released.

A modern variation, used in the New World, is called the Transfer method. Here, the second fermentation takes place in a bottle, the finished wine is emptied under pressure into a tank, filtered, and re-bottled under pressure: all the advantages of wine absorbing flavour from the yeasts without the complications of riddling.

Decisions in the glass
The difference between Drinking and Tasting is Thinking. When you understand the amount

of work and expertise invested in the glass of wine now in your hand, you will want to derive from it as much information and pleasure as possible. Tasting technique will enable you to find more flavours in the glass as well as assess its quality.

Tasting is straightforward: all you need is a sense of taste, a clean suitable glass and some wine, and plenty of practice.

It is on the tip of my tongue

Let us start with taste: try this simple experiment. Dab some sugar on to your finger and dot it over your tongue – the sides, back and front – and you will find that you taste the sugar on the tip of your tongue. Now for acidity – suck a piece of lemon and the sides of your tongue will tingle. Cold, stewed, strong tea will coat the sides of the mouth and your gums with the dry taste of tannin, which you find in red wine. These are the important components in wine which need to be in balance with fruity flavours for real enjoyment.

Building your taste vocabulary

Finding words for flavours can seem difficult – try describing the taste of a strawberry or the smell of a rose. You will probably resort to making comparisons with familiar or remembered aromas and that is just what happens in wine tasting. We easily accept 'citrus notes' in a perfume so we should not feel embarrassed about saying a wine smells of gooseberries, crushed blackcurrant leaves and nettles.

Just remember a few guidelines when building up your taste vocabulary:
- Think, think, think. The difference between Drinking and Tasting is Thinking.
- Use words and phrases which mean something to you – not just copied from a friend or professional commentator.
- Write down your thoughts whenever you can – it helps you remember the wine.
- The most effective tasting notes are so clear, straightforward and to the point that someone else could identify the wine from the description alone.
- There are some tasting terms which really cannot be bettered and get as close as one can to describing particular grape varieties.
- Some descriptions have been accepted as 'industry norms'; for example, 'blackcurrant' for Cabernet Sauvignon or 'steely' for Riesling. It is useful to be aware of those as they are used widely, frequently and, most importantly, they ring true.

What the wine in the glass can tell you

APPEARANCE

Tilt the glass away from you, holding it by the foot or the stem. Now look at the colour – it is best to do so against a light background like a sheet of white paper.

LOOKING AT WHITE WINE FIRST

Is it pale? If so, the wine is probably from a cool climate, perhaps a cool region of Northern Europe, but do not forget countries like New Zealand. Conversely, a more golden hue will suggest a warm or hot area. Acidity gives a wine brilliance and little bubbles in what is not a sparkling wine can either be carbon dioxide keeping a New World wine zippy or secondary fermentation, which is a serious fault.

Red wines can vary in colour from the colour of strawberry juice (a cool climate) to an almost opaque red – warm climate, or hot vintage. Grape varieties also have their own colour characteristics to complicate matters a little. A purple wine is youthful and a brown wine is too old, or if just blackish at the rim, mature.

Swirl the wine round in the glass (sometimes it helps to keep the glass flat on the table) and you will notice that some wines cling to the sides of the glass, like sherry or port. These rivulets are called 'legs' and mean high alcohol – so a hot climate or a ripe vintage.

Whilst you are swirling you are ready for sniffing – the most informative stage of tasting.

SMELL

You cannot taste without a sense of smell – anyone with a cold will tell you that, so if you get the hang of sniffing you are well on the way to being a wine taster. Swirl the glass to aerate the wine and inhale deeply ... What are you looking for? First of all, cleanliness: detecting of smells will guide you to the wine's state of health; secondly, the grape variety. The grape variety will give important clues to the wine's origin; the depth of intensity of the aromas indicate the age and quality of the wine. Some wines are very evocative for the aromas just leap out of the glass and descriptions easily spring to mind. However, with other wines you sometimes have to work a little harder, though the effort is often worthwhile. Very good, but immature wines are often 'closed' or 'dumb', not smelling of much at all, but with time they will open out. As a rough rule of thumb, simple basic wines have least to offer in terms of aroma and flavour; complexity means quality.

TASTE

We have probably all watched wine tasters swishing and spitting and wondered – what is it all for and how do I do that without feeling very silly? There is a serious and valid point to the palaver – the chewing and swishing is to aerate the wine, releasing the aromas and distributing the wine all over the tongue and round the mouth.

Take a good mouthful of wine but do not swallow – swish the wine around and then chew it, just as you would a mouthwash. Now for the important stage – think seriously about the taste and answer for yourself the following questions:

- Is the wine dry or sweet?
- Is the acidity high or low? This can indicate grape variety, age, origin or style – high acidity suggests underripe grapes, certain grape varieties, cool climate, youth.
- What is the body weight of the wine in the mouth? A fuller style indicates alcohol.
- What about the tannin in red wines? Some grapes are naturally high in tannin (Cabernet Sauvignon) but a lot of tannin is found in youthful wines which then soften with age.

The balance between all the separate elements, the length of time the flavour lingers in the mouth and the intensity of these flavours all add up to quality.

Quality in wine, as with food or clothes or literature, is indefinable, but you know it when you meet it and you certainly do not need to be an expert to recognize it.

How wines differ

There are some grape varieties which have found their ideal site and never seem to want to make good wine anywhere else. There are others which lack wide appeal so few vineyard owners attempt to grow them outside their traditional home. However, there is a third category, of international varieties that can create classy wine practically anywhere.

The most famous of the third category are Chardonnay and Cabernet Sauvignon, grown in almost every wine region in the world, followed at a distance by Sauvignon Blanc and Merlot. Riesling is widely planted and produces wines of the highest quality, but is woefully underrated. Extensively grown but occasionally showing real class are Semillon and Chenin Blanc. Conversely, Sangiovese and Nebbiolo are of undoubtedly fine pedigree and generally confined to their Italian homeland. Pinot Noir is gradually taking a few steps out of Burgundy, but it is a very difficult grape to grow; Gamay is best grown in Beaujolais; and Syrah has solid roots in the Rhône, or, as Shiraz, in Australia.

This would help to explain why wine drinkers in the United Kingdom in the last few years have latched on to Chardonnay and Cabernet Sauvignon – put these names on the label and you sell wine.

We like the soft, buttery, fairly neutral character of Chardonnay and its moderate acidity. In Cabernet Sauvignon we are drinking, quite frankly, the best red grape of them all with flavours ranging from minty crème de cassis in Australia to the astonishing complexity and class of mature red Bordeaux. Why look elsewhere? Because variety is the spice of life and because different wines can bring out different flavours in your food.

New World v Old World

At the end of the 1970s a British wine drinker would be hardly aware that wines could be made anywhere other than Europe. The classic regions of Bordeaux, Burgundy, Loire and Champagne in France; the Rhine and the Mosel in Germany; port, madeira and sherry – they defined the known wine world. But soon, a revolution took place. Australian wines burst upon the scene – big, bold and full of fruit – and in one short decade they have completely changed our drinking tastes and habits.

In 1989 8 per cent of the UK's consumption of wine was from the New World; in 1997 that share increased to nearly 23 per cent and all the indicators suggest that by the year 2000 30 per cent of all the wine we drink will be from the New World. Within 'New World' the biggest player is Australia and despite anticipated shortages, it is expected that in the year 2000 Australia will be the third biggest wine exporter to the UK behind France and Germany, knocking Germany off the No. 2 position a year later.

Techniques Covered
Special diets
Costing

Recipes
Chicken breasts with ginger
Spicy fish curry
Hot winter fruit salad

Special diets

All special diets require modification of one or more components of the diet. It is essential that professional help and advice are sought when preparing special diets for medical conditions. Changes in the diet need expert supervision to ensure that all nutrients continue to be provided.

A few of the most common diets are outlined below. Local hospital Dietetic Departments can give further advice on the cooking modifications needed for these and other therapeutic diets.

WEIGHT-REDUCING, DIABETIC AND LIPID-LOWERING DIETS

All medical conditions which need these diets require a change to a healthy lifestyle, which includes a diet based on fresh foods and high in fibre and low in fat. The emphasis should be on wholegrain bread and cereals, fresh fruit and vegetables, with moderate portions of lean meat and fish. These dietary modifications are all based on healthy eating principles, and as such can easily be followed by partners and the rest of the family. Drastic changes should be avoided, as this generally means the diet is difficult to keep to. The appropriate changes made to diet and lifestyle can be incorporated into the normal diet permanently.

GLUTEN-FREE DIET

This diet is specifically for the treatment of coeliac disease. It requires complete avoidance of gluten, a protein found in wheat, rye, barley and oats. All foods containing these, even in small amounts, must be avoided. Gluten-free flour, bread, pasta and biscuits are available on prescription and from chemists: the flour can be used to make gluten-free versions of many foods. Rice, soya, corn and potato flour are naturally gluten-free, and can also be used. Gluten is the component of flour which gives it stretchiness and air-holding qualities. It takes time to adapt to gluten-free flours.

Many manufactured products contain gluten, and labels must be carefully checked. If in doubt, omit it.

Dietary change on religious and moral grounds

Many people choose to follow a specific set of dietary rules for ethnic, cultural, moral and religious reasons. These may be dictated by religious texts, such as the Koran for Muslims. They may also involve special methods of preparation and/or slaughter of animals, or the avoidance of certain foods together at the same meal. It is very important when cooking for other people to find out if they have any such dietary restrictions, and to adhere strictly to them.

The information given below outlines the generally accepted guidelines for the most widely used of these diets. There are also a number of religious festivals, which may provide the opportunity for special foods, or fasting for periods of time.

HINDU

Orthodox or strict Hindus are vegetarian. Many, particularly women, do not eat eggs, and will only eat vegetarian cheese, which does not contain animal rennet. Hindus never eat beef, as the cow is considered a sacred animal. Some non-Orthodox Hindus may eat chicken, mutton and occasionally fish. Milk, yoghurt and butter are permitted.

MUSLIM

Muslims can only eat meat which is halal and has been killed according to Islamic law. This can be obtained from a halal butcher. Pork is strictly forbidden, as are all of its products. Care must be taken with cooking fats, which must be of vegetable origin, or from halal sources.

Fish, eggs, milk and dairy products are allowed. Alcohol is strictly avoided by most Muslims, and should not be used in cooking.

At certain times of the Islamic calendar, such as Ramadan, Muslims will fast during the hours of daylight, and eat late at night and early in the morning. There are a number of important festivals, which are celebrated by special food customs.

JEWISH

Jews can only eat meat from animals which have been ritually slaughtered and prepared to render them kosher. Pork is forbidden, but kosher lamb, beef and goat are acceptable.

Fish which have fins and scales are allowed, but shellfish are not. Chicken, turkey, duck, goose, partridge and pheasant are allowed, but other game birds are not.

The other important aspect of the Jewish diet is that meat and dairy foods must be kept

apart in cooking, and must not be eaten at the same meal.

VEGETARIAN

Some people choose not to eat meat, poultry or fish in their diet. Within this group, there are a number of variations. Protein foods need to be combined in vegetarian meals, to provide all the essential amino acids.

Demi-vegetarians, while not strictly vegetarian, will eat fish, but not meat.

Lacto-vegetarians will eat milk, cheese and dairy products. Cheese should not be made with animal rennet. Seemingly vegetarian foods, such as vegetable soups made with meat stock, are not acceptable.

Lacto-ovo-vegetarians eat eggs in addition to the above foods.

VEGAN

A vegan diet avoids animal foods of any sort, including dairy foods, and relies entirely on plant foods. Protein is obtained from foods such as soya beans and nuts. A vegan diet is deficient in Vitamin B12, which is only present in animal products, or in synthetic form. A number of yeast extracts fortified with Vitamin B12 are available, which can be used in a variety of ways to fortify the diet.

Food additives

Many people express concern about additives in food. Certainly, a diet based mainly on a variety of fresh ingredients, well prepared and freshly cooked, is ideal. However, many food products rely on some form of additives, such as preservatives, to ensure that they are safe to eat. The range of foods available would be severely restricted if these were not used in moderation. Similarly, many foods would look unpalatable after processing if some colouring were not added to them.

The legislation governing additives in the UK is extensive, and all foods containing additives are labelled as such. 'E' numbers show that an additive is accepted as safe throughout the European Community. Many of these are derivatives of natural products, like red colouring derived from beetroot (E162).

The key is to base the diet on fresh foods, using processed foods in moderation.

Excellent information on additives and food labelling is available from the Ministry of Agriculture, Fisheries and Food.

Conclusion

For all its life-giving and therapeutic properties, food is to be enjoyed. If a variety of food is eaten, chosen from a range of food groups, in appropriate portions, anyone's diet can provide for both the body's fundamental physical requirements and the important psychological aspects of the enjoyment of food. The recipes in this book are designed to provide a happy balance of these two interlinked roles of food in our lives.

REFERENCES
1. Dietary Reference Values for Food Energy and Nutrients for the United Kingdom; Department of Health. 1991.
2. Ibid.
3. Ibid.
4. Ministry of Agriculture Fisheries and Food: information of food matters available from Food Sense, London SE99 7TT.

COSTING

If you are cooking commercially it is essential to be able to cost a menu in order to establish the correct selling price and thus make some money. When you start cooking for small dinner parties it is perfectly sensible simply to charge your customers a fee plus expenses. Discuss with your customers what your expenses will be e.g. food, transport etc. Once you start to cook for large numbers you have to become rather more professional and more specific.

System 1

To calculate your fee, establish what you think is a fair hourly rate and then try to work out how long you think the job will take. To begin with you might decide to charge £5 an hour plus expenses. As you get faster the rate can be increased. With experience you will be able to give future customers a rough idea of how much your fee and expenses will be. When you invoice using this rather simple system (see page 147), any raw ingredients that you have not used, but have charged in expenses, should be left in the customer's house. For example, if you bought a dozen eggs but only used 8, the remaining 4 should be left in the refrigerator.

System 2

If you are cooking for large numbers of guests you will be expected to give your client a very specific quotation in advance. Your final invoice (see page 148) should be the same as the original quotation. If by any chance there are to be any extras, for example if your client suddenly asks for another pudding, give them a revised quotation.

Once your quotation has been accepted it is possible to ask for a 10 per cent deposit.

Your quotation should include everything that you will be charging for on top of the food. The extras may be many and varied but could include some of the following:

TABLES AND CHAIRS

Chairs Allow 1 chair per head – if there is to be dancing check that the chairs are stackable.
Tables For long tables allow 45–60cm/18–24in dining space per head

For round tables, imperial: the simple rule is to double the diameter, i.e. a 4ft table seats 8 people and a 5ft table seats 10 people.

For metric: multiply the diameter by 0.06, i.e. a 120 cm table will seat 8 people and a 150 cm table will seat 10 people.

You might need to advise on spacing:

- for a sit-down dinner allow 10–12 sq. ft per head.
- for a stand-up reception allow 6 sq. ft per head.

(Remember to discount space with pillars, etc.).

A simple rule is that you divide the square footage by 10: thus in a 600 sq. ft room 60 people will be able to sit down to dinner.

When arranging the tables you will need to allow space between them. Allow 45cm/18in for chairs and 30–45cm/12–18in for the passage of waitresses. Thus a 5ft diameter table will fit in a 10ft diameter space.

CROCKERY, ETC.

China Work out the number of plates etc. that you need and then allow an extra 10 sets per 200 people. Order plates for crumbing down (for the waitresses to clean on to halfway through service).

Cutlery Order an extra 10 sets per 200 people: do not forget service sets and bread knives.

Serving dishes Always order a few extra dishes.

Butter dishes Allow 2 per table of 10.

Salt, pepper and mustard pots Allow 2 sets per table of 10. Do not forget to take salt, pepper and mustard in case the pots are empty.

Ashtrays Allow 3 per table (so that they can be constantly changed) and plenty for the bar.

Glasses For the reception allow 1½ glasses per head. For the dinner 2 wine glasses each plus 1 water glass each. Order an extra 10 of each per 100 people.

Bread baskets 1 per table of 10.

Napkins 1 per head plus an extra 10 per 100 plus 1 per 10 for crumbing down.

Tablecloths 1 per table plus an extra 1 per 10 tables. Order plenty for the bar, tombola stand, etc. Take advice as to the right size cloth for round tables.

Waitress/service cloths 2 per waitress.

Service trays 1 per waitress.

Drinks trays 1 per 30 guests.

EXTRA EQUIPMENT
Do not forget:
ice bins (make sure the hire arrives
  before the ice)
extra ovens if necessary or hot cupboards
extension leads
coat rails and hangers
easel and board
menu holders
cake stand
coffee urns, for a big party
table mats
water jugs
corkscrews
coffee pots, milk jugs, sugar bowls,
teaspoons
punch bowl and ladle
candlesticks

plate rings (for stacking plates)
sound system
stand for the seating plan
fruit baskets
knife and board for lemons
drugget (cloth for floor behind the bar)
ice buckets

*STAFF (for notes on service see
  entertaining, page 176)*
Food:
- silver service: 1 waitress per 6 guests
- butler service: 1 waitress per 10 guests
- buffet party: 1 waitress per 25 guests
- canapé party: 1 waitress per 35 guests

Bar:
- full bar: 1 butler per 30 guests
- simple bar: 1 butler per 50 guests

Supervisor 1 per 80 guests

Porter 1 per 100 guests

    You may also need to arrange for a master of ceremonies.

WINE
Generally allow a bottle of wine per head – order the wine on sale or return. Never chill wine on ice if you are not sure that it will all be drunk – the labels will fall off and you will not be able to return it.

OTHER DRINKS
As required, e.g. orange juice, whisky, water. Generally allow ½ bottle of water per head.

ICE
1 x 10kg/25lb bag of ice will cool 2 cases of champagne or 3 cases of white wine (champagne is generally served cooler than wine).

Other things to take into account:
- MARQUEE
- BAND Note the band generally eats the
    same dinner as the guests. .
- PHOTOGRAPHER
- BALLOONS
- FLOWERS

Selling price

Generally if you are subcontracting (such as hire equipment) we recommend that you negotiate a discount with the subcontractor and then charge the customer the full price – i.e. the difference between the discounted price and the selling price is your profit. You must tell your customer that he/she will be charged for any losses and breakages.

EXAMPLE:	Price of hire	£2,000
	discount for you	£ 200
	∴ price for you	£1,800
	price for the customers	£2,000
	profit on hire	£ 200

The only exceptions to this rule are

a) *the supply of alcohol* – the mark-up here varies enormously. Caterers will multiply the cost by anything from 1.5 to 3. In other words a customer may be charged, for a £4.00 cost price bottle of wine, anything from £6.00 to £12.00. You have to decide what your market will take.

b) *the supply of staff* – generally staff are invoiced at the cost price – you may well charge for a few extra waitresses in case of last-minute changes.

TO ESTABLISH THE SELLING PRICE OF FOOD

The normal practice in the catering industry is to multiply the cost of the food by 3 in order to make a gross profit of 67 per cent.

EXAMPLE:	cost of food	= £20.00
	selling price	= 20 x 3
		= £60.00
	gross profit	= £40.00
	gross profit	= $\frac{40}{60}$
		= 67 per cent

Naturally not all the £40.00 is profit – you will have plenty of expenses other than the food such as:

- Cook's wages
- Travel
- Heating
- Laundry

Once these expenses have been taken into account you should probably have a net profit of about 15–20 per cent (this does not take corporation tax into account).

EXAMPLE:	selling price	= £60.00
	cost of food	= £20.00
	expenses	= £31.00
	profit	= $\frac{9}{60}$
		= 15 per cent

If making a very sophisticated meal using cheap ingredients but taking a long time to cook you can multiply by 4 or even 5. Conversely, if making a very simple meal using very expensive ingredients – say lobster or crab – it is possible to multiply by 2. You must also take your market into account. For example, you will probably be charged more in London than in Scotland.

Costing a recipe

- Always cost the full recipe.
- Always have a rough idea of the answer, e.g. 1 kg mushrooms = £2.50/kg so you will know that if a recipe calls for 250g the cost will be about 60p.
- Weigh everything before cooking. If a recipe calls for one aubergine and you have the price per kilo you can work out the price if you know the weight.
- We take the incidental costs (e.g. flour for rolling out pastry, fried breadcrumbs, etc.) to be 15p per head per full 3-course meal.
- When working in metric, to divide by 1000 just move the decimal point three places to the left e.g.: 244 ÷ 1000 = 0.244

Useful information

1 kilo: 1000g: 2.2lb	1 average bottle wine : 75cl/750ml
1lb: 450g	1 average bottle spirits : 70cl/700ml
1 litre : 1000ml: 100cl: 10dl	1 head celery = 10 sticks
1 imperial pint: 20 fl oz	1 bulb garlic = 10 cloves
1 American pint: 16 fl oz	1 tablespoon chopped parsley = 10p
1 tablespoon: 3 teaspoons	1 tablespoon chopped mint = 15p
1 rounded tablespoon flour, sugar etc.: 30g/1oz	150ml/¼ pint stock = 10p

TO COST A RECIPE LAY IT OUT AS BELOW
The basic rule is <u>Price</u> x quantity = cost
                        Unit

In imperial

CHICKEN CASSEROLE: SERVES 4

INGREDIENTS	WEIGHT	PRICE	MATHS	RESULT
butter	1oz	1.56/lb	156÷16	9.75
onion	6oz	25p/lb	25÷16x6	9.37
chicken	3lb 3oz	1.25/lb	(3x125)+(125÷16x3)	398.44
stock	½ pint	10p/¼ pint	10x2	20
carrot	3oz	19p/lb	19÷16x3	3.56
2 tomatoes	6oz	45p/lb	45÷16x6	16.88
flour	1oz	14p/lb	Incidental	I
garlic	1 clove	30p/bulb	30÷10	3.
			TOTAL	£4.61
			Price per head	÷4
				£1.15

In metric

KIDNEYS TURBIGO: SERVES 4

INGREDIENTS	WEIGHT	PRICE	MATHS	RESULT
lamb's kidneys	425g	380p/kg	380÷1000x425	161.50
sausages	225g	262p/kg	262÷1000x225	58.95
button onions	185g	143p/kg	143÷1000x185	26.45
mushrooms	225g	330p/kg	330÷1000x225	74.25
butter for frying	30g	344p/kg	344÷1000x30	10.32
2 tbsp sherry	30ml	600p/750ml	600÷750x30	24
stock	450ml	10p/150ml	10x3	30
bouquet garni	I	I	Incidental	–
butter	30g	344/kg	as above	10.32
flour	30g	31p/kg	Incidental	–
soured cream	1 carton	57p carton	57x1	57
			TOTAL	452.79
			Price per head	÷4
				£1.13

Having costed out all the recipes in a menu you can then establish the cost price per head of a particular menu.

e.g.	Recipe	Cost per head
	mushroom soup	50p
	steak and kidney pie	70p
	potatoes	7p
	carrots	15p
	vanilla ice cream	30p
plus incidentals @ 15p a head per full 3-course meal		15p
	TOTAL	**£1.87**

The selling price per head would therefore become 1.87 x 3 = £5.61
You would probably round this up to £5.65.

VAT

If you have been catering for some time it may well be that you will have to register for VAT. Check with your local VAT office (under HM Customs and Excise in the telephone directory). Once your turnover has exceeded a prescribed figure (currently £47,500 per annum) you will have to add VAT on to all your bills. Turnover is the total of money coming in to the business. It has nothing to do with profit. The VAT charged in England is currently $17\frac{1}{2}$ per cent of the selling price.

VAT is an indirect tax (unlike income tax) and people have the choice of paying the tax by buying the goods. Food is free of VAT (zero rated) when you buy it but once a service has been applied then it is VATable. Once VAT registered you will probably become a VAT collector for the government. Any VAT charged has to be given to HM Customs and Excise. Any VAT paid (e.g. when buying chairs, cookers, etc.) is claimed back.

VAT returns are generally done every 3 months. You simply add up the VAT paid (called inputs) and any VAT received (called outputs) and either claim back or pay the difference.

To add on VAT:

example	cost price	= £40.00
	selling price	= £40 x 3 = £120.00
	= VAT @ $17^1/_2$ per cent	= £120 + (120 x $17^1/_2$)

$$= £120 + \frac{(120 \times 17^1/_2)}{100}$$

$$= £120 + £21.00$$

$$= £141.00$$

You would probably not charge customers £141. You will probably want to round up the price to something like £145.

By doing this you inevitably charge the VAT element included in the price so you now have to re-establish VAT.

To do this you have to multiply $\frac{7}{47}$ or $\frac{17^1/_2}{117^1/_2}$

example: £145.00 x $\frac{7}{47}$

= £21.60

Selling price is £145 (including £21.60 VAT)

Billing your customers
Having established your selling price and the VAT element you will then need to send your customers an invoice/statement.
If you are not a company and have not had to register for VAT lay out your invoices as follows:

your name and address
telephone no:
fax no:

Date
Client's name and address

INVOICE
£

For catering – agreed fee	200.00
Travel expenses (at 28p a mile)	30.00
Food supplied (receipts attached)	80.00
TOTAL	**310.00**

Please make cheques payable to ....
Invoice is payable on receipt

If you are not a limited company but you have had to register for VAT lay out your invoice as follows:

Your name and address
Telephone number
Fax number

Date of invoice
Name and address of client

INVOICE AND STATEMENT

	VAT	Fee
For: catering	35.00	200.00
Travel expenses	5.25	30.00
Food supplied	14.00	80.00
(receipts attached)		
plus VAT @ 17½ per cent		54.25
TOTAL AMOUNT DUE		**364.25**

Please make cheques payable to ....
Invoice is payable on receipt.

VAT no: ....

If you are a registered company and registered for VAT you must show:
- The Company's name
- The Company's place of registration e.g. Registered in England
- The Company's registration number
- The address of the registered office – if the invoice has more than one address it is essential to state which of the addresses is the registered office address.
- Your VAT registration number
- Your invoice number

The names of the directors need not be on an invoice, but if you choose to put them in, you must state the names of all the directors. In other words a company cannot be selective about which directors' names it shows – it must show all of them or none of them.

If you are a limited company and registered for VAT lay out your invoices as follows:

Your Company name and address, telephone no:
fax no:

Date of invoice
Name and address of client   Invoice No:

	VAT	Fee
For food supplied for 400 people @ £10 a head	700.00	4,000.00
For marquee supplied	1,750.00	10,000.00
For staff supplied		
14 waitresses @ £20 each	49.00	280.00
1 MC @ £40	7.00	40.00
For wine supplied	70.00	400.00
For orange juice supplied	7.00	40.00
For hire equipment	140.00	800.00
Less deposit received		(400.00)
Plus VAT @ 17½ per cent		2,723.00
TOTAL		17,883.00

Please make cheques payable to ....
Invoice is payable on receipt.
Names of directors ....
Registered at the above address in England
Registration no: .... VAT no: ....

When organizing a large event remember to think also about:

Insurance	Both public liability and employees' liability. Also hired-in equipment is rarely insured.
Liquor licence	If selling alcohol you will have to apply to the local magistrates court well in advance of the event.
Staff	Your staff are very important – if they are happy the customers will be happy; arrange for them to have tea and sandwiches and plenty of breaks.
Van	You may well need to order a refrigerated van.
Loos	Do not forget to make sure that the loos look very good – order loo paper, flowers, soap and towels.
Cloakroom lady	Organize a cloakroom lady with pins and cloakroom tickets (do not forget tea and sandwiches for her).
Security guards and car park attendants	Do not forget they too need feeding.

CHICKEN BREASTS WITH GINGER

SERVES 4

4 chicken breasts, boned and skinned

1 onion, very finely chopped

2 cloves of garlic, crushed

5cm/2 in fresh ginger, peeled and very finely chopped

5 cardamom pods, cracked

1 teaspoon ground turmeric

2 tablespoons light soy sauce

2 tablespoons dry sherry (optional)

1. Place the chicken breasts in a bowl with the onion, garlic, ginger, cardamom pods, turmeric, soy sauce and sherry. Cover the bowl and leave for about 2 hours so that the chicken can absorb the flavour. Turn the chicken once or twice.
2. Preheat the oven to 200°C/400°F/gas mark 6.
3. Line a flat baking dish with kitchen foil and arrange the breasts on it. Pour over the marinade and seal the chicken tightly in the foil so that none of the juice can escape.
4. Bake in the preheated oven for 30 minutes.

SPICY FISH CURRY

Any firm white fish will do for this curry. Be very careful not to overcook the fish or it will begin to fall apart and look unattractive. This is a fairly mild curry but can be made hotter by using an extra green chilli pepper. Remove the seeds of the green chilli under cold running water.

SERVES 4

675g/1¹/₂lb monkfish, filleted and skinned

1 large onion, chopped

1 green pepper, cored, deseeded and sliced

1 green chilli, deseeded and chopped

sunflower oil

1 x 1cm/¹/₂ in fresh ginger, peeled and cut into slivers

1 clove of garlic, crushed

1 teaspoon ground cumin

1 teaspoon ground coriander

1 teaspoon ground cinnamon

1 teaspoon ground turmeric

450ml/³/₄ pint water

salt and freshly ground black pepper

110g/4oz Greek yoghurt

To garnish

roughly chopped fresh mint

1. Cut the monkfish into 2.5cm/1in cubes.
2. Fry the onion, pepper and chilli in a little oil in a frying pan and allow to soften without browning for 2–3 minutes. Add the ginger, garlic and dry spices and cook for a further 2 minutes. Stir regularly and

add a little extra oil if the mixture is getting too dry.

3. Remove the pan off the heat. Add the water and bring to the boil. Season well with salt and pepper. Add the fish and simmer for 10 minutes. Remove the fish with a slotted spoon. Reduce the sauce, by boiling rapidly, to a syrupy consistency.
4. Beat the yoghurt with a little water, add some of the hot fish juices, mix well and return to the pan. Do not allow to get too hot. Return the fish to the pan.
5. Pile into a warmed serving dish and serve garnished with the mint.

HOT WINTER FRUIT SALAD
SERVES 4

450g/1lb good-quality mixed dried fruits, such as prunes, apricots, figs and apples
1 tablespoon Calvados
cold tea
4 tablespoons fresh orange juice
3–4 cloves
1 x 5cm/2 in cinnamon stick
1/4 teaspoon ground mixed spice
thinly pared zest of 1 lemon
1 star anise

1. Soak the mixed dried fruits in the Calvados and enough tea just to cover. Leave overnight.
2. Pour into a saucepan and add the orange juice, cloves, cinnamon, mixed spice, lemon zest and star anise. Bring to the boil, then simmer slowly until the fruits are soft (about 20 minutes).
3. Remove the cloves, cinnamon, lemon zest and star anise. Serve hot or cold.

FISH II AND SUPPER DISHES

CHAPTER 18

Techniques Covered
Poaching fish
Preparing prawns
Making a beurre noisette
Preparing mussels
Chinese stir-fry

❓ Cookery terms
Beurre noisette: Butter browned over heat to a nut colour.
Supreme: Choice piece of poultry (usually from the breast).

Recipes
Skate with brown butter and capers
Prawn pilaf
Thai fish soup
Potato tart
Stir-fried chicken with cashews
Sticky toffee pudding

SHELLFISH
Edible shellfish can be divided into two main categories:
Crustaceans: lobsters, crabs, crawfish, langoustines, prawns and shrimps, which have 5 pairs of legs and live encased in a jointed, multi-hinged shell;
Molluscs: *Gastropods* (univalves) or single-shelled creatures, including whelks and winkles, and *bivalves* or double-hinged shelled creatures, such as mussels, oysters and scallops. These are also known as filter-feeders;
Cephalods: creatures with tentacles and a modified internal shell – octopus, squid and cuttlefish.

The shellfish industry is a multi-million-pound business and is growing. Molluscan shellfish can only be marketed and sold commercially in the EU if harvested from an area in the UK that has met with government approval and has been designated as safe by scientific research. It is unwise to gather these species yourself from any area you are not completely confident about. This is particularly important where bivalves or filter-feeders are concerned as they filter a considerable amount of water through their systems each day and in doing so they can pick up any toxins and bacteria in the water. This does not affect the shellfish but, if the water is polluted, could have an adverse effect on the consumer.

Freshness is of paramount importance in shellfish, so always buy from a reputable supplier.

Debearding and cleaning mussels
It is not a good idea to soak shellfish in cold water, particularly filter feeders, or bivalve molluscs, such as mussels and clams, if you want them to stay alive. When mussels are harvested they go through several screening stages, which filters out any unwanted matter and

Skate With Brown Butter

cleans them thoroughly, leaving them sterilized. They do, however, need a little preparation before cooking. First scrub the mussels to remove any barnacles. Pull away the 'beard' or byssus thread, the stringy thread on the outside of the shell which helps the mussel attach itself to rocks and other surfaces. If the mussel is open and will not close on sharp tapping, it is dead and should be discarded before cooking. Also throw away any that feel heavy or have a shattered or cracked shell. Use as required.

SKATE WITH BROWN BUTTER AND CAPERS

SERVES 4

900g/2lb skate wing
570ml/1 pint court bouillon
  (see page 53)
75g/3oz unsalted butter
1 tablespoon lemon juice
1 tablespoon capers, rinsed and
  roughly chopped

1. Wash the skate and divide into 4 portions.
2. Place the skate in the cold court bouillon in a shallow pan. Cover with a lid and bring slowly to the boil. Poach very gently for 15–20 minutes.
3. Remove the fish and drain on absorbent kitchen paper. Gently scrape away any skin. Place the skate on a warmed serving dish and keep warm in a low oven while you make the sauce.
4. Pour off the court bouillon, reheat the pan and melt the butter. When the butter is foaming and a rich golden brown, remove the pan from the heat, add the lemon juice and capers and pour over the skate.

PRAWN PILAF

SERVES 4

790g/1¾lb cooked shell-on prawns
570ml/1 pint water
100ml/3½fl oz dry white wine
salt and freshly ground black pepper
1 slice of lemon
lemon juice
3–4 parsley stalks
110g/4oz butter
1 medium onion, finely chopped
225g/8oz long-grain rice, washed
2 hardboiled eggs, chopped
To garnish
1 tablespoon chopped fresh parsley

1. Peel all but 3 of the prawns. Reserve the prawns and put the shells into a saucepan with the water, wine, salt, pepper, lemon slice and parsley stalks. Bring to the boil, then simmer for 15 minutes. Strain and reserve the liquor.
2. Melt 85g/3oz of the butter in a saucepan and cook the onion gently until soft. Add the rice and fry slowly until it looks opaque. Add the reserved liquor. Bring to the boil, stirring with a fork. Cover and simmer gently for 25 minutes, until the rice is tender and the liquid absorbed.
3. Meanwhile, melt the remaining butter, add the peeled prawns and eggs and heat through. Season with salt, pepper and lemon juice. Fork the shelled prawns and eggs into the pilaf rice. Pile into a warmed serving dish and sprinkle with plenty of parsley. Put the unshelled prawns on top and serve.

Peeling a raw prawn
Remove the prawn's head by pulling gently from the body. Carefully peel away the body shell.

Deveining a prawn
Using a sharp knife, make a small incision the length of the back of the prawn.

Carefully pull away the dark intestinal vein, which can be gritty and bitter.

After preparing shellfish and other fish, to avoid retaining its odour on your hands, rinse first under running cold water, then wash thoroughly with detergent in hot water.

THAI FISH SOUP

SERVES 4

1 litre/1¾ pints strong fish stock
   (see page 52)
2 sticks of lemon grass, finely chopped
salt and freshly ground black pepper
5cm/2in galangal, peeled and chopped
2 red chillies, finely chopped
4 kaffir lime leaves, finely chopped
   (see Note)
2 curry leaves, chopped
8 raw tiger prawns, peeled and deveined
   (see above)
2 squid, prepared and thinly sliced
   (see page 155)
2 lettuce leaves, finely shredded
juice of 1 lime

1. Put the stock into a large saucepan and add the lemon grass. Bring to the boil, then reduce the heat and simmer very gently for 15 minutes. Season with salt and pepper. Strain the stock into a clean saucepan.
2. Add the galangal, chillies, kaffir lime and curry leaves. Bring back to the boil and simmer for 10 further minutes.
3. Add the prawns, squid and lettuce to the hot stock and cook for 2 further minutes or until the prawns are pink and the squid opaque. Season to taste with salt and pepper.
4. Add the lime juice and serve immediately.
NOTE: The ingredients for the fish stock can be bought from larger supermarkets or specialist grocers, as can kaffir lime leaves. Kaffir lime leaves, also called *makrut*, come from a tree of the lime family and are a typical ingredient in many Thai and Indonesian dishes. They have a distinctive flavour.

This soup is quite hot; adding a little coconut milk to the finished soup makes it more subtle.

Preparing squid
Most squid in this country comes ready-prepared, but if you wish to tackle it yourself it is quite easy, though rather messy.

Remove the tentacles, and with them the blood (ink) sac and entrails, by pulling away from the body. Remove the clear, plastic-like piece of cartilage (quill) that runs inside the length of the body. Cut the head, which is next to the ink sac and has two large eyes, away from the tentacles. Scrape away the fine pink membrane from the outside of the body. Wash the body and tentacles to remove all traces of ink: you should now have a perfectly clear, white, empty squid tube with tentacles. Use as required.

POTATO TART
This doesn't sound very exciting but is in fact a truly delicious tart.
SERVES 6–8
225g/8oz plain flour
a pinch of salt
110g/4oz butter
1 egg yolk
very cold water
For the tomato filling
3 tablespoons olive oil
1 onion, finely chopped
8 medium tomatoes, peeled, deseeded and chopped
1 tablespoon tomato purée
1 sprig of fresh thyme
a pinch of caster sugar
salt and freshly ground black pepper
For the potato filling
6 waxy potatoes, peeled and cut into even chunks
2 tablespoons olive oil
For the onion filling
85g/3oz unsalted butter
5 medium onions, thinly sliced

To serve
150ml/¼ pint crème fraîche
freshly grated nutmeg

1. Preheat the oven to 200°C/400°F/gas mark 6.
2. Sift the flour with the salt into a large bowl. Rub in the butter until the mixture resembles breadcrumbs.
3. Mix the egg yolk with 3 tablespoons water and add to the mixture. Mix to a firm dough, first with a knife and then with one hand, adding more water if necessary.
4. Roll the pastry out and use to line a 25cm/10in flan ring (see page 24). Chill in the refrigerator for 20 minutes, then bake blind (see page 24) in the preheated oven for 15 minutes.
5. Make the tomato filling: heat the oil in a saucepan over a low heat and cook the onion gently for about 10 minutes. Add the tomatoes, tomato purée, thyme, sugar, salt and pepper. Increase the heat and cook until all the liquid evaporates (about 35 minutes).
6. Brush the potatoes with oil and sprinkle with salt. Roast in the preheated oven for about 1 hour, until tender Cut into 5mm/¼in slices. Turn the oven temperature up to 230°C/450°F/gas mark 8.
7. Make the onion filling: melt the butter in a frying pan, add the onions and cook over a low heat for about 30 minutes until soft and creamy.
8. Spread the onions on the pastry base and cover with the tomato filling, then arrange the sliced potatoes around the top. Cover with the crème fraîche and sprinkle with nutmeg. Bake in the preheated oven for 15 minutes, or until brown. Serve at room temperature.

STIR-FRIED CHICKEN WITH CASHEWS
SERVES 4
450g/1lb boneless chicken meat, skinned, or 4 chicken breasts, skinned

2.5cm/1in fresh ginger,
  peeled and sliced
2 small cloves garlic, peeled and sliced
2 teaspoons cornflour
1 tablespoon soy sauce
1 tablespoon dry sherry
150ml/¼ pint white stock, made with
  chicken bones (see page 52)
1 tablespoon sunflower or grapeseed oil
To garnish
55g/2oz unsalted cashew nuts
2 spring onions, sliced on the diagonal

1. Trim the chicken of all fat and cut into
   even-sized pieces.
2. Put into a bowl with the ginger and garlic,
   cover and leave to stand.
3. Mix the cornflour with the soy sauce,
   sherry and stock. Set aside.
4. Heat the oil in a wok. Add the cashew
   nuts and stir-fry until lightly browned.
   Remove with a slotted spoon.
5. Add the chicken to the wok with the ginger
   and garlic and stir-fry until the chicken is
   cooked and tender (4–5 minutes).

6. Add the liquid ingredients and stir until well
   blended and thickened. Add a little water if
   it seems too thick. Check the seasoning.
   Pile into a warmed serving dish and sprinkle
   with the cashew nuts and spring onions.

STICKY TOFFEE PUDDING
serves 4–6
225g/8oz dates, chopped
290ml/½ pint tea
110g/4oz butter
170g/6oz caster sugar
3 eggs
225g/8oz self-raising flour, sifted
1 teaspoon bicarbonate of soda
1 teaspoon vanilla essence
1 teaspoon strong coffee
For the toffee sauce
4 tablespoons brandy
225g/8oz butter
110g/4oz demerara sugar
4 tablespoons double cream

1. Preheat the oven to 180°C/350°F/gas
   mark 4.

2. Soak the dates in the hot tea for 15 minutes.
3. Oil a moule-à-manqué cake tin and line the base with a circle of oiled greaseproof paper.
4. Cream together the butter and sugar until pale.
5. Beat in the eggs, one at a time, and then fold in the sifted flour.
6. Add the soda, vanilla essence and coffee to the date/tea water and then fold into the cake mixture.
7. Turn into the prepared moule-à-manqué tin and bake in the middle of the oven for 1–1 1/2 hours, or until a skewer inserted into the centre of the cake comes out clean.
8. Meanwhile, make the toffee sauce: place all the ingredients in a saucepan and heat until melted. Bring to the boil and allow to thicken slightly.
9. Pour the warm toffee sauce over the hot pudding and serve immediately.

Causes of Failure
Gritty mussels: Not cleaned thoroughly.
Skate tasting of ammonia:
Fish not fresh enough.

GAME

CHAPTER 19

Techniques Covered

Plucking game birds

Drawing game birds

Roasting game birds

Preparation of classic game garnishes

Preparing a venison steak

❓ Cookery Terms

Bard: To tie bacon or pork fat over a joint of meat, game bird or poultry, to be roasted. This helps to prevent the flesh from drying out.

Beurre manié: Butter and flour in equal quantities worked together to a soft paste, and used as a liaison or thickening for liquids. Small pieces are whisked into boiling liquid. As the butter melts it disperses the flour evenly through the liquid, thereby thickening it without causing lumps.

Croûte: Literally crust. Sometimes a pastry case, as in fillet of beef en croûte, sometimes toasted or fried bread, as in Scotch woodcock or scrambled eggs on toast.

Jus or jus de viande: 'God's gravy', i.e. juices that occur naturally in cooking, not a made-up sauce.

Jus lié: Thickened gravy.

Lardons: Small strips or cubes of pork fat or bacon generally used as a garnish.

Recipes

Roast pheasant

Game chips

Game chip baskets filled with chestnuts

Croûtes for roast game birds

Fried crumbs for roast game birds

Brussel sprouts and chestnuts

Peppered venison steak

Pigeon and cracked wheat salad with cranberry dressing

GAME

To prepare and draw a game bird for the oven

Some birds are easier to pluck than others, ducks being notoriously tedious. All birds are easier to pluck if still warm when tackled. Work away from draughts, as the feathers fly about, and pluck straight into a dustbin. Tug the feathers, working from the tail to the head, pulling against the way the feathers grow. If the bird is very young or if there is a lot of fat, pull downwards towards the tail to avoid tearing the flesh.

Once plucked, the bird should be singed. This can be done with a burning taper, or directly over a gas flame, but care should be taken to singe only the down and small feathers, and not to blacken the flesh. The bird should then be rubbed with a clean tea-towel to remove any remaining stubble. It is now ready for drawing.

Surprisingly, birds keep better, when hanging, with their insides intact. Once eviscerated they must be cooked within a day or two. So when you are ready to cook the bird, take it down, and proceed as follows.

1. Pluck it.
2. Cut round the feet, at the drumstick joint, but do not cut right through the tendons. Pull the legs off the bird, drawing the tendons out with them. If the bird is small this is easy enough – just bend the foot back until it snaps, and pull, perhaps over the edge of a table. Turkeys are more difficult: snap the feet at the drumstick joint by bending them over the end of the table, then hang the bird up by the feet from a stout hook, and pull on the bird. The feet plus tendons will be left on the hook, the turkey in your arms. All too often birds are sold with the tendons in the legs, making the drumsticks tough when cooked.
3. Now for the head and neck. Lay the bird breast side down on a board. Make a slit through the neck skin from the body to the head. Cut off the head and throw it away. Pull back the split neck skin, leaving it attached to the body of the bird (it will come in useful to close the gap if you are stuffing the bird). Cut the neck off as close to the body as you can.
4. Put a finger into the neck hole, to the side of the stump of neck left on the bird, and move the finger right round, loosening the innards from the neck. If you do not do this you will find them difficult to pull out from the other end.

5. With a sharp knife slit the bird open from the vent to the parson's (or pope's) nose, making a hole large enough to just get your hand in. Put your hand in, working it so the back of your hand is up against the arch of the breastbone, and carefully loosen the entrails from the sides of the body cavity, all the way round. Pull them out, taking care not to break the gall bladder, the contents of which would embitter any flesh they touched. Covering the gutting hand with a cloth helps extract the intestines intact. The first time you do this it is unlikely that you will get everything out in one motion, so check that the lungs and kidneys come too. Have another go if necessary. Once the bird is empty, wipe any traces of blood off with a clean damp cloth.

The neck and feet go into the stockpot with the heart and the cleaned gizzard. To clean the gizzard, carefully cut the outside wall along the natural seam so that you can peel it away from the inner bag of grit. Throw the grit bag away, with the intestines and the gall bladder. Do not put the liver in the stockpot: it may make the stock bitter. It may be fried and served with the dish, or fried, chopped and added to the sauce, or kept frozen until enough poultry liver has been collected to make pâté. But if the liver is to be used, carefully cut away the discoloured portion of it where it lay against the gall bladder (it will be bitter) and trim off any membranes.

SEASONAL TABLE FOR GAME

Grouse	12 August–10 December
Partridge	1 September–1 February
Pheasant	1 October–1 February
Pigeon and squab	In season all year round
Quail	Available all year round
Snipe	August–January
Wild duck, teal and widgeon	Various, starting in August and finishing in March
Woodcock	October–January
Venison	Seasons are complicated; however, frozen venison is often available all year round
Rabbit	Wild or farmed available all year
Hare	September–March

ROASTING TABLE FOR GAME

If using a fan (convection) oven, reduce the cooking times by 15 per cent or lower the oven temperature by 20°C/40°F.

Meat	Temperature			Cooking time
	°C	°F	Gas	
Pigeon and squab	200	400	6	25–35 minutes
Grouse	190	375	5	25–35 minutes
Guinea fowl	190	375	5	70 minutes
Partridge	190	375	5	20–25 minutes
Pheasant	190	375	5	45–60 minutes
Wild duck, teal and widgeon	200	400	6	40 minutes
Woodcock	190	375	5	20–30 minutes
Quail	180	350	4	20 minutes
Snipe	190	375	5	15–20 minutes

ROAST PHEASANT

A piece of apple can be placed in the pheasant cavity, to help keep the flesh moist and improve the flavour.

SERVES 4

2 medium oven-ready pheasants
salt and freshly ground black pepper
2 strips of pork fat
butter
For the gravy
1 teaspoon plain flour
1 tablespoon ruby port
1 teaspoon redcurrant jelly

1. Wipe the pheasants and remove any remaining feathers.
2. Preheat the oven to 200°C/400°F/gas mark 6.
3. Season the birds inside.
4. Tie the pork fat over the breasts (this is called barding and is to prevent drying out during cooking).
5. Spread a little butter over the rest of the birds and season with salt and pepper.
6. Place in a roasting pan, pour 5mm/¼in water into the pan and cook in the preheated oven for about 40–50 minutes, basting frequently.
7. When cooked, lift the pheasants out of the pan and keep warm while you make the gravy.
8. Sprinkle the flour into the roasting juices and add the port and redcurrant jelly.
9. Place the roasting pan over heat and stir and scrape the bottom until the liquid boils.
10. Add a little more water or stock if it is too thick. Boil for 2 minutes, then season well and strain into a warmed gravyboat.
11. Serve the pheasants on a warmed serving platter. Serve the gravy separately.

GAME CHIPS

SERVES 4

450g/1lb large potatoes
oil for deep-frying
salt

1. Wash and peel the potatoes. If you want even-sized chips trim each potato into a cylinder shape.
2. Slice them very thinly across the cylinder, preferably on a mandolin. Soak in cold water for 30 minutes to remove the excess starch – this will prevent them from discolouring or sticking together.
3. Heat oil in a deep-fryer until a crumb will sizzle vigorously in it.
4. Dry the chips very thoroughly on a tea-towel.
5. Lower a basket of chips into the hot oil. They are cooked when they rise to the surface and are golden-brown.

6. Drain on absorbent kitchen paper, sprinkle
   with salt and serve immediately.
NOTE: Commercial plain potato crisps will
do very well as game chips. Simply heat
them, uncovered, in a moderate oven.

GAME CHIP BASKETS FILLED WITH CHESTNUTS

SERVES 4

675g/1¹/₂lb potatoes
oil for deep-frying
45g/1¹/₂oz butter
30g/1oz pinenuts
1 x 400g/14oz can of whole unsweetened
    chestnuts
a handful of raisins
1 small bunch of white grapes, halved
    and any pips removed

1. Peel the potatoes. Slice thinly, using a
   mandolin or a patterned cutter so that the
   finished basket will look like woven straw.
2. Dip a small wire strainer or sieve into
   the oil to get it well greased. Heat oil in a
   deep-fryer until a crumb will sizzle
   vigorously in it.
3. Line the strainer with potato slices
   overlapping each other. Using a small
   ladle to prevent the chips floating away
   from the strainer as you cook them, deep-
   fry the 'basket' until golden and crisp.
4. Drain well on absorbent kitchen paper.
5. Melt the butter and add the
   pinenuts. Brown them lightly, then
   add the chestnuts, raisins and grapes.
   Fry until hot.
6. Fill the baskets with this mixture just
   before serving.
NOTE: A gadget for making the baskets
is available in shops selling to the
catering trade, but the sieve and ladle
method works perfectly well.

CROÛTES FOR ROAST GAME BIRDS

When roasting small game birds, such as snipe or woodcock, the 'trail', or entrails, is left inside and only the gizzard removed. After roasting, the liver and juices are spread on the uncooked side of a slice of bread which has been fried or toasted on one side only. The roasted bird is served on this croûte.

Larger birds like pheasant and grouse are drawn before roasting, but the liver may be returned to the body cavity to cook with the bird. This, plus any other scrapings from the inside of the bird, is spread on the uncooked side of the croûte, which is then cut in half on the diagonal and served as a garnish to the whole roast bird.

FRIED CRUMBS FOR ROAST GAME BIRDS

SERVES 4
55g/2oz butter
4 tablespoons dried while breadcrumbs

Melt the butter and fry the crumbs very slowly until they have absorbed most of it, and are golden and crisp. Serve in a warmed bowl, handed with the sauce or sauces.
NOTE: Fresh white breadcrumbs can be used, but rather more butter will be needed as they are very absorbent, and great care should be taken to fry slowly so that the crumbs become crisp before they turn brown.

BRUSSELS SPROUTS AND CHESTNUTS

SERVES 4
450g/1lb very small Brussels sprouts
225g/8oz fresh chestnuts
30g/1oz butter
salt and freshly ground black pepper
freshly grated nutmeg

1. Wash and trim the sprouts, paring the stalks and removing the outside leaves if necessary.
2. Make a slit in the skin of each chestnut and put them into a saucepan of cold water. Bring to the boil, then simmer for

15 minutes and remove from the heat. Remove 1–2 nuts at a time and peel. The skins come off easily if the chestnuts are hot but not too well cooked.
3. Melt the butter in a frying pan, and slowly fry the chestnuts, which will break up a little, until brown.
4. Bring a large saucepan of salted water to the boil, and tip in the sprouts. Boil fairly fast until they are cooked, but not soggy: their flavour changes disastrously if they are boiled too long. Drain them well.
5. Mix the sprouts and chestnuts together gently, adding the butter from the frying pan. Season with salt, pepper and nutmeg.

PEPPERED VENISON STEAK

SERVES 4
4 x 140g/5oz venison collops (steaks) cut from the fillet
2 tablespoons black peppercorns
1 tablespoon oil (preferably olive)
30g/1oz unsalted butter
2 tablespoons brandy
150ml/1/4 pint double cream
salt

1. Wipe the steaks and trim off any gristle.
2. Crush the peppercorns coarsely in a mortar or under a rolling pin and press them into the surface of the meat on both sides.
3. Cover the steaks and leave them for 2 hours at room temperature for the flavour to penetrate the meat.
4. Heat the oil in a heavy pan, add the butter and when it is foaming fry the steaks as fast as possible until done to your liking (about 2 minutes per side for blue, 3 minutes for rare, 3 1/2 minutes for medium and 4 minutes for well done).
5. Pour in the brandy and set it alight. Add the cream and a pinch of salt. Mix the contents of the pan thoroughly, scraping up any sediment stuck to the bottom.
6. Place the steaks on a warmed serving platter.

7. Boil up the sauce again, then simmer to a syrupy consistency and pour over the meat. Serve immediately.

NOTE: If the venison is very fresh and you want a gamier taste, marinate it for 2 days in equal quantities of red wine and oil, flavoured with a sliced onion, 6 juniper berries and a bay leaf. Dry well before frying.

PIGEON AND CRACKED WHEAT SALAD WITH CRANBERRY DRESSING
SERVES 4

8 pigeon breasts, skinned and boned
For the marinade
4 tablespoons cranberry juice
2 sprigs of thyme
2 tablespoons hazelnut oil
freshly ground black pepper
For the salad
85g/3oz cranberries
2 tablespoons sugar
1 tablespoon water
225g/8oz cracked wheat
110g/4oz hazelnuts
30ml/2 tablespoons thyme, finely chopped
For the dressing
150ml/ 1/4 pint cranberry juice
6 tablespoons hazelnut oil
1 teaspoon grain mustard
salt and freshly ground black pepper

For the garnish
2 spring onions, finely sliced on the diagonal

1. Combine the marinade ingredients in a bowl and add the pigeon breasts. Marinate overnight.
2. Make the salad: cook the cranberries until just tender in a small saucepan with the sugar and water.
3. Rinse the cracked wheat under running cold water and then cook in 860ml/1½ pints salted water for about 15 minutes or until just soft.
4. Toast the hazelnuts in a hot oven. When brown, rub in a dry cloth to remove the skins.
5. Make the dressing: reduce the cranberry juice by boiling rapidly to 3 tablespoons. Liquidize the juice with the oil and mustard and season to taste.
6. Take the pigeon breasts out of the marinade and pat them dry. Brush a frying pan with a little oil and fry the breasts for 2–3 minutes on each side. They should be served pink. Remove from the pan and toss the spring onions briefly in the hot pan.
7. Mix the cracked wheat, cranberries and hazelnuts together with the dressing and divide the salad between 4 plates. Slice the pigeon breasts on the diagonal and put on top of the cracked wheat mixture.
8. To serve: garnish with the spring onions.

NOTE: Cranberry juice is sold in cartons in most large supermarkets.

Causes of Failure
Cooked game tastes dry: Overcooked or not enough fat used in cooking. An old bird or animal may have been cooked by a method only suitable for a young one.
Game bird flesh is green: Birds were not hung in a cool, well-ventilated area soon after being shot.
Lead shot found in flesh: Badly shot bird – not unusual.

CLASSIC FIRST COURSES AND WINE II
CHAPTER 20

Techniques Covered
How to present some classic foods
Marinated raw fish
Shucking an oyster
Wine continued

❓ Cookery Term
Hors d'oeuvre: Usually simply means first course. Sometimes used to denote a variety or selection of many savoury titbits served with drinks, or a mixed first course (hors d'oeuvres variés).

Recipes
Caviar
Oysters
Asparagus
Globe artichokes
Ceviche

CAVIAR
30g/1oz per person

Leave the caviar in its pot. Chill, and stand on a napkin. Serve 1 teaspoon on each individual plate, and offer, from another platter, wedges of lemon, chopped hardboiled egg white and sieved yolk (in separate piles), chopped fresh parsley and very finely chopped raw onions. Serve with hot toast.

OYSTERS
9 or 12 per person

Serve 6 each if there is a big meal to come, but oyster lovers like a lot! Order the oysters and ask for them to be opened only when you collect them, or as late as possible. Keep refrigerated until serving. If the fishmonger has not loosened the oysters from the bottom shell, do so with a sharp knife. Check that there are no bits of shell or grit on the saucer-shaped bottom shells, but leave any sea water or juices with them. Discard the top shells. Put the oysters on to oyster plates, or failing them, on to dinner plates covered by a napkin to keep them from tipping or rolling. Hand Tabasco sauce, or chilli pepper, freshly ground black pepper, white pepper, wedges of lemon and vinegar separately, and serve with brown bread and butter. The diner eats the oysters with a fork, and drinks the juice from the shell as from a cup.

Shucking an oyster
Holding the oyster in a cloth, insert a shucking knife at the hinge of the shell. Twist the knife and prise open the shell. Work above a bowl, to catch as much of the juice as possible. Take great care with this tricky operation as it can cause a nasty injury if the knife slips.

ASPARAGUS
6 fat or 12 thin spears per person

Cut off the woody ends. Peel the fibrous stalks. Wash well. Tie in bundles. Boil in an asparagus cooker (the stalks stand in the water, the tips cook in the steam), or simmer lying down in salted water in a frying pan, until the stalk is tender halfway down. Drain well. Serve from a platter lined with a napkin to absorb the moisture. Hand melted clarified butter, hollandaise or beurre blanc separately if hot; vinaigrette if cold.

GLOBE ARTICHOKES
1 per person

Twist and pull the stalk off the artichoke very close to the base so that it will stand without rolling. Trim the tips of the bottom few rows of leaves off straight if they are hard or cracked and if the tip spines are prickly. Leave the smaller higher leaves. Boil for 45 minutes in salted water with a cut-up lemon and 1 tablespoon oil. When an inner leaf will pull out easily, drain the artichokes upside down. When cool enough to handle, prise open the middle leaves and lift out the central cluster of tiny leaves. Using a teaspoon, scrape out the fibrous choke and discard it. Serve the artichokes on individual plates on a folded napkin. Give each guest a small pot of clarified melted butter if the artichokes are hot, or vinaigrette dressing if cold. The guest pulls the leaves off the flowerhead, dips the flesh end into the butter or sauce, eats the softer part with his fingers and discards the leaves.

CEVICHE
SERVES 4

450g/1lb fillet of monkfish, halibut or
*   salmon, skinned and cut into thin slices*
*   or small strips (optional)*
1 onion, sliced
juice of 2 lemons or 4 limes
1 tablespoon good-quality olive oil
a pinch of cayenne pepper

1 fresh chilli pepper, deseeded and cut into
strips (optional)
1 tablespoon chopped fresh dill or chives
salt and freshly ground black pepper
1 avocado, peeled and sliced
1 tomato, peeled and cut into fine strips
1/2 yellow pepper, cut into fine strips

1. Put the fish, onion, lemon or lime juice, oil, cayenne pepper, chilli, if using, and half the dill or chives into a dish and leave in a cool place for 6 hours, giving an occasional stir. (If the fish is really thinly sliced, as little as 30 minutes will do; it is ready as soon as it looks 'cooked' – opaque white rather than glassy.)
2. Remove the onion from the marinade.
3. Season with salt and pepper. Arrange on a serving dish with the avocado, tomato and pepper, and sprinkle liberally with the remaining dill or chives.

WINE II
By Philippa Carr M.W.

How Wines Differ
After decades of dominance by France, Germany and Italy, Australia's exciting, fruit-driven, varietally-labelled, consistent, well-priced wines have turned the market around. However, one should not forget entirely the classic areas of Europe which have inspired international wine makers and given a benchmark for quality and style.

The perfectionist Californians wanted to make the best Chardonnays in the world, so have tried to make Burgundy; Australians (who just wanted to have fun) have now tempered the oak and the wines to a more restrained, European style. Paradoxically, the more countries we buy wine from, the greater the choice available, the smaller the world of wine becomes. The interchange of ideas and expertise has undoubtedly created a delicious lake of well-made, fruity wines, but our thirst for an 'international', squeaky-clean style has

driven out the unusual and the idiosyncratic.
Know your grapes
The following grape profiles should help you
expand your knowledge of a grape variety and
its wines as well as introduce you to some
other wines to try.

Chardonnay
TASTING NOTES
Soft, creamy, buttery, baked bread, melons,
tropical fruits. Dry. Neutral. Lowish acidity.
Often oaked (vanilla). River beds (Chablis)
CLASSIC HOME
Côte d'Or, Burgundy (France)
Also Chablis and Champagne
OLD WORLD ELSEWHERE
Practically everywhere – the world's favourite
white grape variety, easy to grow, easy to
make wine from and easy to drink
Northern Spain, Hungary, Bulgaria and Vin
de Pays d'Oc (Southern France)
NEW WORLD
The king of Australia at all levels of quality,
price and style
California, South Africa and South America
Australia, California, New Zealand and South
Africa for sparkling wines
If you like ...
CRISPNESS – Chile, Vin de Pays d'Oc and
Chablis
ACIDITY – Northern Italy, Tasmania and New
Zealand
RICHER AND MORE BUTTERY – California,
Australia and Côte d'Or
OTHER WINES TO TRY – Alsace and Pinot
Blanc are lighter
Bordeaux Blanc (oaked) is heavier
FOOD AND WINE
Fish, cheese and poultry

Sauvignon Blanc
TASTING NOTES
Gooseberries. Nettles. Crushed blackcurrant
leaves. Aromatic. Dry. High acidity.
CLASSIC HOME
Loire Valley – Sancerre and Pouilly Fumé

OLD WORLD ELSEWHERE
Touraine (Loire Valley)
Bordeaux (usually blended with Semillon
giving dry and sweet wines – Sauternes)
Languedoc Roussillon (France)
NEW WORLD
World class from Marlborough, New Zealand,
Casablanca Valley – Chile, South Africa and
California (Fumé Blanc)
If you like ...
PIERCING AND AROMATIC – New Zealand
FULLER – Californian Fumé Blanc
OTHER WINES TO TRY – Muscadet Sur Lie,
Dry Riesling (Alsace, Australia and Germany)
FOOD AND WINE
Use the grape's assertive acidity to temper
citrus flavours in food
Pesto sauce, limes, seafood (unsauced) and
goat's cheese

Riesling
TASTING NOTES
Lavish alcohol. High acidity. Petrol, steel,
limes (Australia), aromatic, flowery
(Germany)
CLASSIC HOME
Germany – Mosel Valley, Rheingau
Underrated and unfashionable – perhaps
because of the decreasing popularity of
German wines
OLD WORLD ELSEWHERE
Alsace. Other areas in Germany
Austria. Friuli (Italy). Central Europe
NEW WORLD
Australian Rhine Riesling
Californian. Johannesburg Riesling (sweet)
New Zealand
If you like ...
FLOWERY, MEDIUM-SWEET – German
Spatlese (single estate)
HONEYED AND SWEET – German Auslese
(single estate)
Californian. Johannesburg Riesling (sweet)
DRY, STEELY – Alsace
Australian Rhine Riesling
German dry Riesling

OTHER WINES TO TRY
Loire Chenin Blanc (Vouvray – medium or sweet); or Bordeaux for either dry or sweet Sauvignon Blanc. Other Alsace varieties (aromatic)
FOOD AND WINE
Fine, sweet German wines should be enjoyed on their own; less sweet with creamily sauced fish
Dry styles – to match acidity in food

Cabernet Sauvignon
TASTING NOTES
Blackcurrants, cedar wood, mint (Australia). Tannin
CLASSIC HOME
Bordeaux, France (aka claret)
OLD WORLD ELSEWHERE
The world's favourite red grape variety
Areas around Bordeaux, Eastern Mediterranean
Languedoc-Roussillon Italy
(very fine in Tuscany)
Central Europe
NEW WORLD
South Africa, California
(particularly Napa Valley)
Chile
Australia (top quality from Coonawarra)

If you like ...
ELEGANCE AND COMPLEXITY – Bordeaux – good vintage
Napa Valley, California
Margaret River and Coonawarra, Australia
SIMPLE, VALUE FOR MONEY – Bulgaria
Vin de Pays d'Oc
OTHER WINES TO TRY
Northern Rhône, Barolo, Merlot
FOOD AND WINE
Young, tannic styles with unsauced red meat
Farmhouse Cheddar
Poultry

Pinot Noir
TASTING NOTES
When young – strawberries, raspberries, light colour, perfumed
Aged – gamey, farmyards, rotting vegetables (not unpleasantly so ...)
CLASSIC HOME
Côte d'Or, Burgundy
Very difficult to cultivate: the 'holy grail' of international wine makers.
OLD WORLD ELSEWHERE
France: Champagne (one of three permitted grapes)
Alsace and Loire (Sancerre)
Southern France

Germany (known as Spätburgunder)
NEW WORLD
New Zealand
California and Oregon, USA
Some cooler areas of Australia (e.g.
Tasmania)
Chile
If you like ...
YOUTHFUL, SOFT FRUITS – Chile, Alsace,
Vin de Pays d'Oc
ROUNDER, COMPLEX – Côte d'Or (very
expensive)
New Zealand (especially Martinborough)
California
OTHER WINES TO TRY
Young and fruity – Beaujolais, Loire reds,
Valpolicella
Barbena d'Asti
Mature – Chianti Classico, Northern Rhône
FOOD AND WINE
Depending on the 'body' of the wine –
poultry or game, duck, good casseroles,
mild cheese

Merlot
TASTING NOTES
Soft, round, fleshy, plums, lowish tannin,
Easy, early drinking. Can balance tannic
varieties in a blend
CLASSIC HOME
Bordeaux – either blended with Cabernet
Sauvignon and others or singly in Pomerol,
St Emilion
OLD WORLD ELSEWHERE
Central Europe – NE Italy
Elsewhere in Gironde area of France
Southern France
NEW WORLD
California, USA
New Zealand
Chile
If you like ...
TOP QUALITY, CLASSIC: Pomerol and St
Emilion
MEDIUM-PRICED, CLASSY: California, New
Zealand

SOFT, EASY-DRINKING: Vin de Pays d'Oc,
Friuli and Trentino – Italy, Bulgaria and
Hungary
OTHER WINES TO TRY
Australian Reds
Wines from the Midi, France
Rioja
FOOD AND WINE
Beef, sausage and mash

Food and wine pairing
There is no such thing as the 'right wine' to
go with a meal. There are no hard and fast
rules to food and wine pairing. There are
some combinations which seem more
successful than others. But you should have
confidence in your own taste and if you love
a sickly sweet wine with steak, then go for it.
If you feel, however, that you would like
some guidance to maximizing the pleasure of
a meal, here are a few helpful hints:
- Match the body of the wine to the
  richness of the food, regardless of whether
  the wine is red or white.
- A sweet wine should always be sweeter
  than the pudding it is served with.
- Acidity in a wine can be tempered by
  some acidity in food, and vice versa.
- If you are not fond of tannin in red wine,
  then eat your red meat unsauced.
  Chewing miraculously softens the mouth-
  drying toughness of young wine.
- If you are really stuck, choose a wine that
  comes from the same region or country as
  the food. For example:
    Beaujolais with andouillettes
    Italian reds with pasta
    Asti Spumante with panettone
    Alsace with choucroute
    Australian Shiraz with kangaroo

Wines in restaurants
Some people feel intimidated in restaurants
and shy about ordering wine.
  If you have ever been bemused by a
lengthy wine list and the whole ritual of a

wine waiter pouring some wine for you to 'try', then relax, you are not alone. Try to make an ally of the wine waiter and do not be embarrassed by any lack of knowledge. None of us are experts in everything and you never stop learning about wine.

So, starting at the beginning. Your guests have chosen the food and that only leaves the wine. You do not recognize many names on the list. However, you would like some white wine and red wine. Which are reliable choices?

WHITE
- Alsace – Except perhaps Gewürztraminer which is very perfumed and does not appeal to everyone
- Australian Chardonnay – wide range of styles and prices available. Also it is consistent
- New Zealand Sauvignon Blanc – great value for a classy wine
- Vin de Pays d'Oc, Chardonnay or Viognier – lovely, nutty wine similar to Chardonnay

RED
- Australian reds, single varieties or blended – soft and fruity
- Rioja Reserva
- Vin de Pays d'Oc, Merlot or Cabernet Sauvignon
- Northern Rhône e.g. Crozes Hermitage – good value

TASTING THE WINE
The wine waiter has brought to your table the *unopened* bottle for you to check that this is what you ordered. Match the year, producer and grape variety to the list then query any discrepancies.

Next, the waiter opens the bottle in front of you and pours a little into your glass to try.

WHAT ARE YOU LOOKING FOR?
In a word, faults. You cannot refuse a wine simply because you do not like it.

Corkiness
A musty smell of damp and dark cellars caused by a tainted cork; it does not mean that there are pieces of cork floating around in the wine.

Oxidation
The wine has been exposed to air too long. A white wine will be dark yellow and a red wine will be a brown colour.

Secondary fermentation
The wine fizzes gently, when it is not supposed to.

Cloudiness
Wine should be clear and bright.

Bringing your wine home
Roughly two-thirds of the wine purchases we make for drinking at home are made in supermarkets and most of that is shared between J Sainsbury and Tesco. Sainsbury's was responsible for introducing most of us to regular wine drinking. Supermarkets in general have helped considerably to popularize wines.

The supermarkets' shelves freed us to make mistakes; to select without embarrassment, to pop a bottle in the trolley and think we were being sneered at. There is a lack of personal advice, but back labels can help and once you have built up your confidence you can venture into wine shops and off-licences to browse.

Shop around, find a friendly manager, a price list that appeals or tune in to the tastes of the market buyer (be warned – personnel move around frequently). The cardinal sin is to say 'I know what I like', when really that means 'I like what I know and I am not prepared to try something different'. Take advantage of the wonderfully wide range of wines that are available to us in Great Britain. Practically all the world's wines are here. The standard also is high because British wine buyers buy on quality, not just on price, and competition is fierce between retailers.

Armed with some basic information about grape varieties, the styles of wines they make and the choices available, you can shop with confidence and most of all, have fun.

ENTERTAINING
CHAPTER 21

Techniques Covered
Summer buffet
Cocktail party
Planning a large party
Cooking for customers

❷ Cookery Terms
Canapé: A small bread or biscuit base, sometimes fried, spread or covered with savoury paste, egg, etc. used for cocktail titbits or as an accompaniment to meat dishes. Sometimes used to denote the base only, as in champignons sur canapé.
Croustade: Bread dipped in butter and baked until crisp. Used to contain hot savoury mixtures for a canapé, savoury or as a garnish.

Recipes
Scallop and rocket salad
Guinea-fowl braised with caramel and
oranges
Pommes Anna
Individual apple charlottes
Chicken Elizabeth
Rice salad
Elizabeth sauce
Herb omelette salad
Creamed cheese with fresh fruit
Taramasalata
Chicken saté with peanut sambal
Toastie cases
Tartlet cases
Cheese sablés
Smoked salmon triangles
Spinach and ricotta strudels

PLANNING A LARGE PARTY
Cooking for a party can be daunting, but if you are well prepared it can also be terrific fun and it is deeply satisfying to look at perfectly presented food and realize that the occasion is going to be a success.

1. Forward planning
- Decide where you are going to have the party, decide on a convenient date and book the venue.
- Decide on the type of party – cocktail party, buffet, sit-down dinner, dancing or disco.
- Work out how many people can come to the party. Allow 3 sq. m/10 sq. ft per person for a sit-down party and 2 sq. m/6 sq. ft for a drinks party.
- If chairs have to be removed to allow space for dancing, make sure that you hire stackable chairs.

- Is the kitchen area big enough? Are there good reheating facilities or should you hire extra ovens?
- Are there adequate toilet facilities or will you need to hire a portacabin?
- Think about the colour scheme, particularly if you are having a marquee that has to be ordered well in advance.
- Get invitations printed – and expect one-third refusals.
- If the party is a commercial event, organize a licence and extend your employer's liability insurance.
- If the party is for charity, set up a committee to organize the tombola, programme advertising, and most importantly the sale of tickets.

2. Medium-term planning
- Plan the menu (see page 58).
- Work out the hire list. See costing (page 140).
- Establish that the hire is returned dirty and agree a delivery time.
- Hire a van to deliver food if necessary – start saving boxes to deliver food in.
- Plan the wine to go with the menu (see page 170). Allow a bottle per head and hope to have some left over. Order on sale or return and only chill wine as you need it so that the labels don't drop off. Many wine firms will supply ready chilled wine and glasses.
- Book a master of ceremonies if necessary.
- Book staff if necessary. The general rule is that for silver service, one waitress can cope with 6 people, and for butler service one waitress can look after 10 people. At a buffet, one waitress can look after 25 people. One barman can cope with 30 people if it is a full bar and with 50 people for a simple bar. Decide whether you need to hire kitchen staff, kitchen porters, cloakroom ladies, security staff or any other help. Decide on the kind of staff you want.
- Think about parking arrangements. Do you need to give car registration numbers to security? Find out from what time you can have access and from what time you can lay the tables. Check what time you need to leave the building and the latest time you can have the hired equipment collected in the morning. Check how the equipment can be delivered to the right place – is there a goods lift, etc?
- Hire and order flower arrangements and table decorations as necessary.
- Order the band, discotheque, casino, etc. Discuss electrical requirements.
- Go to the party venue and make a plan of action so that you can establish if there are any gaps in your forward-planning scheme.

3. A week before the party
- Order the food to arrive 2 days before the party. Don't forget to order sandwiches for the staff.
- Order the ice. Champagne is generally served colder than other wine. Make sure that the containers for ice are delivered before the ice arrives.
- Order other drinks, such as orange juice, mineral water and whisky.
- Talk over the plan of the party with a friend to make sure there are no gaps.

4. A day before the party
- Prepare as much of the food as you can. Separate into small batches to cool as quickly as possible and chill well. The easiest way to cook in large quantities is to do one process

at a time. If making sandwiches make all the fillings, soften all the butter, butter all the bread and then put the sandwiches together.

■ Get all the equipment you need to take, such as:

matches	broom and dustpan and brush
loo paper, cloakroom soap and towels	J-cloths
flowers for loos	plenty of boxes for taking home dirty
clingfilm	equipment
absorbent kitchen paper	first-aid box
kitchen foil	pins
dustbin liners (lots)	screwdriver
knives, whisks, fish slices, etc.	needles and cotton
carving knife and fork	rubber gloves
electric carving knife	chopping boards
oven gloves	scissors
tea-towels	lemons
washing-up liquid	petty cash (for tipping people)
mop and bucket	tea bags, milk, sugar for staff
	cold drinks for staff

5. On the day of the party

■ Get someone to the venue reasonably early to check off the deliveries, sign slips, persuade people to take equipment to the right place and generally organize the setting-up and laying of tables, the seating plan, the flowers, the microphone, the lighting, the table decorations, tidying the cloakroom and warding off potential problems.

■ Meanwhile, finish off all the cooking, pack up the food, undecorated, and deliver it with all the equipment and garnishes.

■ Set up an efficient working kitchen, work tidily and stick to a timeplan.

■ Serve the food by the agreed method and enjoy the party.

Planning a buffet party (see page 121)

COOKING FOR CUSTOMERS

This is a guide for working somewhere other than your own kitchen, e.g. cooking a dinner at someone else's home or at a hired venue, although some of the information, e.g. laying a table correctly, is relevant to home entertaining.

ALL FREELANCE COOKS must have an ansaphone – a mobile is also useful for emergencies. You must also know what your minimum daily rate is. Once you have worked out the minimum you are prepared to work for each week in order to survive (e.g. £35 a day to cover living expenses) you will be able to decide instantly if a job is worth doing or not. If you have a couple of good jobs in a week, you may feel able to take on a cheaper job rather than not working at all.

1. Before the event

■ Discuss as much as possible with the host/hostess, e.g. the menu (take your menu portfolio with you), what you need to bring and what not to bring, e.g. sugar for coffee. Establish a price and the hours, ask how they would like to be invoiced. Discuss expenses, e.g. travelling (28p a mile petrol or public transport).

- Be able to talk confidently about money. Know what your charges are before you meet the client. Know which areas you will be prepared to compromise on. If they don't mention money make sure that you do; make sure they are clear about what you are providing and for how much. Follow this conversation up in writing.
- Ask how large the cooker is – in case your dishes are too big for the oven. Discuss the method of service, how the table is to be laid, and how the evening is to work, for example where the coffee is to be served.
- When travelling allow plenty of time to get to the venue and take a good map with you.
- Make a timeplan for the meal.
- Make a list of things you may need to take with you: knives, kitchen paper, Magimix, clingfilm, rubbish sacks, etc. (see page 174).

2. The event

- Arrive on time – not early or late.
- Wear suitable clothes to serve if necessary.
- Wear a clean white apron, a white shirt and sensible shoes.
- If cooking for large numbers you may be expected to wear chef's kit including hair net and hat.
- Tie hair back.
- Look happy to be there, willing not harassed.
- Check how the cooker works.
- Put a jug of water in the refrigerator.

- Wash your hands when you arrive and be seen to wash your hands as you cook.
- Keep the kitchen very tidy whilst cooking – your customers will probably come to the kitchen and will be disappointed by a mess.
- Do not stroke animals without immediately washing your hands.
- Check how the dishwasher works and what can be put in it.

3. Types of service

- *Butler service* The waiter/waitress moves around the table holding the serving dishes or flats while the customers help themselves.
- *Silver service* The customer is helped to the food quickly by a waiter/waitress who uses a spoon and fork.
- *Family service* A dish is placed on the table and the customers help themselves.
- *Gueriedon* Food is served from a trolley, e.g. flambé or carvery.
- *Plated service* All the food is put on to individual plates in the kitchen and then served to the customer by the waiter/waitress.
- *Buffet/Counter service* The customer takes food from a central point. The food may be ready plated or served on to plates by the waiter/waitress. It might be self-service.

The type of service is determined by price, food and style of occasion, availability, space available and kitchen space. Often a combination of types of service are used, e.g. plated and butler, plated and silver or gueriedon and silver.

4. Preparing to lay the table

Before laying the table think about the positioning of the tables. Is there enough room between the tables and the chairs? If there are several tables make sure that all the folds in the tablecloths are facing the same way, i.e. from 6 o'clock to 12 o'clock. Check that there are no wobbly legs on the table, and carry a piece of card in case it is necessary. Plot the places around the table with side plates. If it is a round table think of it like the face of a clock, i.e. a table for 10 would have a setting every 6 minutes. Put all the glasses on the table upside down and when they have been polished turn them over. Remember that linen napkins crease easily so handle them as little as possible.

All the equipment should be absolutely clean. Dip a corner of your tea-towel in hot water and leave the rest of the towel dry for polishing.

CHINA

Plates need to be polished with a damp cloth, leaving no watermarks. Always check the edges and back of the plates to make sure they are clean.

Cups and saucers: it is important to clean thoroughly for stains both inside and outside. Check for chipped and cracked ones, they cannot be used.

Milk jugs/sauce bowls must be clean inside and outside.

SILVER

Cutlery must be polished, so it is clean and shiny (handles as well). Dip the cutlery in hot water and polish with a dry cloth. The hotter the water the easier it is to shine the cutlery.

GLASSES

Must be free of watermarks; to remove them use an ice bucket with boiling water and a dry tea-towel.

1. Hold the glass at the base with a corner of the tea-towel.
2. Turn the glass upside-down in the ice bucket without touching the water, the glass will

then steam up.

3. Lift the glass out and place two-thirds of the tea-towel in the glass.

4. Holding the base with one hand and placing the other hand's thumb in the glass and the remaining fingers on the outside, rotate the glass.

5. Laying the table

As a rule, cutlery is laid so that the diner works from the outside in – his first-course knife will be furthest from the plate and on the right, because he is to pick it up with his right hand. His first-course fork will be on his left and furthest from his plate. Similarly, if the first course is soup, the soup spoon will be on the right (because most people are right-handed), at the extreme outside of the cutlery collection.

If a knife-and-fork first course is followed by soup, the soup spoon will be in second place, and so on, working inwards to dessert spoon and fork, or cheese knife. Dessert or pudding cutlery is sometimes put across the top of the diner's plate, the spoon above or beyond the fork and the handles pointing towards the hand that will pick them up – i.e. spoon handle towards the right hand, fork handle towards the left hand.

Logic prevails in the same way with glasses, which are set out just beyond the knife tip, in a diagonal row, first one (say for a white wine to go with the first course) a little further away, and the dessert wine glass at the end of the row. The bread plate is placed on the diner's left, to the left of the cutlery. Napkins either go on this plate, or in the middle of the diner's place if the first course is not yet on the table. Individual ashtrays, fingerbowls, salt cellars are placed within comfortable reach.

The commonest mistakes made in laying tables are to fail to leave enough space between the banks of cutlery for the dinner plate to fit comfortably (leaving the guest foraging under his plate for knife or fork), to line up the tips of the cutlery instead of the bases, which gives an untidy unprofessional look (place the bases of the cutlery 2.5 cm/1in from the edge of the table), and to arrange flowers or candles in such a way that diners cannot see each other across the table. Low flowers are best, and candles should be checked to make sure they do not confuse sight lines. Nothing is so irritating as having to peer round an obstruction to carry on a conversation.

6. Serving the food

The person serving the food makes a strong impression on a customer or guest. It is essential that you know exactly what foods and wines you are serving. Also make sure that you know what the vegetarian option is. Many people have allergies, so it is essential to know all the ingredients in the recipes. Make sure that you look approachable and friendly, smile but do not be intrusive, stand up straight and look clean and tidy. Speak clearly, do not use slang, but do not use ridiculously formal language.

A good waiter or waitress anticipates what the customer needs; a good waiter or waitress also has to intuitively know when the customer wants help and when they want to be left in peace. Do remember that the customer is always right; if you cannot deal with a complaint apologize and say that you will get the head waiter/waitress. Always be positive, never say you do not know to the customer, simply say 'I will go and check for you.'

THE ETIQUETTE OF SERVING

At a formal dinner convention holds that women are served before men, starting with the most important female guest and ending with the hostess. Usually the top female guest will be seated on the right of the host. The men are then served, the most important male guest (who will be seated at the right of the hostess) being served first, then the others and, lastly, the host. Once everyone is served the hostess starts to eat which is a signal for everyone else to begin.

HOW MUCH TO SERVE

A daunting plateful tends to take away the appetite, so do not over-help guests to food. Take trouble to arrange things neatly and attractively on the plate. Place the first spoonful (say the meat) to one side, not in the middle, then work round with vegetables and garnishes, keeping them separate. Slops and drips look bad, so take time when spooning a sauce to let any excess run off the spoon before moving away from the main dish, and make sure the serving dish and diner's plate are as close together as possible.

If waiting formally (silver service), by the diner's side, hold the platter with one hand almost over his plate and use a spoon and fork in the other hand to serve him. If the diner is helping himself (butler service), hold the platter very low close to the table and close to his plate, to the side of it, so he can manage the awkward business of turning and wielding spoon and fork. With silver service the server serves food to the diners' left. With butler service diners are offered food to their right. Plates are always cleared from the diners' right. But in awkward or crowded corners it is better to forget convention and do whatever is least likely to disturb conversation.

7. Serving the wine

The wine should be served at the same time as the food, or even before, but not too long afterwards – waiting is a strain and drinking is permitted straight away even if eating is not. The host tastes the wine – if he has not already done so – then everyone is served – ladies first. If you need to handle the glass make sure you hold on to the base not the rim. Hold the bottle in such a way that the customer can read the label.

Good waiters, or hosts, do not constantly top up glasses, but do so positively when they are down to about a third. Glasses should not be filled more than two-thirds full – the idea is to leave room for the drinker to be able to get his nose into the glass to smell it without getting the tip wet! It also means he can swill the wine about, which encourages the release of its bouquet.

8. Housekeeping

You may be required to tidy and clear the drawing-room including: puffing up cushions, cleaning ashtrays, putting more wood on the fire, replenishing the ice, changing the drinks from aperitifs to digestifs, changing the glasses, etc.

Do this quickly between the main course and pudding.

9. Clearing the table

This should happen as unobtrusively as possible. Nothing should be touched until everyone has finished his food and indicated the fact by putting knife and fork firmly together. Then the plates are removed, but not stacked on top of each other or scraped within sight of the diners. Such unattractive operations should be performed out of sight. When the plates are cleared, everything connected with the just-removed course is cleared too – salt and pepper, mustard, sauces, salad dishes and, if the savoury courses are now over, bread plate and bread and butter. Nothing connected with the pudding should go on the table before everything pertaining to the previous course is off it. The same goes for coffee – it should not appear, nor should the bitter mints or petits fours, until the pudding has vanished, with its sauce jugs, cream, etc.

10. Cleaning up

DINING-ROOM

- Clean the mats but don't pile them up on top of each other when wet.
- Don't necessarily wipe the table with a wet cloth, it may be french-polished.
- Clear the table and leave it tidy.

KITCHEN

- Sweep the floor, wipe the door handles, wipe down the surfaces, empty the rubbish. Leave the dishes out rather than put them away in the wrong place.
- Check what is to be done with leftover food.
- Do not be extravagant, e.g. use clingfilm and tin foil sparingly.

11. Client file

Keep a client file. This should contain all contact details, correspondence, menu details, likes and dislikes. Highlight problem areas (no parking, small kitchen, tiny fridge, no freezer, etc.) for future reference. Note which agency gave you the job (for repeat engagements/referral, etc.).

SCALLOP AND ROCKET SALAD
This is a light but elegant and simple
first course.
SERVES 4
12 fresh scallops, cleaned (see page 172)
seasoned plain flour
hazelnut oil

balsamic vinegar
fresh chives
a large handful of rocket, washed

1. Remove the muscular white frill found opposite the scallop roe. Rinse off any black matter. Slice the scallops in half

horizontally, trying to keep the roe attached to the scallop.

2. Dip the scallops into seasoned flour. Heat some oil in a frying pan and fry the scallops quickly on both sides until lightly browned and just cooked. Sprinkle over some vinegar.

3. Tip the scallops on to the rocket leaves. Turn lightly and place on 4 individual plates.

Preparing a scallop

Opening the scallop: prise open the shell with a strong knife and detach the scallop from the lower shell. Scoop out the scallop with a spoon, catching all the juice in a strainer lined with a clean cloth placed over a bowl.

Cleaning the scallop: pull away and discard the membrane or frill and the black stomach parts. Wash the scallop thoroughly under running cold water and pat dry on absorbent paper. Remove the thick white muscle around the outside of the scallop. Separate the coral (roe) from the white meat as required.

GUINEA-FOWL BRAISED WITH CARAMEL AND ORANGES

This makes a very good dinner party dish. It can be made in advance and reheated when ready to serve (see Note).

SERVES 4

2 guinea-fowl
2 teaspoons sunflower oil
55g/2oz shallots, finely chopped
30g/1oz granulated sugar
1 tablespoon wine vinegar
175ml/6fl oz white stock (see page 52)
juice of 2 oranges, strained
salt and freshly ground black pepper
To garnish
1 orange, segmented
1 small bunch of watercress

1. Preheat the oven to 190°C/375°F/gas mark 5.

2. Remove any feathers from the guinea-fowl and wipe clean inside with a damp cloth.

3. Heat the oil in a flameproof casserole. Add the guinea-fowl and brown them all over. Remove them from the casserole.

4. Reduce the heat, add the shallots to the casserole and cook for 2 minutes. Add the sugar and vinegar, dissolving the sugar over a low heat, then boil the liquid until the sugar caramelizes. Pour on the stock – it will hiss and splutter, so take care – and stir over a low heat until the caramel lumps disappear. Add the orange juice. Season well with salt and pepper. Return the guinea-fowl to the casserole and bring the cooking liquor to the boil.

5. Cover the casserole and pot-roast it for 1 hour.

6. Remove the guinea-fowl and joint them as you would a chicken (see pages 44). Arrange the pieces on a warmed serving plate. Skim as much fat as possible from the cooking liquor. Strain it into a clean saucepan, skim it again and boil rapidly for 3 minutes.

7. Garnish the guinea-fowl with orange segments and watercress, and serve the sauce separately in a warmed sauceboat.

NOTE: To reheat from cold pour the sauce over the guinea-fowl. Cover with tin foil and reheat for 30 minutes at 200°C/400°F/gas mark 6. Garnish with the oranges and watercress.

POMMES ANNA

These potatoes are excellent for a dinner party – they can be prepared an hour or two in advance and will keep warm for half an hour or so. Serve them cut into wedges.

SERVES 4

675g/1½lb potatoes, peeled and thinly sliced
55g/2oz clarified butter (see page 192)
salt and freshly ground black pepper
freshly grated nutmeg

1. Preheat the oven to 200°C/400°F/gas mark 6. Brush a heavy ovenproof pan with

the clarified butter.

2. Arrange a neat layer of overlapping potato slices on the bottom of the pan. Brush the potatoes with butter and season well with salt, pepper and nutmeg.

3. Continue to layer the potatoes, butter and seasoning until all the potatoes have been used. Finish with butter and seasoning.

4. Set the pan over direct medium heat for 2 minutes to brown the bottom layer of potatoes.

5. Remove from the heat and cover with greased paper and a lid or kitchen foil. Bake in the preheated oven for about 45 minutes or until the potatoes are tender.

6. Invert a serving plate over the pan and turn the potatoes out so that the neat first layer is on top.

INDIVIDUAL APPLE CHARLOTTES
Apple charlottes make an attractive pudding for a dinner party. They can be prepared in the morning and cooked at the last minute. They are particularly delicious served with Greek yoghurt.
SERVES 4
55g/2oz granulated sugar
5 dessert apples, such as Discovery or Cox's, peeled, cored and sliced
2 tablespoons Calvados
juice of 1 orange
a pinch of ground cinnamon
70g/2 1/2oz butter
8 slices of white bread, crusts removed
For the sauce
55g/2oz granulated sugar
grated zest of 1 orange
1 tablespoon Calvados

1. Put the sugar into a heavy saucepan with 2 tablespoons water and place over a low heat. Allow the sugar to dissolve slowly and become lightly caramelized.

2. Add the apples to the caramel, stir and then add the Calvados, orange juice, cinnamon and 15g/1/2oz of the butter.

Simmer together for 2 minutes.

3. Preheat the oven to 225°C/425°F/gas mark 7.

4. Melt the remaining butter. Flatten the bread slightly with a rolling pin. Cut out 8 rounds and dip them in the melted butter on both sides. Reserve 4 of the rounds and use the remaining 4 to line the base of 4 dariole moulds. Use the remaining bread to line the sides.

5. Drain the apple filling (but reserve the strained liquor) and pile the apple slices into the lined moulds. Cover with the remaining rounds of bread.

6. Put the moulds on to a baking sheet and bake in the preheated oven for 15–20 minutes.

7. Meanwhile, prepare the sauce: reduce the strained apple liquor, by boiling rapidly, to half the original quantity. Set aside.

8. Put the sugar with 2 tablespoons of water into a heavy saucepan and place over a low heat. Allow the sugar to dissolve and then caramelize. When lightly browned add the reduced apple liquor, the orange zest and the Calvados. Simmer for 1 minute.

9. To serve: turn the apple charlottes out on to individual plates and serve with the caramel sauce.

CHICKEN ELIZABETH
The Cordon Bleu School devised this dish for the Coronation celebration in 1953 and it has become a classic.
SERVES 4
1 x 1.35kg/3lb chicken, cleaned but not trussed
white stock, made with chicken bones (see page 52), or water with 1 bay leaf, 6 peppercorns, salt, 2 parsley stalks, 1 lemon slice and 2 teaspoons fresh thyme leaves
225ml/8floz Elizabeth sauce (see page 182)
To serve
rice salad (see page 175)
1 bunch of watercress

1. Place the chicken in a saucepan of simmering stock, or water with the flavourings.
2. Cover the pan and cook gently for 1¼–1½ hours or until the chicken is tender and the drumsticks feel loose and wobbly. Remove the chicken from the stock and set aside to cool.
3. Remove the flesh from the chicken bones, and when quite cold mix with the sauce, reserving a little of it.
4. Pile the chicken into the middle of a serving-dish and coat with the reserved sauce. Surround with the rice salad and garnish with watercress.

NOTE: It is easier to strip chicken flesh from the bones while the bird is still lukewarm. But on no account should the sauce be added to the flesh until the chicken is completely cold.

ELIZABETH SAUCE
This sauce is also deicious made with Greek yoghurt instead of mayonnaise, especially if for a summer buffet party to avoid the danger of giving your guests food poisoning (see eggs, page 18).
1 small onion, chopped
2 teaspoons oil
2 teaspoons curry powder

½ teaspoon tomato purée
3 tablespoons water
1 small bay leaf
4 tablespoons red wine
salt and freshly ground black pepper
2 teaspoons apricot jam
1 slice of lemon
1 teaspoon lemon juice
290ml/½ pint mayonnaise (see page 20)
2 tablespoons double cream

1. Cook the onion gently in the oil for 10 minutes.
2. Add the curry powder and fry gently for 1 minute.
3. Add the tomato purée, water, bay leaf, wine, salt, pepper, jam, lemon slice and juice and simmer for 8 minutes.
4. Strain the mixture, pushing as much as possible through the sieve. Leave to cool.
5. When cold, use this sauce to flavour the mayonnaise to the desired strength.
6. Half-whip the cream and stir into the sauce.

RICE SALAD

Rice salad is a good salad for a buffet party. Try varying the types of rice used. Almost any vegetables can be added to cold cooked rice to make a salad, but it is important to have approximately equal quantities of rice and vegetables, or the result may be lifeless and stodgy. The dressing should moisten, not soak, the dish.

SERVES 8

225g/8oz long-grain rice
110g/4oz frozen peas
½ green pepper, cored, deseeded and chopped
½ red pepper, cored, deseeded and chopped
1 small stick of celery, chopped
¼ cucumber, peeled and chopped
2 tomatoes, peeled and cut into strips
a few black olives, pitted
finely chopped fresh parsley, mint, chives or dill
For the dressing
3 tablespoons salad oil
1 tablespoon vinegar
½ small onion, very finely chopped
salt and freshly ground black pepper

1. Boil the rice in plenty of water until just tender (about 10 minutes). Rinse in boiling water and leave to drain well.
2. Cook the peas.
3. Put all the dressing ingredients into a screw-top jar and shake well.
4. Mix everything together and add salt and pepper if necessary.

NOTE: Rice salad looks pretty when turned out of a ring mould, a jelly mould, or even a mixing bowl. Push it down firmly in the oiled mould, then invert it on to a dish. If simply served in a bowl or on a dish, keep back a few olives and tomato pieces for the top.

HERB OMELETTE SALAD

This makes an attractive summer buffet party dish.

SERVES 2–4

For the omelette
5 eggs
3 tablespoons olive oil
1 tablespoon chopped fresh parsley
salt and freshly ground black pepper
For the salad
2 red peppers, quartered and deseeded
2 large tomatoes, peeled and cut into strips
1 cucumber, peeled, deseeded and cut into strips
1 head of lettuce
1 bunch of fresh chives, roughly chopped
12 fresh basil leaves, chopped
For the dressing
1 clove of garlic, crushed
2 anchovy fillets, mashed
1 teaspoon Dijon mustard
2 tablespoons wine vinegar
8 tablespoons olive oil
salt and freshly ground black pepper
To garnish
10 small black olives, pitted

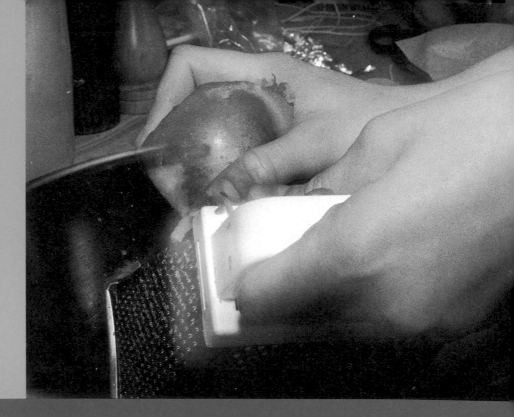

1. Make the omelette: in a bowl, mix together the eggs, 2 tablespoons of the oil, the parsley, salt and pepper.
2. Use the remaining oil to fry the omelette. Lightly grease the base of an omelette pan. When hot, add enough of the omelette mixture to cover the base of the pan. The omelette mixture should be the thickness of a pancake. Cook the omelette for about 1 minute. Slide on to a plate and leave to cool. Continue to cook the remaining omelette mixture in the same way.
3. When cool, cut the omelettes into thin strips.
4. Meanwhile, prepare the salad: place the peppers under a hot grill. When charred, hold under cold running water and scrape off the skin, then cut the flesh into 1cm/½in strips.
5. Prepare the dressing: mix together all the ingredients, and whizz in a blender. Season with salt and pepper.
6. Mix together all the salad ingredients, the omelette strips and the herbs. Add the dressing and toss well.
7. Pile on to a serving dish and scatter over the olives.

CREAMED CHEESE WITH FRESH FRUIT
This dessert is simple to prepare and particularly suitable for a summer buffet party.
SERVES 4–6

225g/8oz cottage cheese
290ml/½pint double cream, lightly whipped
55g/2oz icing sugar, sifted
2 drops of vanilla essence
3 figs, quartered
3 kiwi fruits, peeled and sliced
4 oranges, peeled and sliced

1. Put the cottage cheese into a sieve and drain very well.
2. Push the cheese through the sieve (or process briefly in a food processor or blender) and fold in the cream. Sweeten with the icing sugar and add the vanilla essence.
3. Pile the mixture on to a large oval serving dish and shape into a shallow mound. Arrange the fruit attractively on top of the cheese.

Cocktail party recipes

When planning a party make sure that some of the cooking can be prepared well in advance. Small canapés are time-consuming.

TARAMASALATA

This can be used to fill toast or tartlet cases. Garnish with black olives and Greek parsley.

SERVES 6

1 slice of white bread, crusts removed
225g/8oz fresh smoked soft roe, skinned
1 large clove of garlic, crushed
about 150ml/1/4 pint each sunflower oil
   and olive oil
freshly ground black pepper
juice of 1/2 lemon

1. Hold the bread slice under the tap to wet it. Squeeze dry and put it into a bowl with the cod roe and the garlic. Using a wooden spoon or electric whisk, beat very well.
2. Now add the oils very slowly, almost drop by drop (as with mayonnaise), beating all the time. The idea is to form a smooth emulsion, and adding the oil too fast will result in a rather oily, curdled mixture.
3. The amount of oil added is a matter of personal taste: the more you add, the paler and creamier the mixture becomes and the more delicate the flavour. Stop when you think the right balance is achieved.
4. Add pepper and lemon juice to taste. If the mixture seems too thick or bitter add a little hot water.

CHICKEN SATÉ WITH PEANUT SAMBAL

MAKES 60 COCKTAIL PIECES

5 chicken breasts, skinned
For the marinade
1 medium onion, finely chopped
1 clove garlic, crushed
1 teaspoon ground coriander
1 teaspoon ground ginger
3 tablespoons dark soy sauce
juice of 1 small lemon
2 teaspoons soft dark brown sugar

freshly ground black pepper
For the peanut sambal
1 small onion, finely chopped
1 tablespoon oil
1/2 teaspoon chilli powder
110g/4oz crunchy peanut butter
2 tablespoons dark soy sauce
2 tablespoons lemon juice
200ml/7fl oz cold water
soft dark brown sugar and salt to taste

1. Make the sambal: cook the onion in the oil in a saucepan over a very low heat. Add the chilli powder and cook for 10 seconds.
2. Remove from the heat and add the peanut butter, soy sauce, lemon juice and water.
3. Return to the heat and stir until the sauce is thick and smooth. Season to taste with sugar and salt.
4. Cut each chicken breast into 12 cubes.
5. Mix together the ingredients for the marinade and add the chicken pieces. Leave to infuse for at least 1 hour.
6. Preheat the grill to its highest setting.
7. Skewer the chicken pieces on long wet bamboo sticks and grill for about 3 minutes each side.
8. Serve the peanut sambal as a dip.

NOTE: The bamboo sticks are wetted to prevent them from burning.

TOASTIE CASES

Toastie cases can be filled with any of your favourite dips.

MAKES 20

5 thin slices of bread
butter, melted

1. Preheat the oven to 180°C/350°F/gas mark 4. Stamp out rounds of bread, using a small fluted cutter.
2. Dip into the melted butter and mould into tiny patty tins. Press an empty patty tin on top and bake in the preheated oven until golden-brown and crisp.

TARTLET CASES

Tartlet cases can be filled as required. They are particularly good filled with a little mascarpone cheese and served with a small teaspoonful of keta (salmon roe eggs) and garnished with a sprig of chervil.

MAKES ABOUT 60

225g/8oz quantity rich shortcrust pastry (see page 24)

1. Preheat the oven to 190°C/375°F/gas mark 5.
2. Roll out the pastry 2mm/1/8in thick. Stamp out circles, using a small fluted cutter.
3. Press the circles into tiny patty tins or barquette (boat-shapes) moulds. Chill in the refrigerator for 20 minutes.
4. Bake the tartlet cases blind for about 10 minutes (see page 22), removing the lining paper and beans after 5 minutes.
5. Cool on a wire rack and use as required.

CHEESE SABLÉS

MAKES 24

225g/8oz plain flour
salt and freshly ground black pepper
225g/8oz butter
225g/8oz Gruyère or strong Cheddar cheese, grated
a pinch of dry English mustard
a pinch of cayenne pepper
beaten egg

1. Preheat the oven to 190°C/375°F/gas mark 5. Line 2 baking sheets with greaseproof paper.
2. Sift the flour with a pinch of salt into a bowl. Rub in the butter until the mixture resembles breadcrumbs.
3. Add the cheese, salt, pepper, mustard, cayenne and enough egg just to bind. Work into a paste but do not over-handle or the pastry will become greasy and tough.
4. Roll out on a floured board to a 5mm/1/4in thickness. Cut into rounds or triangles and brush with the remaining beaten egg.

5. Bake in the preheated oven for about 10 minutes until golden-brown. Leave to cool on a wire rack.

SMOKED SALMON TRIANGLES

MAKES 40 SMALL TRIANGLES

5 slices of wholemeal bread
soft butter for spreading
freshly ground black pepper
110g/4oz smoked salmon
lemon juice

1. Butter the bread, sprinkle with black pepper and lay the smoked salmon slices carefully on top.
2. Sprinkle with lemon juice, then cut off the crusts and cut each slice into 8 triangles.

SPINACH AND RICOTTA STRUDELS

MAKES 20

225g/8oz frozen chopped spinach
110g/4oz butter
110g/4oz ricotta cheese
salt and freshly ground black pepper
a good pinch of freshly grated nutneg
4 sheets of filo pastry
1 egg, beaten, to glaze

1. Preheat the oven to 200°C/400°F/gas mark 6.
2. Defrost the spinach. Melt 30g/1oz of the butter and add the spinach, ricotta, salt, pepper and nutmeg.
3. Melt the remaining butter and brush it over the sheets of filo pastry.
4. Cut each sheet of pastry into strips 5cm/2in wide.
5. Place a spoonful of filling at one end of each strip. Form a triangle by folding the right-hand corner to the opposite side, and fold over and then across from the left-hand corner to the right edge. Continue folding until the strip of pastry is used up.
6. Brush the strudels with beaten egg. Place on a greased baking sheet and bake in the preheated oven for about 10 minutes, or until golden brown.

PREPARING LAMB AND GLANCE
FORWARD TO THE INTERMEDIATE TERM
CHAPTER 22

As we approach the end of term we take a glance forward to what the students can expect to learn in term 2 of the 3-term Diploma. In the first term most of the methods of cooking covered are relatively simple. In the next term we will be building on knowledge acquired and teaching more complicated dishes. For example, we have already made mayonnaise which is a cold emulsion sauce which can be prepared in advance and kept in the refrigerator. Next term we will teach hollandaise sauce and all its derivatives. Hollandaise sauce is also an emulsion sauce but it is served hot and is made with butter instead of oil; it has to be made at the last minute and has a cruel tendency to split just as you are ready to serve. We will also be covering all the other methods of making basic sauces and their derivatives.

In term 1 the students will have made both cheese sauce and meringues. In term 2 we will be teaching them how to make a cheese soufflé. A savoury soufflé incorporates two basic methods of cooking – a savoury roux-based sauce and the whisking of egg whites. We will

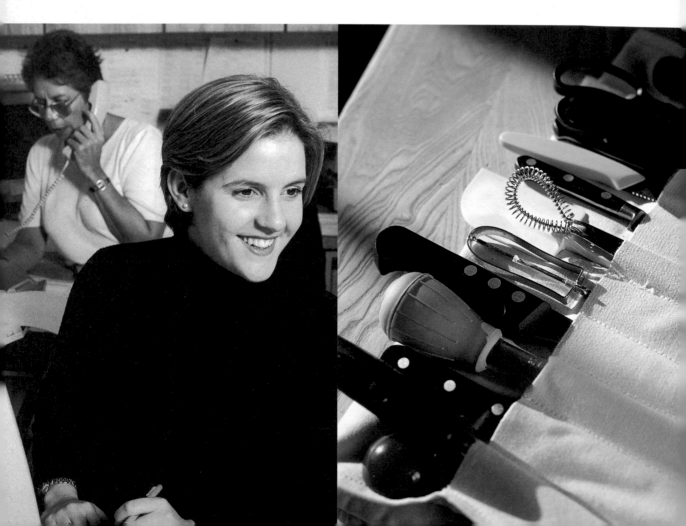

incorporate these two techniques into a delicious hot soufflé and at the same time we will remove the fear and misconception that soufflés are difficult to make and tend to collapse.

Also included at a glance forward to the intermediate term will be making pâte sucrée and using it to make fruit tartlets. Students will have made basic shortcrust pastry and will have learnt how to line a flan ring. In this demonstration we assume that knowledge and teach them how to make far richer pastries using proportionately much more butter to flour. Given the amount of fat used the pastry has to be made by a different method. We will also teach them how to line small boat moulds and tiny tartlet tins. Greater attention to detail is required, the moulds have to be lined absolutely perfectly and they must be baked for precisely the correct time – they burn very easily. The tartlets are then filled with crème pâtissière, decorated with fresh fruit and glazed with apricot glaze. The students have already covered these skills but again greater attention to detail is required and perfectionism is essential.

Techniques Covered

Preparing lamb cutlets

Trimming a pork fillet

Stuffing a shoulder of lamb

Making a hot emulsion sauce

Preparing a hot soufflé

Making pâte sucrée (sweet French pastry)

Crème pâtissière

❷ Cookery Terms

Chine: To remove the backbone from a rack of ribs. Carving is almost impossible if the butcher has not chined the meat.

Collops: Small slices of meat, taken from a tender cut such as neck of lamb.

Lard: To thread strips of bacon fat (or sometimes anchovy) through meat to give it flavour, and, in the case of fat, to make up any deficiency in very lean meat.

Render: To melt solid fat, e.g. beef, pork, slowly in the oven.

Recipes

Lamb cutlets grilled with herbs

Pork fillets in cider

Roast stuffed shoulder of lamb

Hollandaise sauce

Cheese soufflé

Pâte sucrée

French-trimmed best end cutlets

Skin the best end: lift a corner of the skin from the neck end with a small knife, hold it firmly, using a cloth to get a good grip, and peel it off. Chine if the butcher has not already done so. This means sawing carefully through the chine bone (or spine) just where it meets the rib bones. Take care not to saw right through into the eye of the meat. Now remove the chine bone completely. Chop off the cutlet bones so that the length of the remaining bones is not more than twice the length of the eye of the meat. Remove the half-moon-shaped piece of flexible cartilage found buried between the layers of fat and meat at the thinner end of the best end. This is the tip of the shoulder blade. It is simple to work out with a knife and your fingers. Remove the line of gristle to be found under the meat at the thick end.

If thin small cutlets are required, cut between each bone as evenly as possible, splitting the rack into 6–7 small cutlets. If fatter cutlets are required, carefully ease out every other rib bone. Then cut between the remaining bones into thick cutlets. Now trim the fat from the thick end of each cutlet, and scrape the rib bones free of any flesh or skin.

Points to Remember
Hollandaise sauce:

- Do not overheat the egg yolks.
- Direct heat is too fierce for hollandaise. Always use a bain-marie to cook it gently.
- Be prepared for any emergencies, e.g. the eggs getting too hot; have cold water to hand.
- Use unsalted butter.
- The butter must be chilled and cut into small sugar-cube-sized pieces.
- Serve immediately or keep warm for a short time in a warm bain-marie; if it is too hot the sauce may separate.

Soufflés:

- The soufflé dish should be greased with butter and sprinkled evenly with dry breadcrumbs, finely grated Parmesan cheese or caster sugar (depending on whether the soufflé is sweet or savoury) – this helps the soufflé to rise.
- A baking sheet should be placed in the oven when it is lit – this is known as 'bottom heat' and will help the soufflé to rise when it is cooked.
- The base of a soufflé, often a roux-based sauce called a panade, should be the consistency of a thick pouring sauce.
- The base sauce should be over-seasoned in order for the finished soufflé to have good flavour.
- The egg whites should be whisked to a medium peak.
- Fill the soufflé dish two-thirds full and scrape around the inside top edge to remove the crumbs from the top 1cm/1/2in – this will give the soufflé a 'top hat' appearance.
- Cook the soufflé on the hot baking sheet near the top of the oven, making sure there is enough room for it to rise.
- A soufflé is cooked when it has risen well and wobbles – but not alarmingly.

Pâte sucrée:

- Weigh the ingredients carefully.
- The fat must be soft but not melted.
- Blend the yolks with the sugar and butter very carefully by hand, trying not to include air.
- Gently incorporate the sifted flour, taking care not to overwork it or the pastry may become greasy.
- Chill the pastry well before and after rolling out.
- Bake near the top of the oven at 190°C/375°F/gas mark 5.

LAMB CUTLETS GRILLED WITH HERBS
SERVES 4

12 French-trimmed lamb cutlets
(see page 181)
30g/1oz butter, melted
1 tablespoon oil
a selection of chopped fresh herbs,
*   such as thyme, basil, mint, parsley,*
*   marjoram, rosemary*
salt and freshly ground black pepper

1. Preheat the grill to its highest setting.
2. Brush the cutlets with melted butter and oil, sprinkle over half the herbs and season with salt and pepper.
3. Place the cutlets under the grill, about 8cm/3in away from the heat, and cook for 3–4 minutes.
4. Turn them over, baste with the fat from the bottom of the pan and sprinkle over the remaining herbs.
5. Grill for 3–4 minutes (3 minutes each side should give a succulent pink cutlet, 4 minutes a well-done cutlet).
6. Arrange the cutlets on a warmed serving dish and pour over the pan juices. Serve immediately.

PORK FILLETS IN CIDER
SERVES 4

1 tablespoon oil
15g/1/2oz butter

675g/1 1/2 lb pork tenderloin (fillet), trimmed
1 medium onion, finely chopped
290ml/1 1/2 pint cider
1 bay leaf
salt and freshly ground black pepper
1 tablespoon single cream
To garnish
2 dessert apples
butter
caster sugar
chopped fresh parsley

1. Preheat the oven to 180°C/350°F/gas mark 4.
2. Heat the oil in a frying pan. Add the butter and when hot add the pork and brown quickly all over. Remove to a plate. Reduce the heat, add the onion and cook slowly until soft. Return the pork to the pan. Add the cider and bay leaf. Bring to the boil, then tip into a flameproof casserole. Season with salt and pepper, cover and cook in the preheated oven for 10–15 minutes.
3. Peel, and core the apples and cut into wedges. Fry in butter, sprinkled with sugar, until lightly coloured.
4. Take out the pork and keep warm. Strain the cooking liquor, remove the bay leaf from the sieve, and place the onions in a serving dish. Keep warm.
5. Boil the cooking liquor rapidly until reduced to a syrupy consistency. Add the cream. Taste and adjust the seasoning if necessary.
6. Slice the pork thickly, arrange on top of the onions, pour over the sauce and sprinkle with parsley and garnish with the fried apple.

ROAST STUFFED SHOULDER OF LAMB
SERVES 6
1.8kg/4lb boned whole shoulder of lamb
15g/1/2 oz butter
1 large onion, finely chopped
55g/2oz mushrooms, sliced
1 clove of garlic, crushed
1 tablespoon chopped mixed fresh herbs,
such as mint, thyme, parsley, rosemary
a squeeze of orange juice
salt and freshly ground black pepper
1/2 cup cooked rice
2 tablespoons sultanas
For the gravy
2 teaspoons plain flour
1 teaspoon tomato purée
290ml/1/2 pint brown stock (see page 51)
100ml/3 1/2 fl oz red wine
To garnish
1 small bunch of watercress

1. Weigh the lamb and calculate its cooking time: 20 minutes to 450g/1lb plus 20 minutes.
2. Preheat the oven to 190°C/375°F/gas mark 5.
3. Melt the butter in a frying pan and add the onion. Fry over a low heat until soft.
4. Add the mushrooms, garlic, herbs and orange juice. Cook over a low heat until the mushrooms are soft. Season with salt and pepper.
5. Remove from the heat and mix with the cooked rice. Stir in the sultanas.
6. Push this stuffing into the shoulder of lamb, sewing up the edges with thin string. Place in a roasting pan.
7. Roast in the preheated oven for the calculated cooking time.
8. Lift the meat from the roasting pan and keep warm on a serving platter in the turned-off oven.
9. Make the gravy: pour off most of the fat from the roasting pan, then stir in first the flour and then the tomato purée. Cook for 30 seconds.
10. Add the stock and wine, and stir over the heat until the sauce boils, scraping the brown bits from the bottom of the pan as you go. Simmer for 2–3 minutes. Season to taste with salt and pepper. Strain into a warmed gravy-boat.
11. Garnish the lamb with bouquets of watercress and serve with the gravy.

HOLLANDAISE SAUCE
SERVES 4

3 tablespoons wine vinegar
6 black peppercorns
1 bay leaf
1 blade of mace
2 egg yolks
salt
110g/4oz unsalted butter,
*   softened*
lemon juice

1. Place the vinegar, peppercorns, bay leaf and mace in a small heavy saucepan and reduce by simmering to 1 tablespoon.
2. Cream the egg yolks with a pinch of salt and a nut of the butter in a small heatproof bowl. Set over, not in, a saucepan of gently simmering water. Using a wooden spoon, beat the mixture until slightly thickened, taking care that the water immediately around the bowl does not boil. Mix well.
3. Strain on the reduced vinegar. Mix well. Stir over the heat until slightly thickened. Beat in the softened butter bit by bit, increasing the temperature as the sauce thickens and you add more butter, but take care that the water does not boil.
4. When the sauce has become light and thick remove from the heat and beat or whisk for 1 minute. Check the seasoning and add lemon juice, and salt if necessary. Keep warm by standing the bowl in hot water. Serve warm.

NOTE: Hollandaise sauce will set too firmly if allowed to get cold and it will curdle if overheated. It can be made in larger quantities in either a blender or a food processor: simply put the eggs and salt into

the blender and blend lightly. Add the hot reduction and allow to thicken slightly. Set aside. When ready to serve, pour in warm melted butter, slowly allowing the sauce to thicken as you pour.

CHEESE SOUFFLÉ

SERVES 2

40g/1¼ oz butter
dried white breadcrumbs
30g/1oz plain flour
½ teaspoon dry English mustard
a pinch of cayenne pepper
290ml/½ pint milk
85g/3oz strong Cheddar or Gruyère
   cheese, grated
4 eggs, separated
salt and freshly ground black pepper

1. Preheat the oven to 200°C/400°F/gas mark 6. Melt a knob of the butter and brush a 15cm/6in soufflé dish with it. Dust lightly with the breadcrumbs.
2. Melt the remaining butter in a saucepan and stir in the flour, mustard and cayenne pepper. Cook for 45 seconds. Add the milk and cook, stirring vigorously, for 2 minutes. The mixture will get very thick and leave the sides of the pan. Remove from the heat.
3. Stir in the cheese, egg yolks, salt and pepper. Taste; the mixture should be very well seasoned.
4. Whisk the egg whites until stiff but not dry, and mix a spoonful into the cheese mixture. Then fold in the remainder and pour into the soufflé dish, which should be about two-thirds full. Run your finger around the top of the soufflé mixture. This gives a 'top hat' appearance to the cooked soufflé.
5. Bake in the preheated oven for 25–30 minutes and serve immediately. (Do not test to see if the soufflé is done for at least 20 minutes. Then open the oven just wide enough to get your hand in

and give the soufflé a slight shove. If it wobbles alarmingly, cook for a further 5 minutes.)

PÂTE SUCRÉE

170g/6oz plain flour
a pinch of salt
85g/3oz butter, softened
3 egg yolks
85g/3oz sugar
2 drops vanilla essence

1. Sift the flour with the salt on to a board. Make a large well in the centre and put the butter in it. Place the egg yolks and sugar on the butter with the vanilla essence.
2. Using the fingertips of one hand, mix the butter, yolks and sugar together. When mixed to a soft paste, draw in the flour and knead just until the pastry is smooth.
3. If the pastry is very soft, wrap and chill, before rolling or pressing out to the required shape. In any event the pastry must be allowed to relax for 30 minutes either before or after rolling out, but before baking.

CRÈME PÂTISSIÈRE

290ml/½ pint milk
2 egg yolks
55g/2oz caster sugar
20g/¾oz plain flour
20g/¾oz cornflour
vanilla essence

1. Scald the milk by bringing it to just below boiling point in a saucepan.
2. Cream the egg yolks with the sugar and a little of the milk and when pale, mix in the flours. Pour on the milk and mix well.
3. Return the mixture to the pan and bring slowly to the boil, stirring continuously. (It will go alarmingly lumpy, but don't worry, keep stirring vigorously and it will become smooth.) Allow to cool slightly,

GUEST DEMONSTRATIONS
CHAPTER 23

Every term we invite guest chefs or cooks to demonstrate recipes of their own. In the first term we have 3 guests but by the third term we have eight or nine guest lecturers. The topics will range from restaurant cooking to Thai food, butchery, sugar working, cooking with chocolate to recipe development and understanding taste.

The three guests we had in term 1 were Roz Denny, Jane Nemazee and Peter Gordon. Roz has been demonstrating at the school for ten years and kindly wrote the introduction to rice in this book. We have included several of her recipes in the text. Roz takes the students through the many varieties of rice now available and advises them about which type of rice to use with different recipes.

Jane Nemazee is an ex-student of ours whose husband is from the Middle East and the recipes that she demonstrates are recipes that have been handed down in his family. They are not from a specific region, simply an eclectic collection of different ideas.

Peter Gordon, I am sure, needs no introduction: he is the head chef of the Sugar Club restaurant. The Sugar Club was one of the first London restaurants to bring us the idea of fusion food that is, through which fuses the tastes of East and West. The result causes an explosion of flavour. It is sometimes called Pacific Rim cookery. Peter is naturally an excellent chef but he is also a very good teacher and very keen on training – many of our students are given work experience at the Sugar Club.

Techniques Covered
Peter Gordon from the Sugar Club –
Pacific Rim cookery
Jane Nemazee –
Middle Eastern food

Recipes
Grilled scallops with sweet chilli sauce and crème fraîche
Aubergine and potato curry
Lamb fillet with saffron
Aab gosht
Pushpa's South India dahl
Khapoli potatoes

GRILLED SCALLOPS WITH SWEET CHILLI SAUCE AND CRÈME FRAÎCHE

This dish – one of my all-time favourites – is now synonymous with the London Sugar Club. I first put it on the menu in July 1995, and it has only come off when storms have prevented divers collecting scallops. It's also the dish that most reviewers choose when they visit! The crème fraîche softens the strong flavours of the sauce, which in turn cut through the richness of the scallops. The chilli sauce recipe makes more than you need, so keep the surplus in the fridge for other dishes.

SERVES 4

12 large diver-caught scallops, trimmed
sesame oil
salt and freshly ground black pepper
watercress leaves
125ml/4fl oz crème fraîche
Sweet chilli sauce
10 cloves of garlic, peeled
4 large red chillies, stems removed
3 knobs of fresh ginger, peeled and
*   roughly chopped*
1 knob of galangal, peeled and roughly chopped
8 lime leaves
3 lemon-grass stems; remove the two outside
*   leaves, discard the top third of the stem*

and finely slice the remainder
55g/2oz fresh coriander leaves
340g/12oz caster sugar
150m/ ¼ pint cider vinegar
100ml/3 ½fl oz Asian fish sauce
50ml/1 ¾ fl oz tamari

1. Put the first seven ingredients of the chilli sauce in a food processor and purée to a coarse paste.
2. Put the sugar in a saucepan with 4 tablespoons of water and place on a moderate heat, stirring well until the sugar dissolves.

Remove the spoon and turn the heat up to full. Boil for 5–8 minutes without stirring until it has turned a dark caramel colour (but don't allow it to burn). Now stir in the paste, bring the sauce back to the boil and add the last three ingredients. Return to the boil and simmer for 1 minute. Leave to cool before eating.
3. Lightly oil the scallops with sesame oil and season, then grill each side on a char-grill, conventional grill or grill pan for 90 seconds.
4. Place them on a bed of watercress, put a dollop of crème fraîche on top and drizzle generously with sweet chilli sauce.

AUBERGINE AND POTATO CURRY

2 large onions, sliced
sunflower oil
2 cloves garlic, crushed
2.5cm/1in fresh ginger, crushed
1/2 teaspoon ground turmeric
1 teaspoon ground cumin
1–1 1/2 teaspoons panj piran
1/4 teaspoon chilli powder
450g/1lb potatoes, peeled and cubed
2 aubergines, cubed
1 green pepper, deseeded and cubed
1 tablespoon tomato purée
fresh coriander leaves, chopped, to garnish

1. Sweat the onion in oil in a large saucepan until soft.
2. Mix the garlic, ginger and spices together and add a little water to form a paste. Add the paste to the onions in the pan and continue cooking for 2–3 minutes.
3. Add the potatoes, aubergines and pepper, then add the tomato purée, and a little water if required.
4. Cook over a gentle heat until the vegetables are soft. Serve garnished with coriander leaves.

NOTE: Panj piran is a mixture of ground spices available in Indian shops.

LAMB FILLET WITH SAFFRON

1 lamb fillet per person, trimmed
olive oil
1/2 large onion per fillet, thinly sliced
large pinch of saffron
1 small garlic clove, crushed, per fillet
pinch of turmeric
salt and freshly ground black pepper
1 large tomato per fillet, peeled and chopped

1. Marinate the lamb overnight in the oil, onion, saffron, garlic and turmeric, turning occasionally.
2. Remove the fillets from the marinade. Gently fry the marinade ingredients together for 15–20 minutes, add the tomato and continue frying until the onions are very soft and flavours amalgamated.
3. Preheat the grill to high. Grill the lamb fillets for a few minutes on each side. Pour any excess juices into onion and tomato mixture.
4. When the lamb is cooked, slice and serve with the onion and tomato and plain boiled rice.

AAB GOSHT

1kg/2.2lb boned shoulder of lamb, cut into cubes
1kg/2.2lb onions, thinly sliced
pinch of turmeric
pinch of chilli powder
2–3 pieces cinnamon bark
6–8 cloves
4–5 cardamom pods
3 bay leaves
3–4 dried limes
2.5–4cm/1–1 1/2 in fresh ginger, puréed together with 3–4 cloves garlic to form a paste
225g/8oz lentils or split peas, soaked, boiled and puréed
900g/2lb tomatoes, peeled and chopped
5–6 medium potatoes, cut into large chunks
6 extra onions, sliced
salt and freshly ground black pepper
juice of 1 lemon
good handful of fresh coriander leaves, chopped

1. Put the meat and enough water to cover in a large saucepan.
2. Add the 1kg/2.2lb sliced onions, spices, bay leaves, dried limes, ginger and garlic.
3. Simmer gently for about 15–20 minutes. Skim off any foam that rises to the top.
4. Add the puréed lentils or split peas, tomatoes and potatoes.
5. Meanwhile, fry the 6 sliced onions until caramelized.
6. Season with salt and pepper and add the lemon juice, coriander and caramelized